It's Good to Be a Woman

Voices from Bryn Mawr
Class of '62

*To Michelle,
Good luck at Bryn
Mawr & beyond.*

It's Good to Be a Woman

Voices from Bryn Mawr
Class of '62

Alison Baker

Alison Baker

Photography by Anne White

PublishingWorks, Inc.
Exeter • New Hampshire
2007

Printed in the United States.
Published by:
PublishingWorks, Inc.
60 Winter Street
Exeter, NH 03833
603-778-9883
www.publishingworks.com

Orders:
Revolution Booksellers, LLC
60 Winter Street
Exeter, NH 03833
800-738-6603
www.revolutionbooksellers.com

LCCN: 2007921834
ISBN: 1-933002-33-6
ISBN-13: 978-1-933002-33-0

For my father,
Geoffrey Baker

Contents

List of Illustrations

All current photos are by Anne White, except where noted, as is the cover design and back cover author photo. All old photos are from the Bryn Mawr Class of '62 Yearbook, except where noted.

Acknowledgments

First of all, I would like to thank the women of Bryn Mawr's class of '62, more than half of whom participated in this project–all those who made themselves available for (repeated) oral history interviews and photo sessions, those who answered my questions, who engaged in long conversations by e-mail, phone, and letter, those who responded to the 40th (or the 10th or 25th) reunion survey, those who contributed documents, photos, and other memorabilia, those who helped me through numerous revisions, who waited patiently through all the years that it took me to complete this book.

The exigencies of space and focus made it impossible to have more than a few "main characters" in the book, which means that many classmates and others who talked with me are not included, at least not by name. Their contributions were no less important, and I would like to thank them particularly as follows:

Martha Armstrong, Bannon (Marbut) Baker, "Betchen" (Wayland) Barber, Caryl Barnes, Arlene (Belkin) Bernstein, Joelle Bertolet, Elizabeth (Reed) Bramwell, Linda (Davis) Cirino, Mary (Adler) Cohen, Rosalind (Conn) Cohen, Judith (Samuelson) Craig, Alice Davison, Helen (Von Raits) Geagan, Barbara Gormise, Valerie (Schoenfeldt) Greenberg, Martha (Horsley) Hanrott, Rebecca Hazen, Daryl (Hansen) Hiller, Diana (Meyer) Hirsch, Judith (Stuart) Hohman, Lynne Hollander, Carolyn (Smith) Holt, "Pat" Jackson, "Kate" (Yablonsky) Kalil, Jane (Tanner) Kendrick, Isobel Kramen, Helen (Rodnite) Lemay, Carole (Lemon) McMichael, Barbara (Bauman) Morrison, Sandra (Goldberg) Narin, Lisa Pate, Pamela (Sharp) Perrott, "Rob" (Colby) Pierce, Lois Potter, "Heddy" (Fairbank) Reid, Martha (Fruit) Rohr, Nick Rubashkin, "Sasha" Siemel, Carolyn Stark,

Janice (Richman) Sufrin, Apu Sohoni, Abigail Trafford, Margaret (Norman) Venator, Martha Webb, Elizabeth (Jones) Wehr, Louise (Weingartner) Wiener, and Stefanie (Tashjian) Woodbridge.

Bryn Mawr alumnae from other classes have also contributed, as have members of the faculty, staff, and students currently at the College. Special thanks to Alison Cook-Sather, director of the Bryn Mawr/ Haverford Education Program, to college archivist Loretta Treese, and to staff members at the Alumnae Office and at the Alumnae Bulletin.

I started writing *It's Good to Be a Woman* at the Norcroft Writers' Colony in Lutsen, Minnesota. Thanks to Joan Drury for creating Norcroft, to Kay Grindland for making it work, and to Rosalva Hernandez, Ladette Randolph, and Zoe Zolbrod, fellow "Norcrofters," for their continuing friendship and support. Thanks to Rachel Devlin, Ann Jones, Kim Robinson, Julia Schnakenberg, Kio Stark, and Laura Wolf-Powers, for their thoughtful reading and critique. Finally, thanks to Patricia Lee Lewis and members of the 2004–2005 Patchwork Farm Manuscript Group– Marianne Banks, Carolyn Benson, Portia Cornell, Sophia Craze, Mary Fussell, Sara Dalmas Jonsberg, and Ann McNeal. Without their constant encouragement, I might never have finished the book.

I am grateful to classmates Betsy (Barber) Gould, who designed the 40th Reunion Survey, and has written demographic notes to provide a context for the oral histories in the book, and Ellen Zetzel Lambert, who read and critiqued the manuscript not just once, but several times, in its crucial, final stages. The book is much the better for all these readers' comments and critiques; whatever deficiencies of content or style persist are my own responsibility.

Like many of my most recent projects (building a house, for one), this book has been a family affair. Special thanks and love to my father, Geoffrey Baker, the masterbuilder, who gave lots of good advice on text and design; and to my sister, Anne White, who took all the current photos (except where noted). My niece, Alison Pena, did proofreading and editing. Thanks and love to my children, Eleanor, Caroline, and Ted, and their spouses, who made important contributions and generally cheered me on, and to my five wonderful grandchildren, Huey, Isaac, Ava, Benjamin, and Celia.

Introduction

> *If you want to see a picture of social change during the latter part of the twentieth century, follow the lives of the class of 1962. Raised during the prosperity following World War Two, entering college at the peak of the Baby Boom, nurtured on the ideal of the nuclear family with Mom in the kitchen and Dad bringing home the bacon, we have been at the cutting edge of a revolution in the role of women.*

> [*Bryn Mawr Class of '62—25th Reunion Survey Report,* by Elizabeth Gould]

It's Good to Be a Woman traces a small number of particular and representative lives, women from the Bryn Mawr College class of '62. These are not celebrities; they are ordinary people in extraordinary times, women who have led productive and successful lives, but not necessarily on a grand scale. In 1962 (a year before the publication of Betty Friedan's *The Feminine Mystique*), most college-educated women still expected their lives to revolve around marriage and family. But these women had larger ambitions. Bryn Mawr had given them the support of a kind of old-school feminism, the idea that women are capable, that it's good to be a woman. They were determined to have lives of their own, to find meaningful work, to make a difference. The question they all ask, again and again, is: "Who am I, and what do I want to do with my life?" In a world in flux, each woman had to create her own particular path through life, to find her own way. We follow these stubborn, can-do optimists as they navigate the turbulence of the sixties and early seventies, confront crisis (divorce, sickness, getting fired), and build lives and careers, charting new territory for women in the professions.

As a group, these women are important because they were in the vanguard of the feminist movement, breaking down barriers for women entering the professions. By following their lives, *It's Good to Be a Woman* fills in a missing piece in the history of the women's movement. Finally, it was these women, and others of their generation, who turned out to be the wave of the future. The absence of well-defined career tracks, the need to be creative in seizing opportunities, the problem of balancing work and family—these are now true for all educated women, and even some men.

In 1987, I went back to Bryn Mawr for my 25th class reunion, curious to know what had become of my classmates. I discovered that at least a few had succeeded in traditionally male professions, often as "the first woman" to reach the highest levels—the first woman to make partner in a big New York law firm, the first woman brain surgeon and professor of neurosurgery at Stanford University medical school. Others were still searching, trying various lines of work, not yet satisfied that they had found their real vocation. By that time in my life, I had gone through marriage, divorce, and a rather episodic career in college administration. In conversations with classmates, I discovered that I was not alone. Many of us were divorced, and most had moved around a lot, from job to job, not necessarily by choice. I talked with classmates about career setbacks, about getting fired, stopping to have children, balancing work and family. While many of the conversations were about failure, there was always an undercurrent of optimism. We talked about what we had learned from failure, about different definitions of success, about the meaning of our lives so far.

I heard so many stories. I met, or reconnected with, so many vibrant, interesting women. And I felt, even back in 1987, that what I was hearing was more than a collection of individual stories, however compelling; that there was something intriguing and important about these women as a group. Those reunion conversations stayed in my mind, along with a lot of questions, even as my own life took a new direction. I began working in oral history, spent time in Morocco, and wrote my first book, about Moroccan women (*Voices of Resistance,* SUNY Press, 1998). Ten years passed before I came back to the subject of Bryn Mawr's class of '62.

As a member of the class, I have had unusual access. More than fifty classmates generously shared their life stories with me in tape-recorded interviews; not interviews really, more like conversations. Over half the class responded to a 40th reunion questionnaire. More than half (not necessarily the same people) responded to my requests for information, sending papers, clippings, photos, notes, letters, and e-mail. I consulted a wide variety of historical sources, as well as materials from the college archives and personal collections.

In the course of five or six years of talking with classmates, I found lots of interesting stories, compelling personalities. I was thrown off, at first, by the low-key, self-deprecating tone taken by these very accomplished women. When I suggested that they had come out of Bryn Mawr full of confidence, several said, "No, not really." Classmates talked about times when they might have given up, when it all might have gone another way. Many talked about being "lucky" in their lives and careers. I began to realize how brave these women were, how strong, to go ahead in spite of real barriers (sex discrimination was perfectly legal before the Civil Rights Act of 1964) and even self-doubt. They showed remarkable resilience, and never an ounce of self-pity, even when times were tough.

A theme began to emerge. I realized that we were the spearhead of a mass movement of women going into the professions. And I realized that we were ideally positioned to be that fighting wedge precisely because we were privileged—economically, socially, and in our education. We could not have stayed out there in front without having a certain level of economic privilege and a core of inner confidence. When we graduated from Bryn Mawr, professional positions and career ladders were not there for women. We had to be able to try out different things, to take time, to dither around a bit, to take risks. You have to be strong to break down walls, and these Bryn Mawr graduates had the sort of stubborn optimism, even arrogance, that was essential. They didn't give up.

The 192 girls who entered Bryn Mawr as freshmen in the fall of 1958 were not typical of their generation. Almost half the class came from private schools, at a time when the vast majority of Americans went to public school. Three-quarters of the class identified their mothers as "homemakers," at a time when women held more than a third of jobs in the United States. This was clearly a group that came from economic privilege. Even girls from more or less modest home circumstances were privileged just by being at Bryn Mawr. As a group, these women had choices and opportunities that were not the norm for most American women coming of age in the early sixties.

Most of the girls who went to Bryn Mawr could just as easily have ended up at one of the other "seven sisters" women's colleges. But the fact that they went to Bryn Mawr made a difference. Not only was Bryn Mawr the most self-consciously academic of the women's colleges; it also had a strong feminist tradition. The College expected its graduates to go on and do something serious in the world, and that was different from other women's colleges at the time.

Born in the war years, we attended college right on the cusp between the conservative fifties and the explosive sixties, and came of age with Martin Luther King, Jr., and the civil rights movement, President Kennedy, and the New Frontier. These were heady times, with an extraordinary sense of possibility. "I wanted to save the world," said one classmate, a journalist, "I thought you could do that." The message we got from Bryn Mawr was one of can-do optimism mixed with a strong sense of responsibility. Knowing that we were privileged, we were determined to do something with our lives, to make a contribution.

To be a vanguard, it is not enough to break down barriers. You have to have someone, indeed large numbers of people, who will follow in your footsteps. Most of us were born in 1940, just six years before the start of the postwar baby boom. That meant that after our generation had broken down the walls, several waves of women from the baby boom were there, ready to surge through the breach. The baby boomers have dominated the conversation, through sheer force of numbers, ever since they grew up to become the sixties generation, defined by their opposition to the Vietnam War. Meanwhile, the class of '62 has gone through life more quietly, always just one step ahead, part of a little-known "in-between" generation, neither hippies nor housewives, difficult to define, more reticent than the boomers who followed, less angry, more confused, perhaps more thoughtful.

Very few of the narratives in *It's Good to Be a Woman* deal with someone who found both love and vocation early on. Most experienced a real searching in these two vital areas. And while these women were pioneers in trying to do serious work and have a family, they were also probably the last generation of women who followed their husbands' career moves, without any discussion or debate. A lot of classmates told of being uprooted, their professional lives interrupted, not just once but again and again. This has made their lives rather quirky and episodic, but also more interesting.

It is the right time for such a book. More than forty years out of Bryn Mawr, we can see the full arc of these women's lives. Several classmates told me they had already been thinking along the same lines, cleaning out parents' attics, getting ready to write their own memoirs, looking back to try to understand themselves in relation to the times, musing on roads not taken, the "what-ifs," and looking forward to the next chapter.

Part I
The Class of '62
at Bryn Mawr

Chapter One

Bryn Mawr College
and the Class of 1962

Bryn Mawr College – May 1987

It wasn't nostalgia that brought me back. I'm glad I went to Bryn Mawr. I remember living my four years there very intensively. But I'd never felt any urge to run back to visit. Then a classmate called, and talked about going to our 25th reunion. I began thinking about other women from the class of '62. What stories lay behind those cryptic class notes in the *Alumnae Bulletin?* How had their lives gone forward from that particular time we shared at Bryn Mawr?

Classmates drifted in, one by one, on Friday of the reunion weekend. I recognized Stephanie (Condon) Shoemaker and Barbara (Paul) Robinson, huddled in animated conversation. Both were much as I remembered them–Stephanie grounded and serene, Barbara smart and capable–but both were somehow more defined, more themselves, altogether more beautiful. Barbara had become the first woman to make partner at Debevoise & Plimpton, a big New York law firm, I had heard, while Stephanie, with her youngest child just heading off to college, was still trying to figure out what she wanted to do with her life.

Years later, Stephanie told me her memories of that day: "There was Barbara," she said, "looking as she had when she was eighteen. Looking gorgeous. I can still see her in that pink linen dress. Everything was perfect. And I thought, 'I've done nothing in my life; I'm not going to be able to talk to Barbara.' And then Boom! She came flying down, and threw her arms around me. 'Stephanie! Oh gee!' We were so glad to see each other. Everything else just melted away."

Ellen Zetzel Lambert was also back for the 25th reunion, and spent time with old friends from Haverford (the neighboring men's college), as well as with her Bryn Mawr classmates. Ellen was struck by the differences between the two groups. "The Haverford conversations were all quest narratives," she told me. "It was all about where they had been and what they had done. And how much money they made and how important they were. It was all about power. The Bryn Mawr stories weren't about power at all. There was a lot of talk about failure and insight gained from failure. We had much more honest conversations, about the meaning of our lives. And the meaning of your life was not at all about how far you had gotten."

The Bryn Mawr Class of '62

One hundred and ninety-two girls entered Bryn Mawr as freshmen in the fall of 1958; one hundred and fifty-nine graduated in the spring of 1962, and approximately one hundred and seventy count themselves as Bryn Mawr class of '62 alumnae. My subject here is mainly this last, self-selected group.

The girls who became the Bryn Mawr class of '62 were overwhelmingly white, largely middle class, about 70 percent Protestant, 20 percent Jewish, and 10 percent Catholic, from families living mainly in the Mid-Atlantic and New England states, especially from the greater Philadelphia, New York, and Boston areas. There were sixteen Bryn Mawr alumnae daughters, several international students from Europe and from Hong Kong, one African-American (one of only four in the entire undergraduate college), and a handful of girls from working-class families.

Almost half the class came to Bryn Mawr from private school, at a time when private "prep" schools, like private colleges and universities, were mostly single-sex. These schools didn't have much social diversity, but they *were* places where adolescent girls were encouraged and taken seriously, a sanctuary from the rigid sex roles of fifties culture. Several classmates told me how important it was to them, for eight years, through high school and college, to be able to grow up without any sense that they were supposed to take a lesser role in life *vis-à-vis* men.

At the beginning of freshman year, you could see some differences between the girls who went to private prep schools (mostly upper-class WASPs), and those who went to public school (including most of the Jewish girls). Girls from private schools had a veneer of sophistication. There were cliques–girls who hung around together, played bridge, drank coffee, smoked, and talked about "coming out" at debutante balls. "I felt like such an outsider," said one classmate, a Jewish public school graduate. "I didn't know how to play bridge, and I didn't drink coffee." And more poignantly: "I was one of the strivers. And those girls, the WASPs who stayed in their own little cliques, didn't even see me." In general, girls who were poorer noticed who was rich; girls who felt like outsiders–Catholics, girls from Hong Kong, even Midwesterners–noticed who was "inside."

Girls from public schools often didn't feel as well prepared, and that, paradoxically, made coming to Bryn Mawr more exciting. One classmate, who grew up in a small town, told me,

> *I was very naive when I came to Bryn Mawr, and very uneducated, really. I just came from this little local high school. At Bryn Mawr, I had the sense that everyone else had read so much more, and knew so much more. Any time anyone mentioned anything, I would run out and read it, or listen to it. I think a lot of kids who had better educations found it less of a jolt, less of an excitement to be there. But for me it was this flowering, just exhilarating!*

Another classmate talked about the mixed messages she got, growing up. Her parents wanted her to follow in their footsteps and become a doctor. Her father insisted that she take physics in her senior year in high school, and in those days, she said, "girls just didn't take physics." Other girls were cheerleaders, but she always felt different. Then she came to Bryn Mawr, and it was like the ugly duckling in the fairy tale. "All of a sudden everybody was a swan!" she said. "All of a sudden I discovered all these young women . . . like me!"

Of course, not everyone was happy at Bryn Mawr, especially at first. Some were overwhelmed by the academic demands. Some found the "old girls" atmosphere stuffy and oppressive, dull and pedantic. Alumnae daughters often had a particularly hard time. "My mother had so loved Bryn Mawr," said one, "and I was so unhappy there." One classmate, from a family with several generations of loyal Bryn Mawr graduates, still feels bitter and betrayed by the College. And while some students were happy to be left alone, others felt cast adrift, and could have used some friendly counseling and advice.

I was a "prep school kid," happy to leave home at age fourteen, and happy to be left alone at Bryn Mawr. I went to the Putney School, a progressive, coeducational high school on a farm in Vermont, founded in the thirties by Carmelita Hinton, a Bryn Mawr graduate. (It was at Putney that I had my own ugly-duckling-to-swan experience.) Then I took a year off, studying German, violin, and voice in Munich, Germany. By the time I got to Bryn Mawr, in the fall of 1958, I was a year older than most of my classmates, impatient with rules and curfews. I participated in lots of activities, especially theater and music, and began writing for the *College News.* But really, I was quite unsure of myself. Others in the class seemed so much more at ease, so much more serious and substantive. In comparison, I felt awkward, unformed.

While some classmates talked about discovering people just like themselves at Bryn Mawr, others talked about the differences they found. Our class was not diverse in any of the ways that we now measure diversity—race, ethnicity, class, even geography. But perceptions of diversity depended on where you came from. For one classmate, who had grown up in Washington, D.C., diversity was not just the foreign students, but also girls from New York and Boston, and "people just not like anyone [she] had ever met." Another noted that Bryn Mawr was the sort of place where a Texas "hick" and a European countess could become best friends.

One classmate, from a middle-class Jewish family in Newark, New Jersey, was "stunned by class" when she got to Bryn Mawr. "Where I grew up, I barely ever saw just a plain WASP," she said. "What most people take to be the standard type, to me was the most exotic thing in the world." Another, coming from a very upper-crust private school in Boston, told me that at Bryn Mawr, for the first time in her life, she met people who were not so privileged, and that was a wonderful experience for her. "They were on scholarship," she said. "They came out of a whole different part of America."

Influences, Growing Up

Our earliest memories are of the war years, living in female-headed households, seeing women in charge, while the men were off at war. In the postwar prosperity, we were raised on the ideal of the nuclear family, our mothers mostly "homemakers," while our fathers went out to work. On the whole, we were good girls, with happy childhoods. One classmate told me of being bratty in elementary school, "too smart for [her] own good." Another talked of stealing the family car and taking it out for a spin when her parents were away. Nothing big. In those early years, we were all good girls really. Through the fifties, we wore bobby socks and saddle shoes, swing skirts, blouses with Peter Pan collars, and cardigan sweaters turned backward. When we did begin to rebel, we sulked and brooded; the real turmoil was inside us. A number of classmates looked back on their early teenage years as a very dark period. "I was really shy," said one, "my body hormonally out of control, would *never* talk to a boy, no social skills whatsoever, *loved* to read, kind of a classic portrait of a Bryn Mawr girl."

Our mothers loomed large in our lives, for good or ill. (One classmate, in a 40th reunion survey, listed her mother's occupation as "housewife/prima donna.") Most of our mothers were at home through the years when we were growing up. Many also worked in their communities as volunteers. These women were the mainstay of nonprofit organizations, working for social and political reform. Perceptions varied. One classmate referred to her mother's "groundbreaking work" in education, housing, and health care, while another noted that her mother's volunteer work consisted mostly of giving lunches. My own mother, a Bryn Mawr graduate (Elizabeth Fain, class of '34), taught French in a private school for a few years after college, then stayed home while my sister and I were growing up. She also volunteered with the local League of Women Voters chapter and the NAACP (National Association for the Advancement of Colored People), and worked on the Bryn Mawr book sale (to raise money for scholarships). It seemed to me that lunches were a large part of what she did, but I also got the very strong message that it was important to do something to give back to the community, to help make the world a better place.

That was also a message we got from Bryn Mawr. We came out of college eager to make a difference, confident that every problem has a solution if you just think hard enough. But while our mothers expressed this restless idealism mostly in volunteer work, we took it into the workforce and the professions. That has made all the difference. We came up against the larger society in a way that most of our mothers never did, and we were pathbreakers for the next generation.

On the whole, my classmates spoke of their mothers with affection, even admiration. "My mother was a very positive role model," said one. "She grew up on a farm, got a college degree in 1933 in math and chemistry, taught school before she got married, and did some graduate work in math at the University of Michigan. She had a yearning to do more, but my father didn't want her to work. In the end, she was an underachiever." Other accounts echoed that same, rather poignant sense of early promise followed by unlived life and thwarted ambitions. We didn't want that to happen to us. Many of us looked to our fathers as role models—they seemed more curious, more engaged in the world.

In some ways we remember our actual childhoods less vividly than the lives we lived in our imagination. One classmate talked about seeing Moira Shearer in *The Red Shoes,* and imagining herself a ballerina, on the New York stage. At the age of ten or eleven or twelve, we were reading the Nancy Drew mysteries. Nancy Drew was appealing, even a little subversive, for girls of our generation, especially if you had a housewife mother. She was independent (driving her own blue roadster), daring, and had a talent for *getting in the thick of things.* "I just devoured Nancy Drew," said one classmate. "She was smart, pretty, independent, and she solved mysteries."

Classmate Sue Johnson's heroes were the Rockford Peaches, her home team in the All-American Girls Baseball League. From the time she was about ten years old, Sue went to their games, hung around at fan picnics, and clipped all the articles about the Peaches from the sports pages. "It was so fabulous to see women playing sports," Sue remembered, "working hard, getting dirty, playing to win." Some forty years later, Sue decided to write a book about the League,[1] and her scrapbooks, which she had saved through all those years, were the jumping-off point.

Bryn Mawr seems to have attracted the bookworms and the dreamers. One classmate, who described her parents as "boring, straight-arrow capitalists," told me she used to imagine herself sitting in a café, arguing about socialism, drinking tea from a glass, a sugar cube between her teeth. A lot of classmates describe themselves as "lucky" in their lives and careers. Perhaps that is because all the "possible" lives that we could imagine for ourselves seemed so dull. So much of what we achieved and became was the stuff of dreams when we were growing up—romantic, impossible.

Elvis, Sputnik, and Tea Sets

Our consciousness was formed largely in reaction to the quiescent, "normal" decade of the fifties. For many of us it was the music that first caught our attention: Pete Seeger and the Weavers, rhythm and blues, Elvis, and rock 'n' roll. One classmate recalled the night that Elvis made his first appearance on the Ed Sullivan show, in the fall of 1956: "We were mesmerized watching this—all that sex—really, before Elvis there was nothing!"

On October 4, 1957, just as we were all writing our applications to Bryn Mawr, the Russians put a satellite they called Sputnik into orbit. Until this event, girls generally had been discouraged from doing math or science. The thing about Sputnik—and the ensuing drive to improve science education—was that there was no distinction made between boys and girls. To compete in the cold war, *all* American schoolchildren had to learn more math and science, and that included girls. "The idea permeated the national consciousness," said classmate Marion (Coen) Katzive, "and fit right into our ideas about what was right for us."

Speaking at the class 40th reunion, Marion began her story of our Bryn Mawr days in 1957 with Sputnik, and ended it in 1963, a year after graduation, with the assassination of John Kennedy. "In between," she said, "was a very special time of high expectations and challenges that allowed us to get a good grip on our capabilities and our ideals." We came of age in this special time, and have carried its imprint through the rest of our lives—idealism and stubborn optimism, along with a lot of mixed messages.

In the summer of 1958, we received the Bryn Mawr College Handbook, with lists of clubs and activities and lots of advice. "This still being the fifties," said Marion, "we weren't surprised to read that 'For the various activities of Freshman Week, including a reception given by Miss McBride . . . a suit or wool dress, stockings and gloves (no hat) are the accepted costume.' And, there was another noteworthy directive: 'Bring a tea set. It's almost part of Bryn Mawr tradition to have tea on particular occasions.'" We were not quite the last class to be told to bring a tea set, but the tradition seems to have waned soon after us. When the class of '65 entered three years later, the same handbook suggested merely that a tea set might be "useful."

President Katharine McBride, in her introduction to the Handbook, gave us a very different message, with a spirit that owed more to Sputnik than to tea sets. "Freshmen starting college in 1958 strike an important year for education in the United States," she said. She pronounced us "ready for new and rapid progress," and encouraged us to set our sights high. She also cautioned us that, while she and others at Bryn Mawr were ready to help, our progress would be determined largely by our own "initiative and perseverance."

The messages in the Handbook, Marion noted, were "part of a bigger message we've been getting all of our lives and that we've all learned to live with: be smart, be committed, be diligent, be insightful, and bring a tea set."

While we were at Bryn Mawr, the Eisenhower fifties turned into the New Frontier sixties. We watched the Kennedy-Nixon debates on one of the few television sets in each hall, and we watched the inauguration, seeing poet Robert Frost, who had visited Bryn Mawr the previous March, sitting on the platform next to our new, young president. "When Kennedy said, 'Ask not what your country can do for you, but what you can do for your country,'" Marion recalled, "some of us began the process of figuring out what we'd be doing with our lives."

In concluding her 40th reunion talk, Marion got right to the heart of what made our Bryn Mawr class a little different, even back then in the spring of 1962. This is so important—it's what defines us as an in-between, hinge generation, and the key to all that followed. "Notwithstanding the constant mixed messages that we all got—often from parents—we knew we *had* lives," said Marion. "We had opportunities, challenges, and role models that were not the norm for women in America. Even if the choices seemed to be graduate school or learn to type, we did not expect to find our lifetime satisfaction in somebody else's career. We generally wanted to work, and the struggle was to figure out a way to find work that would be meaningful and that would allow us to make a difference."

Why Bryn Mawr?

In those days, Harvard, Yale, and the rest of the Ivy League colleges were still all-male. For girls, women's colleges were the jewels, especially the "seven sisters" in the Northeast—Bryn Mawr, Radcliffe, Wellesley, Smith, Vassar, Mount Holyoke, and Barnard. Of course this whole Ivy League world was rather small and rarefied, upper-class and concentrated on the East Coast. Most girls in the fifties didn't go to college at all, and those who did went mainly to their local state colleges and universities. Several classmates told me that it was pure chance, a series of coincidences, that got them to Bryn Mawr. One was selected for an academic track in high school in Chicago, which led her to take the SATs. After she scored high on the SATs, the college counselor told her to apply to Bryn Mawr. Another, whose mother was a sewing machine operator, was told to apply to one large public university and one small women's college. She chose "Bryan Mao-er" because it was the smallest of the seven sisters.

In the Ivy League world, Bryn Mawr had a reputation as the most serious and intellectual of the seven sisters. Several classmates told me they were influenced by a *Chicago Tribune* report that came out in the spring of 1958, ranking all the colleges, with Bryn Mawr as the top women's college. Wellesley was generally considered the most social of the seven sisters, and Radcliffe was really Harvard, the center of the world. But decisions on where to go to college seem to have been governed as much by chance as by deliberate choice. Most of the girls in our class at Bryn Mawr could just as easily have ended up somewhere else. Why did they choose Bryn Mawr, I wondered, and what difference did it make in their lives?

Talking about the decision to come to Bryn Mawr, some made it sound like a stroke of fate—one classmate was on her way to the post office to mail her acceptance letter to another college, when she ran into someone from Princeton who told her to tear up that letter and go to Bryn Mawr instead. Others made it sound quite whimsical. "I didn't like Wellesley much, for some reason," said one. "Then I went to Bryn Mawr, and it was spring and everything was blooming, and I thought, well, this is it." Yet everyone seemed to feel, in retrospect, that their lives would have been significantly different had they gone somewhere other than Bryn Mawr.

"At Radcliffe, the big agenda was boys, from Harvard," said one classmate. "You were really learning how to be a second-class citizen. At Bryn Mawr, you're brought up with the idea that it's good to be a woman. There's nothing second class about being a woman." Others echoed this. "One very positive outcome of my experience at Bryn Mawr was I never doubted that women were capable, never even considered that women might be inferior to men intellectually," said classmate Josie Donovan, a women's studies professor. "Unfortunately, that is still not an uncommon idea, even in the year 2000. Students today are still wrestling with that idea, and to me it's off the map; it's not even an issue. I just know there are many, many brilliant women." Another classmate noted that Bryn Mawr encouraged its students to go on to graduate and professional school, to do something serious in the world, unlike most women's colleges at that time.

The Story of Two Presidents

M. Carey Thomas was Bryn Mawr's first dean (1885–94) and second president (1894–1922), and dominated the life of the college over its first forty years. The shape of the College, as we knew it, was largely her legacy—the rigorous academic program, the strong student self-government, the imposing architecture. We lived, dined, and studied in massive stone buildings modeled on the great universities of England, built in theatrical Jacobean style, replete with towers, battlements, arches, turrets, and carved stone ornamentation. Thomas Library, which bore her name, had a cloister at its center, and a vast reading room modeled after the dining hall of Wadham College at Oxford University in England.

Taylor Hall, the original college building, stands in the main quad right across from the library, its Quaker modesty a reminder of what

Bryn Mawr might have been, a small undergraduate college, a "female Haverford" for "young women or girls of the higher and more refined classes of society," with preference to Quakers. But M. Carey Thomas took Johns Hopkins University as her model, not Haverford College, and although she herself was a Quaker, modesty was not her style.

For us as students, Thomas was rather a daunting figure in college myth and history. We studied in the Thomas Library, and walked in the cloisters, where she was buried. By all accounts, she was a difficult, brilliant woman, with strong opinions and an autocratic style. An 1885 photo of the college's first students, faculty, and administration, gathered on the steps of Taylor Hall, shows Thomas as a young woman, not yet thirty years old, serious and determined. In photos taken later, after she became president of Bryn Mawr, she is a formidable figure, rather stout and all trussed up in corsets, skirts, and bustle. One or two show her in blurred motion, with a faint smile. People who knew Thomas describe her as an "explosive" personality, with a strong sense of the dramatic. She lived on campus in a grand, rambling mansion known as the Deanery (used as a guest house when we were at college), in opulent style, and in a relationship with a woman, Mary Garrett.

Thomas wanted to give women access to the kind of higher education that was then reserved for men—rigorous, on the German university model—all the way up to the PhD level. She was convinced that women needed a place of their own, a place where women would hold power. At a woman's college, she said, there's a different feeling in the air. Students know that they don't come second to the table, that in their own colleges, "everything exists for women students and is theirs by right and not by favor."

At Bryn Mawr in our day, women were in charge—the president and dean were women, as were a good number of the faculty. These were vibrant, independent women, who obviously loved what they were doing. And it was not just the women currently at Bryn Mawr, but a whole continuum of remarkable women: M. Carey Thomas herself, and others like legendary geologist Florence Bascom. "This is *the life*," wrote Bascom, "to plunge into the welcome isolation of the field, to return to the stimulating association of Bryn Mawr." Two of the College's best-known alumnae were poet Marianne Moore ('09) and actress Katharine

PRESIDENT KATHARINE MCBRIDE

Hepburn ('28), both of them strong, original characters.

Katharine McBride was president of Bryn Mawr while we were there as students. Her tenure lasted almost thirty years, from 1942 to 1970, an era that spanned three separate wars as well as the McCarthy years. Marianne Moore once wrote a piece in praise of McBride, noting "her exceptional unpresidential constant: a liking for people as they are," a citation later engraved under a stone lion rampant, which guards the McBride Gateway at the entrance to the College. McBride was just thirty-seven when she became president of Bryn Mawr. But we knew her when she was in her fifties, toward the end of her tenure, and most of us, as students, found "Miss McBride" rather intimidating. "She scared me," said one classmate. "She seemed very distant, the kind of person who's given her life to an institution. I didn't identify with her at all."

Miss McBride represented all that was best and worst about the college when we were there. She exhorted us to reach high, to pursue excellence, and to make a difference in the world, but she seemed incapable of—or not interested in—relating to the confusion of our actual lives. Classmates who complain that the only role model we got at Bryn Mawr was the totally career-oriented academic woman, completely in the masculine-success mode, point to Miss McBride. She embodied a Bryn Mawr ethos that was essentially individualistic, elitist, encouraging us to achieve and to contribute to the world, but not necessarily to change it.

The Graduate School

The graduate programs were what most distinguished Bryn Mawr from other good, small liberal arts colleges. While we were at Bryn Mawr, graduate students accounted for more than a quarter of the total college enrollment, and at least two programs—in classical and Near Eastern archaeology, and in geology—had national (even international) reputations. Because of the graduate school, the tone of the College was more like a university, with a certain tweedy, British style. Original research was the standard, for undergraduates and PhD students alike. Almost everyone in the class felt that there were brilliant people at Bryn Mawr, both teachers and students, but almost no one felt that they personally were among this exalted group. "I felt quite ordinary," said one classmate. Most of us did.

The College was small then, with only about seven hundred undergraduates—by the year 2000, undergraduate enrollment had more than doubled—and President McBride and Dean Dorothy Marshall apparently knew each one of us. We were fortunate to have our teachers living nearby. We would occasionally invite them for tea in the dorms. Nonetheless, relations with faculty and administration were generally quite formal. I remember a running discussion in the *College News,* while I was an editor, on student-faculty relations. It started with some students complaining that teachers were inaccessible. Others countered that this was not their experience, and "if a student needs guidance, it is up to her to seek it." Finally, history professor Caroline Robbins weighed in with a brisk retort, saying that for students to expect the faculty to discuss their personal development was "egotism run mad." At the time, Robbins' comment seemed to me quite reasonable. Now, writing it down, I think, "Ouch!"

Bryn Mawr had international connections from the very beginning and, in the thirties and forties, the College played an important role in welcoming refugee scholars, those "undesirable elements" driven out of Europe by the Fascists and Nazis. These were extraordinary men and women. Among them was Emmy Noether, a brilliant mathematician, who taught at Bryn Mawr from 1933 to 1935. One source describes Noether as a "likable character" who wore "baggy clothes and short hair, swam at a 'men only' pool, was overweight, refused to take housework seriously, and ate out every day."[2] Noether apparently spoke very little English, and her work was so specialized that only a very few advanced graduate students and faculty members could understand it. She taught at Bryn Mawr for just two years, but her reputation endures. The father of a recent Bryn

Mawr graduate, himself a mathematician, told me that he had encouraged his daughter to apply to Bryn Mawr "because of Emmy Noether."

"Only Our Failures Wed"

"Only our failures wed" is the quote that M. Carey Thomas is remembered for. Thomas herself later claimed that what she really had said was, "our failures *only* wed," implying that her scorn did not extend to those who married and worked outside the home. That more forgiving, revisionist version never caught on. *The College News,* in our time at Bryn Mawr, listed student engagement and marriage announcements under the heading "Our failures . . . " Even now, more than forty years after graduation, this is the nub of our continuing conversation about Bryn Mawr.

"I think there was a deficiency in the Bryn Mawr dogma that underlies the confusion about that famous quip," wrote one classmate in a 40th reunion booklet. "Either way, this quip had the effect of making the topic of real women, living real lives, virtually undiscussable . . . . It put off discussion about the intersection between our public lives as women professionals and our private lives, where love, marriage, children dwell . . . . Was this silence because no one back then was having such discussions? Was it a conscious decision on the part of the college or simply a blind spot that prevented them?"

Girls at the other women's colleges in the late fifties and early sixties were being given practical advice about how they might combine "homemaking" with careers. At Mount Holyoke College in 1957, an incoming (male) president described a three-phased life pattern for the college-educated, "uncommon" woman: a period of schooling, a score of years occupied primarily by homemaking, and a third phase working outside the home, in a career. At Barnard College, circa 1962, President Millicent McIntosh, a Bryn Mawr graduate and mother of five, told students, "Have your babies while you're young. Afterward you can fulfill your intellectual ambitions." But at Bryn Mawr, there was no official talk about how we might combine professional and private lives, and it wasn't something we discussed among ourselves. Now, it seems quite amazing that we never had those discussions. But those were different times. We didn't have the language of feminism yet, and we had no experience of the world.

Here again we are an in-between generation, a generation on the cusp. We graduated a full year before Betty Friedan's book *The Feminine Mystique,* came out—and in any case, most of us didn't identify with Friedan's suburban housewives—and seven years before the start of the second-wave women's movement. Simone de Beauvoir's *The Second Sex* was first published in 1949, but most of us didn't discover de Beauvoir until much later, in the early seventies, after "the woman question" had been taken up by American second-wave feminists.

In fact, M. Carey Thomas herself spoke and wrote a good deal about "the woman question," mainly in the period from 1900 to 1922, in the context of the suffrage movement. With the vote, she said, women would have the power to change their condition, to act in their own self-interest. She even talked about a second revolution, which would bring about the economic independence of women, following the first revolution, of giving women access to higher education. But we knew nothing of all this, just as we knew nothing of Simone de Beauvoir. The idea that women might constitute a class/group with common interests and grievances did not occur to most of us until some years later, in the period leading up to the women's movement. Graduating from Bryn Mawr, we felt privileged, not disadvantaged. We had high expectations. We wanted to do something with our lives.

Feminism and Bryn Mawr

Ten years after graduation, Bryn Mawr '62 graduates looked much like other college-educated women of their generation in patterns of marriage and family. A reunion survey showed 80 percent of respondents married, with (among those who were married) an average of two children. But unlike most of their peers, the Bryn Mawr graduates were also quite successful in professional life—most had gotten at least a toehold in careers. It looked as though the class of '62, the pioneers, really were managing to "have it all."

But there was a lot going on that didn't show up in the survey. I think of my own situation in 1972: my first college teaching job was just ending,

DEAN DOROTHY NEPPER MARSHALL

with no real prospects for the future; my marriage was falling apart; I had three small children—the oldest just five years old—and I was struggling to finish a PhD dissertation, seven years after starting in graduate school. It certainly didn't feel like "having it all"; it was more like trying to "do it all," and mostly failing. It was just then, around the time of the 10th reunion, that I met up with Dorothy Marshall.

Bryn Mawr gave us a lot of strong, independent women as role models, but there were not many we could identify with, not many who were life-sized, or who had both a family and a professional life. Dorothy Marshall was one exception. While Miss McBride was tall, imposing, and single, Mrs. Marshall was small and approachable, and had a husband and child. Of course, Mrs. Marshall shared the general view in the college administration that if you needed advice, you should ask for it. I, for one, never asked.

In the early seventies, I was living in the Boston area, my life in some disarray, as I have just described. I was reading the *Boston Globe* one day, and saw that Dorothy Marshall had just been appointed vice chancellor for academic affairs at the University of Massachusetts at Boston. I called to say hello, she invited me to her office to talk, and I ended up with a job as her assistant. In that first interview, I had told her about the unfinished PhD dissertation. By that time I was quite discouraged, ready to give up.

But Mrs. Marshall would have none of that. She just assumed that I would finish, and gave me every Friday off to work on the dissertation. It was the kind of no-nonsense approach that I remembered from Bryn Mawr–"Of course you can do it"–not sympathy really, and certainly no special pleading because you were a woman and life was not fair, and women were oppressed. Just the practical support of a day off every week, and, most of all, an infusion of grit and confidence. After that, I wouldn't have dared not to write the dissertation, and I did get it done in fairly short order. "Bryn Mawr women are slow learners," Mrs. Marshall once told me. "While everyone else knows that there are lots of things that women can't and shouldn't do, we just blunder along and do them anyway."

That was the sort of old-school feminism that we got from Bryn Mawr. When we graduated, we thought that women in general were smart and capable, Bryn Mawr women especially so, and that we could do anything we set our minds to. We didn't want our mothers' lives, centered on husband, house, and children. We were determined to have our own lives, our own careers. Not feminism, exactly, but a kind of optimistic, pro-woman view.

By 1972, the women's movement was running strong. A rash of feminist books were coming out, starting with the understanding that "the personal was political." Many of us joined women's consciousness-raising groups. By that time we had been out in the world of work and had discovered that in most places, women were still outsiders, even in academia, where we thought we would feel at home. The professions–law, medicine, journalism, academia–were especially hostile to women. It was such a different world then, hard to imagine now. Help Wanted ads were listed separately for men and for women. In most jobs, if you got pregnant, you were fired. When several Southern congressmen added a ban on sex discrimination to the 1964 Civil Rights Act, they meant it as a joke. A page-one article in *The New York Times* in 1965 debated whether the law would require executives to let a "'dizzy blonde'" drive a tugboat or pitch for the Mets.

A 10th reunion survey asked whether we had encountered "sexism" (a new term coined by the women's movement) in our lives and/or our work, and whether we thought there had been a "failure of feminism" at Bryn Mawr. Two-thirds of respondents answered Yes and Yes. They were angry that Bryn Mawr had not prepared them for the problems they would encounter as women in a sexist society, that there had been no explicit discussion of women's roles and conditions of oppression, and that no one had told them it would be so hard. "I graduated from Bryn Mawr totally unconscious of male/female roles, going merrily on my way," wrote one classmate, "not understanding that many potential problems would develop which I, of course, blamed on personal failings and inadequacies rather than social programming. It's taken a while to work it out. Bryn Mawr could have helped."

At the same time, several classmates who responded to the 1972 survey credited Bryn Mawr with giving them a strong and enduring confidence in themselves and their own abilities that sustained them through all the trials and tribulations of life in a sexist society. One wrote that "Bryn Mawr was the only place that I was not self-conscious about being a woman; it freed me to be myself–after a sexist high school and before the ordeal of male law school and confronting life." Another was grateful to the college for giving her "the unique opportunity to be a 'whole person'–excellent preparation for liberation."

By the time of the 25th class reunion, in 1987, we were in mid-career, with a lot of the bumpiness behind us. There was a general tone of optimism in the 25th reunion survey results, and opinions on the women's movement were mainly positive. "I am a committed feminist," said one classmate. "As long as it's inclusive of all," said another. "Solidarity with women in poverty is essential." Several spoke more as observers than participants: "While I'm glad I didn't do it, I'm glad someone did." And, as always, there were dissenting voices. "Although I firmly believe in equal opportunity, I find the whole concept of preferential treatment or affirmative action degrading," said one. Others criticized the "strident, man-hating" aspects of the movement.

In 2002, in a 40th reunion survey, there were several questions relating to feminism and the women's movement. Looking back, there is none of the anger that we saw at the 10th reunion. On the whole, we are grateful for the kind of no-nonsense feminism we got from Bryn Mawr, grateful for having caught the second wave of the women's movement. "The women's movement changed my life," said one classmate. "I feel as though I was on the leading edge of the feminist movement," said another. "The choices for women have changed so dramatically in our lifetime."

Two-thirds of respondents identified themselves as feminists. The remaining third did not, or said they couldn't be sure. A few identified feminism as "a political movement that works to better conditions for women by ending patterns of discrimination and abuse." Most had a broader, less political definition. "Yes, I'm a feminist," said one classmate, "not avid, but there." To be a feminist, she said, was to be "pro-woman." (Another said, "fiercely pro-woman.") One wrote that feminism "encouraged people to contribute to society according to individual talents and leanings rather than preconceived stereotypes." This is not the "self-fulfillment" or "choice" feminism that is so much in the news as we enter the twenty-first century. It is a sterner brand of feminism that still owes a lot to Bryn Mawr, talking about "contributing to society," asking for "equality for women, not special favors and not restrictions against women." Feminism, said one classmate, means "equal rights, equal work, equal pay. Helping our sisters too." There is a certain generosity concerning other women. Several classmates told me they wished that young women would stick together more, would support one another. But most were still reluctant to identify women as a class or a group with common interests and grievances. Those who did not identify themselves as feminists—even a few who did—felt somewhat out of tune with the contemporary feminist movement, saying it was too radical, too "strident, asking for help where one should make one's own way."

The Wave of the Future

The women in Bryn Mawr's Class of '62 were pioneers in trying to do serious work and also have a family. Work, for most of us, was vocation, making a contribution. Marriage and family seemed inevitable. We put them together as best we could. Almost none of us followed a well-defined career track. Most married (in spite of M. Carey Thomas), in an era when a married woman's professional life was secondary to her husband's, and most of us followed our husbands' career moves, without any question. But there was also an assumption that the husband had primary responsibility for supporting the family, especially when there were children. This gave us some flexibility, enabled us to try out different kinds of work, to take our time figuring out what we wanted to do. Perhaps we would have achieved more if we hadn't been slowed down by periods of discontinuity and divided energy. But many classmates would argue that it has been nice *not* to be on a track. It meant they had to be more creative in what they did, sometimes to let fate intervene.

Women's expectations have changed dramatically over the forty-five years since we graduated from Bryn Mawr. Girls growing up now are told that they can be anything they want to be, and can have a marriage and family or not, as they choose. Yet somehow the structures of family and work have not changed that much, and women's "choices" are not quite what they seem. In a 2000 book titled *Flux: Women on Sex, Work, Kids, Love and Life in a Half-Changed World,* author Peggy Orenstein talks about the moment in every young woman's life, sometime in her early to mid-thirties, when "no matter what she does—whether she is single or married, avidly pursues a career or scales back, has children or does not—the contradiction between a woman's vision of equality and the tug of tradition will get her right in the gut."[3] In a 2004 book titled *Midlife Crisis at 30,* thirty-something authors Lia Macko and Kerry Rubin talk about the "New Glass Ceiling—one that keeps women who want a life outside of work from getting ahead and doesn't allow women who are getting ahead to have a life outside the office."[4]

In this world in flux, the experience of Bryn Mawr's class of '62 has new relevance, for new generations of women. Many of us have daughters who are part of the first post–baby-boom generation (born 1958 to early seventies). They grew up in the Carter, Reagan, and GHW Bush presidencies, learning their feminism at school and through the popular media. My eldest daughter, born in 1966, told me that when she was in high school, in the eighties, feminism (if anyone thought of it at all) seemed irrelevant ("It had nothing to do with us; it was our mothers' thing, very uncool") and unattractive (feminists didn't shave their legs, would never get a man). The eighties saw a narrowing and watering-down of feminism. It became more and more about self-control and "choice," less and less about empowerment, solidarity with other women, or any broader vision of social change.

In a 1991 book titled *Backlash,* feminist author Susan Faludi writes about an "undeclared war against American women" that started in the late seventies, an insidious backlash, amplified by the popular media, that "convinced the public that women's 'liberation' was the true contemporary American scourge, the source of an endless laundry list of personal, social, and economic problems."[5] Essayist Katha Pollitt, in a column that appeared in the November 28, 2005, issue of the *Nation,* reels off a long list of "backlash lit." She starts with a 1986 Harvard-Yale study (falsely) comparing women's chances of marrying after 40 to the likelihood of being killed by a terrorist, and goes on to cite Sylvia Ann Hewlett (ambitious women stay single or childless), Lisa Belkin (mothers give up their careers), Louise Story (even undergraduates understand this now), "and other purveyors of the view that achievement and romance/ family are incompatible for women." Small wonder that so many high school and college women today say that "feminism" is a dirty word.

Meanwhile, the first post–baby-boom generation has grown up. Many of our daughters are married now, with young children. In her 2005 best seller *Perfect Madness,* Judith Warner, herself a young mother, talks about the "*master narrative,* if you will–that we tell now about women's progress and the problems of motherhood."

> *That story is that our [post–baby-boom] generation grew up with the greatest number of choices of any generation before and continues to enjoy that wealth of choices in motherhood. We can choose to work or stay at home or do some combination of the two, and we are free to do this largely because we have liberated ourselves from the yoke of feminism, which pushed so many women before us to feel they* had *to keep on striving in the workplace.*[6]

It is time to reclaim the history of American feminism, to broaden it, to find different models. We have heard a good deal about fifties housewives, the angry rebels of the baby-boom generation, and feminist leaders such as Bella Abzug and Gloria Steinem. But most young women today don't identify with any of these. And the media fixation on women who have opted out of high-powered careers to stay home with their children is at best irrelevant. For the 75 percent of married and single mothers who are out in the workforce, these stories perpetuate a cruel hoax, the idea that mothers can "choose" to work or to stay at home, in a world in which public policy and workplace structures remain unchanged. Perhaps it is time to hear from a quieter, in-between generation, not housewives, not angry rebels, not feminist leaders, just ordinary women trying to find satisfying lives and careers in times of flux and mixed messages.

The field of women's history developed in the seventies at least in part as a response to the largely ahistorical analysis of women's place in society in Betty Friedan's *The Feminine Mystique* and in some of the early pamphlet literature of the women's liberation movement.[7] Warner, Orenstein, and others have given us a fresh analysis of women's roles and dilemmas in contemporary society. In response, it may be useful to take a fresh look at American women's history as it played out through the second half of the twentieth century.

The graduates of Bryn Mawr's class of '62 were pioneers in opening doors for women in the professions. They are also real women living real lives. They tell what it was like to come of age in the early sixties, the enormous sense of possibility and the mixed messages. These stories from the class of '62 take us across the full arc of women's lives. They tell us what women were doing, and how they were doing it. They give us women's own view of their place in history.

Chapter Two

From a Fetish for Decorum to Marching on the Picket Line

This is the story of a transformation in student attitudes that occurred while we were at Bryn Mawr, something that most of us were only dimly aware of at the time. Most of all, it is about the process of change, including all the hesitancies, contradictions, and countercurrents. And it is about remembering–about how people experienced what happened and how they remember (or don't remember) particular events. The slow pace of the narrative, the endless musing and discussion–these all reflect an elusive quality that defines the Bryn Mawr class of '62, a curious mix of caution and rebelliousness, uncertainty and confidence, and always scrupulous honesty. Whenever I tried to move things along, or to paint the characters and events of those years in bolder colors, my classmates would draw me back. "No, it wasn't like that," they would say. "I didn't want to change the world. I didn't have that kind of confidence. And now, looking back, I'm not even sure I was there. I have no real 'body memory' of marching on the picket line."

When we came in as freshmen, in the fall of 1958, the tone on campus was set by seniors and juniors of the fifties generation, cautious and conservative, focused on academic work and campus life. We represented a new generation–a little more rebellious, more willing to question authority, more involved with the outside world. Over the next four years, as members of the class of '62 moved into positions of leadership in the college, the tone on campus began to change. Race and civil rights were the focus. In the spring of 1960, Bryn Mawr students picketed the local Woolworth's in support of the lunch counter sit-ins happening in the

South. In the fall of 1961, they began to raise questions about the status of black maids and porters at Bryn Mawr. Our class was in the thick of things. Indeed, several classmates were key players. At the time, none of these events seemed especially significant. It is only now, in retrospect, that what happened at Bryn Mawr takes on new meaning as part of a larger national narrative. We were among those who took the first steps.

Most white students at Bryn Mawr had grown up with no real contact with African-Americans, except perhaps with household servants in the South. In the North, blacks and whites lived in separate neighborhoods, attended separate churches, and didn't mix socially. In public high schools in the North, there was often *de facto* segregation—blacks and whites were on different tracks, took different courses, and sat at separate tables in the lunchroom. Interracial dating was almost unheard of. In those days, even Jewish-Christian dating was rare.

Most American households had television in the fifties, but there was no CNN, no Internet, no twenty-four-hour news cycle. White girls growing up in the North in those years were generally not much aware of events in the South. When the Supreme Court outlawed school segregation, in May of 1954, we were in the eighth grade. We were in high school when Emmett Till was murdered in Mississippi, and when Rosa Parks refused to give up her seat on the bus and sparked the Montgomery, Alabama, bus boycott. What most classmates remembered from those years was Elvis and Sputnik, not Rosa Parks or Emmett Till. (The story of Rosa Parks was carried in a slim column on page 31 of the next day's *New York Times,* and photos of Till's grotesquely mutilated face were published in Jet magazine, not in the mainstream, white press.) Then, just a year before we entered Bryn Mawr, in September 1957, the first black students tried to enter Central High School, in Little Rock, Arkansas. We saw these students, just about our own age, running a gauntlet of jeering white people. That was the first awareness, for most of us, of the violence of racism in the South.

The story of our four years at Bryn Mawr is pieced together from my own memory and the memories of others who were there, and where those memories were lacking, from the weekly student newspaper, the *College News.* Articles from the *News* helped me to reconstruct events, while editorials, opinion pieces, and letters to the editor were useful in tracing changing concerns and attitudes. The paper finally emerged as one of the main characters in the story, along with a succession of three student editors: Ellie Winsor (Leach) (class of '59), who was editor in the 1958 fall semester; Betsy Levering (Morgan) ('61), editor in 1959; and especially Marion Coen (Katzive) ('62), editor in 1960. The editor was the one who decided what to put in the paper, gave out reporting assignments, and wrote most of the editorials, after sometimes heated discussion with the editorial board. Above all, she set the tone.

In the fall of 1958, *College News* editor Ellie Winsor (Leach) was starting her senior year, writing an honors paper on literary criticism. She herself had no particular interest in social issues, but she decided that it would be useful, four years after the Supreme Court decision on segregation, for the News to do a report on southern attitudes toward school integration. Ellie had asked several students from southern states to do some research and write articles over the summer. (Of course, these were all white students and reported only on white southern attitudes.) The articles appeared as a special section in the October 8, 1958, issue of the News, right at the start of our freshman year.

Susan Downey ('60), from Jackson, Mississippi, reported that, in her state, there was "a widespread belief that the Negroes were an inferior race and that therefore integration would lower the academic level of the schools." Betsy Levering (Morgan) wrote about the situation in Virginia, where she said there was "a real and abiding fear of intermarriage, and the humiliation of hundreds of thousands of white farmers and mill workers who will be déclassé." She identified segregation as a caste system, and said that, if it were obliterated, there would be "a large, poor, white population stripped of the pride of being white, faced with the reality of being poor." Betsy was surprised and hurt when she discovered later that people thought that these were her own opinions. "It wasn't *my* point of view," she explained, "rather what I thought intelligent, decent southerners would say. I see now that I was distinctly naive and incautious."

Betsy grew up not so much in the South proper as in Appalachia, in a county in the mountains of Virginia that tried to secede from the Southern cause (like West Virginia, which sent guerrillas against the Southern armies and has been solidly Republican ever since). She was and is Quaker, and her views are more Quaker than Southern. She went to high school at

Westtown, a Quaker boarding school outside of Philadelphia, and while her parents were integrationists, their focus was more on international issues. But the segregated South was all around them in Virginia—Betsy remembers riding the school bus past the black school to get to the white school. Like many southerners, she was annoyed at northerners' "parade of moral superiority" and demonizing of the South. "My sense is that the orthodoxy at Bryn Mawr was that legal oppression of African-Americans, as practiced in the South, was wrong and should change," she said, "but that this was a distant matter that didn't really involve northerners."

While most of the *News* articles were written with objective, and perhaps defensive, detachment, as a report on other people's views—standard Southern views at that time—there was one that had a very different tone. Hanna Woods ('61), from Little Rock, Arkansas, gave a cry from the heart. "It shouldn't have happened in Little Rock!" she wrote. "The stage seemed set for quiet and peaceful acceptance of integration; the city bus system had been integrated without incident or furor. There was no evidence that there would be any real trouble until the unmistakable villain of the story, [Arkansas Governor] Faubus, moved."

College students in the North were just beginning to get involved in supporting school integration in the fall of 1958. A Youth March for Integrated Schools, held in Washington, D.C., in November, drew an extraordinary turnout, estimated at ten thousand students, both black and white. A few weeks earlier, the *College News* ran an editorial titled "On Disdain and a Demonstration." The editors asserted that the upcoming youth march was "repugnant to nine out of ten students here on campus," and went on to say that they assumed that "boredom with the segregation-integration issue was widespread." But student views on integration were not the main focus of the editorial. The editors' overwhelming concern was that the march would take the form of "a demonstration, a purposeful creation of a disturbance . . . something from which we shrink instinctively." The editors themselves seemed troubled by this stance, almost apologetic. "We are unable to explain easily the fetish for decorum," they write, "the unwillingness to become actively involved in such matters that we think prevalent in our generation."

Ellie was editor, but when I asked her about this editorial, she disclaimed authorship, except possibly by collaboration. "I just can't imagine having had so well-articulated a social consciousness at the time," she said. "In that respect, I was very late fifties." She suggested that Betsy Levering, "Quaker by background and historian by disposition," must have been the author. Betsy demurred, saying that she couldn't possibly have written the editorial, "though who knows what one's younger self was like." Her guess was that Ellie wrote it, and that it reflected a heated discussion in the editorial board, which had come down on the side of demonstrations, but not unanimously and not with Ellie's wholehearted concurrence. "I would have been on the pro-demonstration side," said Betsy, "and incapable, I think, of writing a phrase like 'repugnant to nine of ten students here on campus.'"

The editors' views did not go unchallenged. 1961's Dee Wheelwright (Moon) participated in the Youth March, which she characterized as "a quiet, dignified and solemn procession," and wrote a letter to the editor taking issue with the *News* editorial. "I get the impression that you are for integration, but against demonstrations—in other words, you believe the river should be crossed, but you are afraid to get your feet wet. I am surprised by your wide-eyed assertion that the demonstration would be 'repugnant to nine out of ten students on campus' [that phrase again] and other brief glimpses you give into the mind of the average Bryn Mawr girl. . . . No! Let us not be bored, prissy, or blasé."

In January of 1959, Betsy Levering (Morgan) took over as editor, and the *College News* began to focus more on campus issues, with a series of editorials taking students to task for their lack of interest in campus organizations and affairs. By this time, several members of the class of '62 had joined the News writing and editorial staff, including Marion Coen (Katzive), who would succeed Betsy as editor. Marion had an intense, serious air, a probing curiosity about world affairs, and a concern for social justice. Early in the 1959 fall semester, she wrote an opinion piece

MARION COEN

on "campus apathy," an issue that had been much in the *News*. Marion was trying to move the discussion forward, to open up the much broader question of how Bryn Mawr students could or should relate to the world outside the college. "If there is a lack of interest in campus issues," she wrote, "may this not mean a concentration of concern on what is beyond the campus, a preference for world problems to campus projects? Or . . . an intensity of academic excitement, intellectual exploration which leaves little energy for immediate social concerns but better prepares the mind for those it will handle after the period of formal education?"

The question that Marion raised about students' roles in relation to events in the outside world seemed to be in the air just then, springing up almost simultaneously on several college campuses. At Yale, a group of students initiated "Challenge," a program of student-generated lectures and discussions on current topics, to try to bridge the gulf that seemed to separate students' academic life from that of the world community. The idea caught fire. It provided an outlet for students to articulate their anxieties about the world—an intermediate step between passive awareness and active protest that was just right for the times. A first weekend conference was held in the fall of 1959, and a second one was planned for March 1960 on the subject of "Twentieth Century Democracy: Myth or Reality?"

As college students in the North were beginning to consider getting more involved in the outside world, students in the South went ahead and took action. On February 1, 1960, in Greensboro, North Carolina, four black college students sat in at a local Woolworth's lunch counter, protesting segregation. Within days of the first sit-in, hundreds of other students took similar actions. Soon sit-ins were taking place throughout the South. With the sit-ins, students began to play a major role in the civil rights movement.

Soon after Marion became editor of the *College News*, in January 1960, she brought an announcement of the upcoming Yale colloquium to the editorial board for discussion. I was a member of the board by then, along with several others from our class. "I thought this might be a useful way of getting some perspective on the issue that was with us," said Marion, "our roles as students in relation to world events." So Marion, Susan Nelson, Judy Stuart (Hohman) and I, all from the *News* and the class of '62, got funding from the Student Undergraduate Association and took the train up to New Haven. The Yale conference was organized around two "challenges" to American democracy: "the need to recognize national goals based on principles other than the profit motive, and the need to achieve full integration and equal rights for the Negro." For us, integration and equal rights were the focus.

Big-name speakers were there, representing opposite poles of the political spectrum: conservative Republican Senator (and 1964 presidential candidate) Barry Goldwater, NAACP lawyer (later Supreme Court Justice) Thurgood Marshall, and AFL-CIO Vice-President A. Philip Randolph. Pete Seeger (a longtime singer and activist, and part of the Weavers folk group) and Odetta (a black woman folk singer with close-cropped hair and a deep, powerful voice) gave a sing-along concert.

It was two younger activists, just back from the South, who connected most strongly with students at the colloquium. Allard Lowenstein, a lawyer and freelance social activist, impressed us with his gentleness and informal manner—we were all calling him "Al" before the session was out. He talked about African-Americans in Montgomery, Alabama, living in an atmosphere of terror. Paul DuBrul, a representative of the National Student Association, was just back from participating in the lunch counter sit-ins. We were interested in what he had to say but put off by his dogmatic pronouncements and his aggressive, hard-edged style. Some students were suspicious of DuBrul's "emotional involvement" with the issue of integration and pressed him to talk about "the broad philosophical bases underlying his standpoint." It was an extraordinary moment—arrogant, naive nineteen-year-old college students confronting a seasoned activist, who had been out there on the front lines.

We were inspired by Lowenstein, but DuBrul helped us to think about the next steps, alerting us to a specific, active role that students could play to support the lunch counter sit-ins in the South. DuBrul said that there should be a picket line around every Woolworth's in every college town. This was something that college students should do. The concreteness of it was what made the difference. It helped us in figuring out what it meant to be an activist. We came back from Yale with a cause we could identify with, and an idea of what we, as students, might do to participate. The struggle for integration and equal rights was the perfect

"We did not expect to find our lifetime satisfaction in somebody else's career."

cause for us. Other issues were too hard to grasp–labor issues seemed too complicated, peace and disarmament much too complicated. How do you disarm and still protect yourself? But this was a clear issue of social justice, right and wrong. "It's interesting that our notion of civil rights was supporting integration in the South," said Marion. "It was supporting someone else in a struggle that was happening somewhere else."

Girls from Vassar, Smith, and Bennington who had attended the Challenge weekend went right out and picketed their local Woolworth's, rallying large groups of fellow students and carrying signs of protest: *Don't Buy from Woolworth's–It discriminates in the South.* Students at Harvard and Yale formed action groups (though I'm not sure they took any action). At Bryn Mawr, the immediate response was more considered and complex.

The next issue of the *News* carried reports on the Yale colloquium and an editorial by Susan Nelson titled *A Talk With Yourself,* challenging Bryn Mawr students to "look deeply into their own feelings," and consider what they were prepared to do to support the cause of integration. "Some would sit in who refuse to picket," wrote Susan. "Others would picket who would not date a person of another race." She concluded that "It is only fair to the cause of abolishing racial discrimination to look into our feelings and attitudes and get to know them, whatever they are, to see where they contradict themselves, where they are strong, where limited."

What can we make of this editorial? What did it mean at the time, and what is its significance now, in retrospect? Susan doesn't remember writing the editorial, nor does she remember the trip to Yale or the Woolworth's demonstration. She explained to me that none of these issues were new to her—in her family, civil rights was the ordinary stuff of dinner-table conversation. Her parents were both college professors in New York City. Her mother, a social psychologist, had worked on the Supreme Court school desegregation case with Thurgood Marshall of the NAACP. Susan herself had become fascinated with art history, and that's what she remembers from Bryn Mawr, not the *News* or the picket line.

I showed Susan's editorial to another classmate for comment, and she gave me a quick, scathing response: "That sounds like a Bryn Mawr approach, doesn't it? Don't go out and picket. Let's think about it." The idea of rallying groups of students to picket Woolworth's was certainly at odds with a campus culture that valued reason, independent thought, and an open-minded consideration of every question. Perhaps the approach exemplified by Susan Nelson's editorial was just a cop-out, a way to avoid taking action. But perhaps this "Bryn Mawr approach" was instead remarkably prescient, even admirable, challenging Bryn Mawr students to take a hard look at themselves and to examine their feelings about the issue of race. The editorial asked us to decide what we would do to advance the cause of civil rights not just in the South, but in our own neighborhoods and in our personal lives. This echoed a Quaker belief in the primacy of individual conscience that was quite familiar to us at Bryn Mawr. It anticipated at least one element of the strategy that Student Nonviolent Coordinating Committee (SNCC) leaders would later develop for the Mississippi Freedom Summer of '64, a strategy that combined personal transformation, direct action, and community mobilization. Personal transformation came first, and, for white students especially, it was a challenging experience. "It had to be premised on an understanding of your whole past, all the limitations of your past," said one Mississippi Freedom Summer volunteer. "Examining your motives. Having these long, excruciating internal inspections of yourself." Susan had this idea back in the spring of 1960, when students were just beginning to get involved in the civil rights movement, and SNCC, which was founded by some of the black college students who organized the lunch counter sit-ins and would soon become the key civil rights organization for the young, was very new.

In the next issue of the *News,* the editors issued a call to action. Finally, two weeks later, after everyone returned from spring vacation, we went out and picketed. Saturday, April 16, 1960, was a balmy day in the wealthy Main Line suburbs south of Philadelphia. Sixty-two students from Bryn Mawr and Haverford colleges came out on the picket line, the Bryn Mawr girls dressed in skirts and flats, the Haverford boys in suits and ties. They were split into three groups, two of which demonstrated in front of Woolworth's stores in Bryn Mawr and in the neighboring town of Ardmore. A third group was made up of students who wanted to protest discrimination, but didn't want to picket Woolworth's. They pointed out that the Bryn Mawr and Ardmore Woolworth's *did* serve and employ Negroes, whereas other stores (i.e., not Woolworth stores) on Philadelphia's Main Line did not. So they set up a third picket line at a busy intersection in the town of Bryn Mawr.

In meetings during the week, student organizers had talked about what to do "if cursed or struck at" by passersby: "Don't be provoked to retaliate; don't interfere with traffic; don't attract unfavorable attention in any way." The picketers walked in a circle, single file, taking hour-and-a-half shifts, holding up signs that read: *We Stand So All May Sit; Until We Can All Sit Together Let's Stand Together; Freedom to Stand Together—To Eat Together.* One person in each group passed out leaflets titled Why We Are Here, explaining that the picketers "believe that discrimination is wrong, and want to focus public opinion on the problem."

The manager of the Bryn Mawr Woolworth's had told his salespeople to offer "no comment." In Ardmore, the manager sent out a salesgirl with a little cart of flowers and a sign *Buy Your Easter Flowers at Woolworth's,* and she wheeled her cart around in a circle along with the picketers for much of the afternoon. Some teenagers shouted out hostile comments as they drove by, calling the picketers "Beatniks," "Intellectuals," "Rabble-rousers." People stopped to talk. Some said there was no need to picket;

"After all, this is the North." Others thought it was a good idea and might help to bring the problem closer to home.

It was the spring semester of our sophomore year when we picketed Woolworth's. Looking back, it is clear that this was the moment when the tide began to turn, when student attitudes began to change. It was the first time that Bryn Mawr students as a group had taken action, and this first action, however tentative, put us in touch with the nascent student movement, as well as the civil rights movement in the South. Young black activists from SNCC and other national student groups began visiting the College, giving speeches and raising money. They created quite a stir on our staid, cloistered campus.

What Bryn Mawr College students did that day in April of 1960 seems, in retrospect, a rather timid gesture of support ("as tame a demo as you can imagine," said one participant), but for us it was a big step, our first experience of direct action and community mobilization. What is interesting is how people remember, or especially how they don't remember the event. Five classmates have five different stories.

"I have a memory of the time we sat in at Woolworth's and picketed," said Barbara (Schieffelin) Powell, "but I don't know whether this is true or if I just made it up. I think I picketed, but sometimes I wonder whether I actually did it or if I just imagined it, made it up." After Bryn Mawr, Barbara taught school in Nyasaland (now Malawi) in Africa. In the summer of '65, she went down to Orlando, Florida, to teach black children and prepare them for going into integrated schools that fall. She would like to think that she participated in the picketing; it would be consistent with who she is and everything that has happened since then.

"Maybe I picketed," said Judy (Stuart) Hohman, "but I remember it being more an intellectual experience than an activist one. I've always felt a bit guilty that we weren't out there picketing, because I was definitely committed to the idea of the equality of people." Judy had grown up in the military, which in the fifties was the only integrated community in America, but she was more involved in the late-sixties antiwar movement. The Vietnam War impinged on Judy directly—her husband was drafted, and her father was in the military and supported the war, while she felt passionately that United States involvement in Vietnam was wrong.

Anna Kimbrough

"I remember the picketing," said Ellen Corcoran, "but I didn't participate, out of principle. In those days, my view was that I had no business imposing my idea of civil rights on someone else." Ellen went to Ghana with the Peace Corps after Bryn Mawr, and later taught African-American children in Roxbury in Massachusetts and Harlem in New York City. She is a little embarrassed about her noninterventionist stance back in 1960.

Lynne Hollander remembered in some detail what happened that day. "I remember we all dressed up," she said. "That was the last picket line I was ever on where we dressed up, a skirt and blouse and stockings and all that. And I remember that the people of the town were so hostile. There was a lot of, 'Go back to Russia' and that kind of stuff." Lynne later joined the Berkeley Free Speech Movement, did civil rights work in Mississippi, and went on to devote much of her life to "the movement."

Anna (Kimbrough) Morris remembers clearly how she came to walk the picket line and also what happened next. As Anna told the story, Liz Lynes (Hollander) ('61) and a bunch of other Bryn Mawrters "had gotten this group together, and they said, 'Come on!' I said, 'Okay, Okay.' They grabbed me by the scruff of my neck and there I go. Because I'm *expected to*. 'You're black, therefore . . . ' I look around, and none of the other black students were there."

Some weeks later, some students from SNCC came and spoke at Bryn Mawr. "They wanted to raise money," said Anna, "and I went around the dorms to raise money. This is when one girl in my dorm wouldn't even open her door! Now these were people who were wonderful, good friends. But they didn't want to deal with that. No one would come anywhere near me. So that's when dividing lines appeared that had never been there before. Being black was never an issue until it became a national issue, and then, of course, the activists on campus *made* it an issue."

Anna was born into a Mississippi sharecropping family as one of more than a dozen children, but raised as an only child by her uncle and aunt in Chicago. There she lived what she described as "a dual existence," moving between the white world of high school, where she was one of four black students selected for a special college-prep program, and the black world of her neighborhood, where she remembers lots of fun and parties, especially the music: R&B and doo-wop–the Dells, the Orioles, and the Moonglows, the Penguins, and the Five Satins.

Anna was very active–and of course very visible–when she first got to Bryn Mawr. She wrote the music for our Freshman Show and was elected as our class "songmistress." Wry humor was her style, with a lot of bravado. By the time of the Woolworth's demonstration, Anna already knew she would have to leave Bryn Mawr–her grades were too low and she lost her scholarship. For years after that she suffered under a burden of guilt–that she didn't complete Bryn Mawr, that her father had taken out loans for her to go there, that she wasn't good enough. Now, in retrospect, she sees it differently. "I was totally unprepared," she said, "on a lot of levels. Mostly I was too young, just seventeen. And once I got behind, I couldn't catch up. In high school, if you started falling back, somebody

"Being black was never an issue until it became a national issue, and then, of course, the activists on campus made it an issue.."

would come and . . . but at Bryn Mawr you were considered an adult—if you need help, you should be able to go and ask. I suffered in silence."

Picketing Woolworth's was central to Anna's life story because it was when everything began to change and new lines began to be drawn. Before that, Anna explained, "My color didn't make a difference; I was part of the body politic. I think that if the black students had made an issue of being the only four at Bryn Mawr and tried to be a lobby, it would have brought attention to us. People would have resented that. But the unfortunate thing about it is that the African-American students at Bryn Mawr, the students there of color, do need a support group. The white students have a club, and it's called 'white.' They don't realize it. They don't understand it."

Anna says she's always been more of an observer than a participant. "I had never felt disenfranchised, so when the civil rights movement took off, I couldn't generate the passion. Protesting and shouting and the rest of that—that's never been my kind of thing. Later, in the corporate world, I made changes in hiring policies. I made it my business to get people of color into jobs and to fight discrimination that way."

The *News* carried a front-page report on the Woolworth's demonstration, complete with photo and a banner headline: *Sixty-two Student Picketers Stand So That All May Sit* (Marion was especially pleased with the headline). In that same issue of the *News*, there was an article by Judy Stuart (Hohman) about racial discrimination in jobs and housing on the Main Line. Judy had gone out into communities on the Main Line, both black and white, and had talked with realtors and members of the minority community. She pointed out that, while African-Americans in the North could use public transportation, eat in public places and go to the movies, "the Negro who lives in Bryn Mawr or Ardmore is often denied rights even more basic in terms of our democratic ideals—the right to have a decent home and equal job opportunities." Judy discovered an urban renewal plan for the area right next to Haverford College, which would have the effect of forcing African-Americans living in the area to move, leaving their workplaces, schools, and churches, thus destroying the community. She ended the article with a plea from the Reverend Jones, minister of the Baptist Church in Ardmore: "Why don't we see more of Bryn Mawr girls? If they have a genuine interest in our problems, why don't they come down and help us, observe the mind, temperament and expression of our people and our problems?"

As far as I know, no one at Bryn Mawr took up the Reverend Jones on his invitation; we were all focused on supporting the struggle against racial discrimination in the South. No one quite remembers how Judy came to write the article.

Campus activists wanted to build on their success in the Woolworth's demonstration, to keep up the momentum. A two-part *News* editorial, with a new, urgent tone, called on Bryn Mawr students to help pass an all-college resolution condemning Southern violations of civil rights, and asked those students who opposed campus action to come forward and state their views.

At that point, Bryn Mawr president McBride summoned the leaders of student organizations to meet with her and other senior members of the administration. Betsy Levering (Morgan) was there in her capacity as president of the Arts Council, and Marion Coen (Katzive) as editor of the *News*. As Betsy told it, Miss McBride objected to the idea of a student resolution "on the grounds that, as Bryn Mawr students, we inevitably dragged the college into it (through the mud), and that this was unfair, since we were only a few students and the rest of the college community had not expressed its views on the issue. The President said we were, in effect, speaking for Bryn Mawr whether this was what we intended or not.

"I've often wondered whether the college administration ever got to the point of feeling some retrospective pride and ownership in that little demo," said Betsy. "Certainly there was nothing then of the commitment to the spirit of the civil rights movement that later came to play a real role on campus and that has left its stamp on the college. The first faint tremors of the earthquake to come had not yet disturbed the college's tranquil sense of its own rectitude (so superbly embodied by Miss McBride)."

Efforts to pass a college resolution did not succeed, and a letter to the editor signed by four seniors sharply condemned student action and *News* coverage of the civil rights issue. As the 1960 spring semester came to an end, so did the drive to get Bryn Mawr students *as a group* involved in the civil rights movement. But while the collegewide resolution had failed, the events of those few months, in the spring of 1960, had succeeded in bringing about a palpable shift in student attitudes. The seniors' letter was the last gasp of student generations of the fifties, with their "fetish for decorum" and "unwillingness to become actively involved." The *News* editorials in the spring of 1960 were the first breath of the new student generations of the sixties, beginning with a "new and revolutionary" understanding "that integration is our problem and action to affect it is *our* responsibility."

As we entered our junior year, in the fall of 1960, the campus was caught up in the Nixon-Kennedy presidential contest. None of us was old enough to vote—in those days twenty-one was the voting age—but we held our own election on campus. The class of '62 led the student body in support of the Kennedy-Johnson ticket, with 55 percent for Kennedy, 37 percent for Nixon, and 8 percent undecided. Several students went out and rented TV sets to watch the election returns, staying up all night until Kennedy squeaked through to a narrow victory.

Our senior year opened with the class of '62 in charge of all the major student organizations. Sue Johnson was president of "Self-Gov," and Barbara Paul (Robinson) was president of "Undergrad"—the two leading student government bodies in a hierarchy too complicated for even an insider to fathom—and both had just returned from a National Student Association (NSA) summer conference. NSA was a political and service organization, with a traditionally liberal slant, which dealt with student government functions. By 1961, they had become more activist, more engaged with national and international questions, taking positions, passing referenda, speaking out against the House Un-American Activities Committee, supporting Civil Rights and Freedom Rides, and condemning the denial of academic freedom under the Castro regime in Cuba. DuBrul, who spoke at the 1960 Yale colloquium, was typical of the new breed of NSA representative, outspoken and activist. For Sue Johnson, the NSA meeting was a real turning point: "I was stunned at what they were talking about, their attitude of challenging authority," said Sue. "Of course we had a strong student government, so it was an easy step to think of doing more. But it was a moment of 'Oh, My God! Everything is not okay!'" Back at Bryn Mawr, Sue called for "the reformulation and reanswering of basic questions" about student government.

Barbara wrote an article that appeared in the *News* at the start of our senior year. She noted that Bryn Mawr students were fortunate to live in an atmosphere where questions of academic and social freedoms were largely academic, where the caliber of scholarship was high in all quarters of the campus, and where the students were dedicated to that scholarship. She went on in a more critical vein, pointing out that "In the absence of pressing issues, the Bryn Mawr campus has settled down to a pleasantly friendly schedule of concentrated scholasticism, but it has lost some of the electricity of conflict." This showed how greatly attitudes had already changed at Bryn Mawr. It is hard to imagine a student leader from the fifties generation yearning for "the electricity of conflict." Barbara was tough and bright, competence personified, a skillful campus politician who knew how to get things done. When she came in as president of a new, more activist Undergrad, it was almost inevitable that she would have a few encounters with Bryn Mawr President, Katharine McBride.

Miss McBride frequently spoke out about national and international affairs. In our freshman year, Bryn Mawr was the first of only three colleges (with Haverford and Swarthmore) to stand up to a federal government demand that students sign a loyalty oath in order to receive federal student aid. Miss McBride testified before a U.S. Congressional committee in the spring of 1959, explaining that there was a bond of trust between the College and its students, and that requiring students to sign a loyalty oath would violate that trust. I remember feeling quite proud then of the College and of President McBride. I think she did trust individual students to have their own views and to make their own choices. As long as they stuck with the traditional issues of student government and student life, Miss McBride did not interfere. But she became very uncomfortable when students wanted to take up larger social and political issues, to speak out as a group, to demonstrate, or in any way to challenge her own authority as president. In her convocation address at the start of our senior year, Miss McBride urged us all to keep national and international crises "at the forefront of [our] thinking" during the coming year, citing the area of civil rights specifically. She could not have anticipated that the next "civil rights" challenge would come so soon and so uncomfortably close to home.

In early October, Barbara raised the question of relations between Bryn Mawr students and the college staff of maids and porters. At the time, almost all Bryn Mawr students were white, lived in spacious single rooms and suites, sat down every evening to a dinner served by maids, and knew maids and porters by their first names only. The maids and porters were older and black, some of them lived in cramped quarters under the eaves, and they addressed us by our last names, as Miss so-and-so. There was a Maids and Porters Committee, with student membership, which had the specific mission of addressing staff concerns and activities, and every year the maids and porters put on a musical show, like the Freshman and Junior class shows or the occasional faculty show.

When I asked Anna (Kimbrough) Morris whether she, as an African-American, had any particular feelings in relation to the maids and porters, her response was, "No. Mea culpa, mea culpa, mea ultima culpa. I guess, in the light of today, I should have. I don't know; they seemed happy." Anna thought for a moment, and then went on to explain: "I think it was because of the cloistered existence there, and because of the times. Black awareness, black power, black activism and all the movements that followed—none of that had happened yet. The maids and porters were just the maids and porters. It was the way it was. Eating family-style at dinner was the way it was. I've talked to students at other colleges that had cafeterias. Bryn Mawr was just totally different, period. But that was the way it was."

Like Anna, most of us hadn't really thought much about the situation of maids and porters at the college. It was Barbara who first made the connection between student support of civil rights in the South and the status of African-Americans on our own campus, and decided that the situation at Bryn Mawr was outdated and wrong. She focused on forms of address. The Undergrad Executive Board, under Barbara's leadership, approved a "recommendation," stating that "the manner of address between maids and porters and students should be consistent with that which governs any relationship between older and younger persons." But Undergrad hadn't consulted with anyone in the administration, to whom the maids and porters were directly responsible, and they hadn't polled any of the maids and porters to discover whether they wanted such a change. "I remember Beulah, the head honcho of Denbigh Hall, being furious," said one classmate. "It wasn't really a question of the maids and porters," said another. "They had good jobs. What it was about was us, and our way of relating to people." Finally, no one was quite sure what a "recommendation" from the Undergrad Executive Board meant, whether it was just an expression of opinion, a recommendation to the student body, or what. The *News* received a flurry of letters to the editor, with opinions pro, con, and confused.

The Undergrad action opened up the whole question of the maids and porters system at Bryn Mawr. Students requested a meeting with Miss McBride and prepared a list of probing questions on hiring, working, and living conditions. Later, things began to go off track. Students suggested that they might be paid to work in the halls, and some of the maids and porters began to worry that their jobs were in danger. (The maids and porters system was phased out a few years later, and many of the maids and porters did lose their jobs.) Eventually the Undergrad recommendation was rejected.

While this particular initiative didn't go anywhere, it started an accelerating process of change on campus. It was the beginning of student activism and a new willingness to question authority. It pushed Bryn Mawr into the sixties. And it launched the class of '62 into the world.

Part II
Navigating the Sixties

Chapter Three

The Sixties (and Seventies): Turbulence and Change

The fifties were our teenage years, a peculiarly dark, inward era when nothing public ever seemed to happen. Then the sixties burst out in living color–like going from Kansas to the land of Oz–full of gaudy characters and outrageous happenings. Suddenly there was an enormous sense of possibility. We felt a seismic shift, even within the cloistered confines of Bryn Mawr. In April of 1960, the Woolworth's demonstration nudged us, stumbling, across the great cultural divide between the passive fifties and the activist sixties. By September, we were in the waning months of the Eisenhower era. In November, John F. Kennedy was elected president.

Josie Donovan was in Geneva, Switzerland, on a junior year abroad when Kennedy was elected. She followed the campaign from a distance, with mounting excitement, a flurry of letters going back and forth between Geneva and Bryn Mawr. "I've always felt that the sixties largely resulted from the Kennedy election," said Josie, "from that sense of heightened expectation that Kennedy brought, those dreams of changing the world and having a real, practical impact on politics."

"I remember hearing Kennedy's call: *Ask not what your country can do for you,*" one classmate told me. "I wanted to be a player, to make a difference." Several from our class were inspired to join the Peace Corps. Others entered law school. I joined the foreign service of the U.S. Information Agency, then headed by Edward R. Murrow, the great CBS radio and TV newsman, who broadcast from London during World War II, and later stood up to political bully, Senator Joe McCarthy.

History seemed to speed up in the sixties. In August of 1963, a crowd of more than 200,000 heard "the melodious and melancholy voice of the Reverend Dr. Martin Luther King, Jr. crying out his dreams to the multitude."[1] A month later, four little black girls were killed in a church bombing in Birmingham, Alabama. Riots followed. In November, President Kennedy was shot and killed in Dallas. We had gone from dreams to despair in a span of less than six months.

Everyone in our class remembers where she was when she heard of Kennedy's assassination. I was in Moulmein, Burma, and got the report by word of mouth. I was sure, at first, that my Burmese friends had it wrong, that it must be some other country, some other president who was shot.

Kennedy's death shattered our world. It marked the end of "our" sixties, that innocent optimism, that sense that we were all on the same side, fighting for social and racial justice, working together to create a better world. After Kennedy's death, things got much more complicated, in American politics and in our own lives.

In the summer of '64, a thousand white volunteers, most of them college students, headed south to join the Mississippi Freedom Summer, inspired and organized by black students from SNCC. The Mississippi Freedom Summer was the spark for all the great social revolutions that followed—the student movement, the antiwar movement, the women's movement, and the gay and lesbian rights movement.

At the University of California, Berkeley, in the fall of '64, everybody was talking about free speech. Students were tired of being talked about; they wanted to speak for themselves, to be heard and taken seriously. Of all the causes of the sixties, free speech was perhaps the purest, the most elemental. The Greek philosopher Diogenes called freedom of speech *the most beautiful thing in the world.* Free Speech Movement (FSM) leader Mario Savio said that freedom of speech, for him, represented "the very dignity of what a human being is ... what marks us off from the stones and the stars ... the thing that marks us as just below the angels."[2] The Berkeley Free Speech Movement became the prototype for other student movements of the sixties, in Europe as well as the United States. They all shared the same anti-authoritarian spirit and the same essential demand for free speech.

All of us were touched in some way by the revolutions of the sixties, and almost all of us participated in *something* along the way. One classmate played a key role in the FSM at Berkeley, and went south to Mississippi in the summer of '65 as a SNCC volunteer in the voting rights campaign. But we were a little older than the "sixties generation" of college students who sang and marched in antiwar protests. We were well into our twenties by then, busy with graduate study, jobs, and young children, most of us too cautious to want to abandon all that and join the revolution.

Experiencing the sixties was largely a matter of being in the right place at the right time, and oddly enough, for a rather quiescent, bookish group, many of the class of '62 did end up being in at least some of the right times and places. Not so surprising, really. After Bryn Mawr, a large number of classmates headed off to first jobs in Washington, D.C., or New York or to university campuses for graduate study or law school—Yale, Harvard, Columbia, the University of Chicago, and especially UC Berkeley and UW–Madison—all the hot spots of the sixties. A couple of classmates even found themselves in Paris in the spring of 1968, at the height of the student rebellion there, again not so surprising for women who were part of a small academic elite.

In the spring of 1968, student rebellions were breaking out all across the world—in Japan, Mexico, Czechoslovakia, and in all the countries of Western Europe. Classmate Helen (Rodnite) Lemay was a graduate student in Paris at the time of *les événements.* "The change in the city made quite an impression on me," she said. "Police and soldiers lined the streets; they sat around in buses all day. It felt like a military occupation. I remember taking the Metro one evening when tear gas had wafted down into the subway. We all came out with our eyes burning and watery."

The movement reached its climax on May 10, the "night of the barricades." Dany Cohn-Bendit, who was a student leader at Nanterre University at the time, described what happened: "It's a moment I shall never forget," he said. "Suddenly, spontaneously, barricades were being thrown up in the streets. People were building up the cobblestones because they wanted—many of them for the first time—to throw themselves into a collective, spontaneous activity. People were releasing all their repressed feelings, expressing them in a festive spirit. Thousands felt the need to communicate with each other, to love one another. That night has made

Paris 1968: *Be young and shut up!*

me forever optimistic about history. Having lived through it, I can't ever say, 'It will never happen . . . '"[3] Students in Paris carried a banner reading, "Long Live Imagination."

In America, the student movement was focused on ending the war in Vietnam, and Students for a Democratic Society (SDS) emerged as the leading student organization. SDS had its roots in the civil rights movement—Tom Hayden, from the original University of Michigan chapter, worked with SNCC in Mississippi in 1964—and made the connection between civil rights, the war in Vietnam, and students' own lives. By 1968, like their counterparts in Europe, American students saw themselves as a revolutionary movement, wanting not just an end to the war, but a whole new society.

The student antiwar movement attracted more and more allies from among first-wave feminists and the peace movement, including a number of women from Bryn Mawr. More than four hundred Bryn Mawr alumnae signed onto a full-page statement, protesting the war in Vietnam, which appeared in the Sunday *New York Times* on April 7, 1968. The heading was in Latin: *atque ubi solitudinem faciunt pacem appellant* . . . . Then, at the very bottom of the page, in exceedingly small letters, a translation: "they make a desolation and they call it peace . . . ." Tacitus, *Agricola* —just in case any *Times* readers might be a little weak in Latin. The text reads, in part:

> *We, the undersigned alumnae of Bryn Mawr College . . . join the rising thousands throughout the country who protest, on grounds of morality, and in the interests of world peace and security, our government's presence and policies in Vietnam.*
>
> *This is a war we cannot win, politically or militarily. We can only 'make a desolation and call it peace.'*

The classical reference, the reasoned analysis, the protest "on grounds of morality and in the interests of world peace"—all these come out of a Bryn Mawr tradition of principled objection, and call to mind the college's Quaker roots and the long history of Quaker women in the peace movement. Signatories are listed by class, starting with the class of 1896, a stirring roll call down through the generations, the class of '62 well represented with thirty-four signatories, including many of the women who appear in this book.

The reasoned argument of the Bryn Mawr alumnae petition and the grassroots democracy and direct action of the student movement were both rooted in a peculiarly American faith in participatory democracy. That faith was badly shaken by the assassination of Martin Luther King in April (and Bobby Kennedy in June) of 1968. "It seemed like there was nobody left," said classmate Isa (Brannon) Spencer. "During the sixties, you felt there were people who were going to lead us out of all this. And then we began to realize it's not about people; nobody is going to do it for you. You're going to have to do it yourself."

In August 1968, the Democratic Party held its national convention in Chicago. Students from various SDS factions went to Chicago to demonstrate against the Vietnam War. Others were there as part of a small countercultural group called the "Yippies" (Youth International Party), led by Abbie Hoffman and Jerry Rubin. People came to Chicago with a lot of different agendas–some to show their support for antiwar presidential candidate Eugene McCarthy, some to protest the war, some to conduct absurdist street theater. ("Rise up and abandon the creeping meatball!" was one Yippie slogan.) No one expected Mayor Richard J. Daley, Chicago's Democratic political boss, and the police forces under his command, to react the way they did. Just as delegates were voting to nominate Hubert Humphrey for president, the police launched a brutal attack on a peaceful street demonstration. We were among the millions across America who saw this live on television–the roll-call vote inside the hall and the riot outside in the streets. It showed a side of American politics that was vicious and violent. After Chicago, many students lost their hope of ending the war through electoral politics.

By the end of 1968, most of the student movements had run their course. The French general elections in June brought a sweeping victory by General Charles de Gaulle and his followers. In August, the Soviets invaded Czechoslovakia, crushing the new democracy that had been born in the Prague Spring. In Mexico, where a mass movement of students had sprung up in July, an October massacre by the police and the army left three hundred students dead. In America, SDS had splintered into

Marxist and Maoist factions, and SNCC had been taken over by Black Power separatists. To many activists, "the movement" seemed dead.

As the old civil rights and student movements disintegrated, there were already signs of something new. In January 1968, a group from Women's Strike for Peace (WSP), calling themselves the Jeannette Rankin Brigade (named after a congresswoman who voted against U.S. entry into both world wars), organized a rally in Washington to protest the Vietnam War. These were mostly "older" women, in their thirties and forties, married, with children. Their idea was to rally masses of women, mothers and housewives, to persuade members of Congress to withdraw their support for U.S. involvement in Vietnam. A group of younger women, calling themselves the New York Radical Feminists (NYRF), got word of the plans for an antiwar rally, and decided to give the event a more radical, feminist twist. The NYRF group sent out black-bordered invitations to a "Burial of Traditional Womanhood" at Arlington Cemetery, conducted a mock burial, and read out a funeral oration: "We must bury Submission alongside Aggression," they said.[4] It was the start of a new movement with a flamboyant, media-savvy style. A few months later, the Sunday *New York Times Magazine* ran an article titled "What do these women want? The Second Feminist Wave." Next, the NYRF and other radical feminist groups organized a protest demonstration at the Miss America Pageant in Atlantic City. They shouted and carried placards, and threw girdles, high heels, and bras into a trash can. The media were there in force, and started the myth of bra burning.

On June 28, 1969, the police raided the Stonewall Inn, a gay bar in New York's Greenwich Village, a routine occurrence. But this time, the people at the bar fought back. This time, the story wouldn't die. A few days later, *The Village Voice* carried two front-page articles on the June 28 riots. A year later, in June of 1970, the first gay pride marches took place—two thousand marched in New York, twelve hundred in Los Angeles, and a few hundred in four or five other American cities. By the following year, there were gay pride celebrations in London and Paris. Stonewall sparked a revolution. After that, gays and lesbians began to insist on being seen and heard, to demand equal rights.

The last year of the sixties was a year of endings and beginnings, the year of Woodstock, "women's lib," and Stonewall—the last big celebration of the hippies and the year that the women's movement and the gay rights movement caught fire. By the early seventies, the first feminist books were out. Before long, there were women's studies programs, feminist bookstores, women's health clinics, and shelters for battered women. The seventies were an exciting period of institution building, led by women, when the ideas of the sixties were spread and absorbed throughout the country.

Classmates Sue Johnson and Josie Donovan were both graduate students at the University of Wisconsin at Madison through much of the SDS-led antiwar movement in the late sixties. In the seventies, Sue was part of a group of women building new feminist institutions in Duluth, Minnesota, while Josie was at the University of Kentucky at Lexington, creating some of the first women's studies courses.

Susan ("Sue") Johnson–There Wasn't a Dyke in the Land

Sue Johnson remembers growing up in the fifties, living a secret life as a lesbian and feeling all alone. It was not until 1973 that Jill Johnston's *Lesbian Nation* finally broke the silence, speaking out about the experience of being a lesbian, celebrating women loving women, and talking about a whole community, a whole nation, of lesbians. *Lesbian Nation* has a chapter

SUSAN ELEANOR JOHNSON

about that long, lonely time growing up in the fifties and sixties, when "there wasn't a dyke in the land." "It wasn't really until the mid-seventies that people talked about lesbianism," said Sue. "That's just been very, very freeing, for me and for everybody else who's gay or lesbian. It's made us visible, we can claim legitimacy and we can advocate for ourselves, instead of being hidden and secret." She paused. "And that's just *breathtaking* to somebody like me who, of course, grew up with a lot of internalized homophobia because of the era in which I was growing up."

Sue and I converged at Bryn Mawr at a college reunion in May of 1998, she from Anchorage, Alaska, and I from New York City. We soon found a quiet place to talk, perched on folding chairs under one of the spacious yellow-and-white-striped tents, which had been staked out on the great lawn ready for the next day's events. I hadn't seen Sue since we graduated, and she still looked much as I remembered her, the same short-cropped hair, open, Midwestern face, and sturdy, athletic form. There's never been any cynicism about Sue.

"There were definite signs that Sue was probably lesbian, but who even thought about it?"

As a child, she became a big fan of women's baseball, rooting for the Rockford Peaches; in junior high she was smitten with rock 'n' roll, and at Bryn Mawr, she just took it all in.

Later, I looked at the candid photo that Sue had picked out for the class of '62 Yearbook, the one where she's wearing jeans, a leather motorcycle jacket and cap, and striking a defiant Marlon Brando pose, thumbs hooked into her pockets. How could we not have guessed that Sue was lesbian? I talked with another classmate, Mary Beebe, who was a good friend of Sue's at Bryn Mawr. "It's amazing to me, but we didn't know," she said. "I spent so much time with Sue Johnson, and we were part of a gang. . . . We used to tease Sue about when she was a *little boy*. There were definite signs that she was probably lesbian, but who even *thought* about it? It amazes me now that it didn't even occur to us. But if it had occurred to me, would we have talked about it? The subject just wasn't ever brought up. As close as we all were as friends . . . looking back on it, it just seems sort of amazing that we didn't at least talk about it."

Sue was a lesbian in her heart when she came to Bryn Mawr, but so completely closeted that she didn't try to find anybody else at the college who might be lesbian. "I didn't even spend very much time thinking about it," she said. "I was so far from actually *doing* anything about it that even thinking about it seemed dangerous." It would be hard to imagine Sue leading a secret, underground life as a lesbian. She was outgoing, visible, did a lot of sports and other student activities, was elected head of student self-government. "I wasn't an underground person," she said, "and that made it even harder to conceive of doing some underground sort of thing. So that worked against my finding other lesbians." All of this may have been completely irrelevant—as far as Sue knows there *were* no active lesbians at Bryn Mawr at that time. Even now, she knows of only one other lesbian who was with us at college, and she only recently found out about her.

When we were at Bryn Mawr, nobody, except perhaps close confidantes, really knew or cared whether you dated or had a sex life. Sue would have had an especially hard time being at a place where there was explicit pressure to be heterosexual. "I did very much appreciate the fact that you didn't have to date at Bryn Mawr," said Sue, "and that was perfectly okay, you didn't have to explain yourself or anything." She paused, then went on. "Actually I did date some. That was my period when I was doing everything. But you didn't have to care about it, right? It was perfectly okay to go through the motions." We both laughed.

Sue's decision to come to a women's college didn't have anything to do with being a lesbian, or at least that wasn't something she thought about when she made the choice. What interested her about Bryn Mawr was the athletics program; sports were very important to her at the time, and she knew that the college had a good varsity athletics program. (That was news to me. I had always thought of Bryn Mawr as supremely *un*athletic.) A competitive swimmer from a public school in the Midwest (three points in her favor), Sue always thought that was what got her into Bryn Mawr. It turned out to be a good choice. "Bryn Mawr was a fabulous place for me," said Sue. "It just completely worked for me, without driving me crazy as it did some people. I could do it." Still, coming from a public high school in Rockford, Illinois, to Bryn Mawr, was a major challenge. Sue remembers her very first day on campus: "Kitsey Cushman and Laning Pepper were

"Bryn Mawr gave us the support of a kind of old-school feminism, like what your mother does, telling you that you're terrific."

walking—I didn't know who they were yet—but they were walking in front of me on campus and they were discussing art history. I thought, Oh My God, *how* am I going to keep up in *this* scene?" She worked harder at Bryn Mawr than ever before in her life, Sue said, and, at the end of it, she felt a strong sense of intellectual independence and self-confidence. Bryn Mawr also gave her the support of a kind of old-school feminism, "like what your mother does," said Sue, "telling you that you're terrific."

Sue's family was highly educated, the women as well as the men, going back several generations. All of her grandparents went to college; there's a story in her family about her great-great-grandfather riding on horseback all the way from Illinois to Pennsylvania to deliver his daughter, Sue's great-grandmother, to school. It was always assumed that Sue would go to college, and although she's the first in her family to get a PhD, both parents had master's degrees, and her brother has a business degree.

Sue had been accepted into the sociology graduate program at Harvard for the fall semester following her graduation from Bryn Mawr, and went home to Rockford for the summer. At that point, feeling exhausted from the pressure to perform at college, she made the mistake of going to see the family psychiatrist. "I told him that I didn't want to be a lesbian anymore," said Sue, "and he, being a traditional kind of psychiatrist, took me at my word, which was absurd!" That was when she first told her parents about being a lesbian, in a context that made it easy for them, because she was presumably trying to get over it. "But of course that didn't take," said Sue. "The psychiatrist was very weird. He told me that, if I read another book, I would go crazy. I was tired and kind of miserable then, but I don't think it was anything that some nice chatting and a couple of weeks of sleep wouldn't have solved." She withdrew from Harvard and spent that year living at home with her parents, made an effort to date men ("It was horrible, horrible!") and worked in Rockford, first at a TV station and then at Rockford College.

After almost a year in Rockford, Sue fell in love with a woman who herself was a lesbian. Then she felt less alone. Before that, she'd always been falling in love with straight women, or women who were going to become straight. "That *never* works and always turns out to be a horrible experience," said Sue. "A lot of people in my era did that." Finding a potential partner who was *also* a lesbian gave Sue the strength to work her way out of the psychiatrist's office. At that point her parents had to come to terms with the fact that she actually was a lesbian. "They were very uncomfortable with it," she said, "though they're good Unitarians and knew they were supposed to be tolerant."

That summer, Sue drove up to Madison, where she was able to get a late admission to the University of Wisconsin graduate program in sociology, on the strength of having studied medical sociology at Bryn Mawr. "They *loved* that at Wisconsin," said Sue. She entered UW–Madison in the fall of '63, and was there when the sixties happened. "That was *wild,*" she remembered, "a distinct turning point in my political life. In fact, it was a really lucky thing that I didn't get to go to Harvard. Harvard would have been much duller, I do believe. Wisconsin was wild and wonderful."

In 1963, Madison, Wisconsin, billed itself as "the all-American town," the "best place to live in America," a city with no industry really, but the vital combination of the university and state government. UW–Madison attracted an unusual mix of students and faculty, many of them from outside Wisconsin and quite political. The history department, in particular, was known as leftist, and had been targeted by McCarthy in the fifties. In the sixties, UW–Madison had the largest percentage of Jewish students of any Big Ten university, including very sophisticated, radical students from New York and Chicago. The first student demonstration against U.S. involvement in Vietnam occurred in mid-October of 1963, just after Sue arrived on campus. But it was after the U.S. bombed North Vietnam, in February of 1965, that the demonstrations really picked up. The Committee to End the War in Vietnam was formed then, a highly mobile, politically sophisticated group that grew out of Students for a Democratic Society. In the spring and summer of '66, there were Vietnam War hearings and draft card burnings. Finally, more than a thousand students took over a UW administration building. While the immediate targets were the draft and the Vietnam War, SDS was also trying to build a mass movement, a whole counterculture. There was a sense of community, of doing things together. (By this time, there were also some defections, black students who were more interested in participating in the Black Power movement.)

By 1967, the whole campus was becoming much more radical. As one activist pointed out, "Once you've carried a sign, once you've taken a step, it's easier the next time." It started when nice, white, middle-class girls, carrying picket signs in the streets of Madison, had people spitting at them, telling them to "go back to Russia where you belong." Then, in October of 1967, there were the "Dow Demonstrations," protesting against Dow Chemical recruiters on campus. (Dow manufactured napalm for use in the war.) The campus police called for reinforcements, and the Madison police came up fast, swinging their billy clubs. They started using tear gas. Suddenly all these privileged students were being tear-gassed and clubbed.

After the Dow episode, and throughout the following spring, the student movement turned into a broader community movement against the war, in the city of Madison and in the state. The presidential candidacy of Eugene McCarthy started in Wisconsin, and it was the Wisconsin delegation to the Democratic Convention in Chicago that took the lead in trying to stop the convention and relocate it. By 1969, both sides were becoming more militant. The police went to break up a block party at the Mifflin Street community, in Madison. They arrested people, and that led to tear gas, barricades, burning, and rubble. (It turned out that the FBI had been working undercover for at least a year to subvert the New Left, and Mifflin Street was one of its targets.) Finally, the governor sent in Wisconsin National Guard troops to occupy the UW–Madison campus.

At this point, Sue was already far enough along in her graduate work to be teaching a class in social organization. "It was *so easy* to teach," she said. "You didn't have to make the abstract point that there's *power* behind these social arrangements that we all just kinda politely go along with, there's power behind it. All you had to do was look out the window. The National Guard was occupying our campus. There was a tank! They were there armed, with bayonets! Fixed bayonets! It was absurd!" After that, Sue was out in the streets, along with everyone else.

"For people of our age," she said, "if you were in the right place at the right time, the sixties were wonderful! They were very radicalizing. They pushed us. Oh, they definitely did." And what a time it was! There were *waves* of social movements—the civil rights movement, the anti–Vietnam War movement, feminism, and then gay and lesbian rights. Sue was the right age and in the right places to catch them all. "There have been four waves of movements that I've been able to be a part of," she said, with emotion. "It's just wonderful! And I miss it, I *really* miss it."

Around 1965, Sue fell in love with a woman who was a recent widow—her husband had just been killed in an automobile accident. "She had been happily married," said Sue. "She didn't have any internalized homophobia, because she hadn't *been* a lesbian before she fell in love with me. So she just thought it was the most wonderful, fabulous thing to be a lesbian, and she wanted to tell *everybody*." Sue laughed. "I thought, 'Oh God, you're *kidding* me!' But she helped me let go of a lot of that internalized homophobia. Because she didn't *have* it, she wasn't reinforcing it in me." Sue and "Carrie" were together for ten years, the first five in Madison and the last five in Duluth, Minnesota. It was during these years with Carrie that Sue found her identity as a lesbian feminist. She had always been a lesbian and fiercely pro-woman, but it wasn't until then that her lesbian and feminist convictions merged.

Carrie and Sue had grown up together in Rockford, Illinois; Carrie was older than Sue by about a year. Both their families are Unitarian and their mothers knew one another. Carrie came to Sue's third birthday party, and in high school, they were part of the same group, though not close personal friends. When they fell in love in Madison in the mid-sixties, it was a time when lesbians were just beginning to find one another, to feel connected to a larger lesbian community. There was a feeling of belonging to some sort of secret society, a kind of lesbian tribalism. Sue and Carrie became friends with a group of lesbians, all graduate students at the university.

In 1970, they moved to Duluth, Minnesota, where both got jobs at the University of Minnesota–Duluth's new medical school, with Sue teaching medical sociology and Carrie in administration. In the seventies, Duluth was a wonderful place to be a lesbian. There was a strong lesbian community and a group of women, both lesbian and straight, who were activists, institution builders. "It was fabulous," said Sue, "a *hugely* exciting period that came straight out of the sixties. I loved it. We were building free clinics, women's centers, and this and that." Some of the people involved had jobs at UM–Duluth, but the institutions they built were all outside, independent of the university. In fact, the university stood against the whole lesbian-feminist agenda; there was a big fight to get a room at the university for gays and lesbians to meet, and Carrie was eventually fired for being too much of an activist. Duluth was always just a step behind the Twin Cities of Minneapolis/St. Paul. By that time, in the early seventies, "the cities" had everything, a whole separate lesbian/feminist world. There were bars where you could meet other lesbians, and a free women's health clinic. (Carrie started a second one in Duluth.) Amazon, the oldest feminist bookstore in the country, was then just starting up in someone's house, and one of the first battered women's shelters opened in St. Paul in 1973.

One day, shortly after arriving in Duluth, Sue was sitting in her office at the university, and a woman knocked on her door. "She came in," said Sue, "and we began this weird conversation. I couldn't figure out whether she was a student or a faculty person; I couldn't figure out what she was doing there. After about twenty minutes of this, I suddenly realized that we were having what we call a 'code conversation.' She was trying to figure out if I was a lesbian, and trying to tell me that she was one, but without saying the words, just in case I might be offended or scared or something." Every semester, this woman would look through the list of new faculty, and if there were single women on that list, she would go and knock on their doors, just the way she did with Sue. She was looking for lesbians to be part of the whole institution-building enterprise. She'd been there quite a few years, and knew everybody, and that was all it took for Sue to get connected. These women did a lot of wonderful work in Duluth, and some of those institutions still exist. "It was the real fruition of sixties radicalism," said Sue, "the continuation of the idea that politics are important and that you can change the world."

Sue and Carrie joined a lesbian consciousness-raising group in Duluth. They began talking with a group of lesbian friends about forming a collective and living together, and rented an island in the boundary waters (up near the Canadian border) with two houses on it, a place where they could go to be together. Carrie once sat down and counted, and figured out that they knew at least a hundred and fifty lesbians, all across the Midwest. There was an active network of lesbians, and news traveled by word of mouth—a huge change from the time when lesbians, like Sue, felt all alone.

Toward the end of her time in Duluth, Sue wrote, "If you had asked me fifteen years ago (1962) what was most special to me about myself, I would have said, 'I'm intelligent.' Had you asked me the same question five years ago (1972), I would have answered, 'I'm a woman.' Ask me now (1977), and 'I'll tell you, 'I'm a Lesbian.' Through the security of long love that I see as my third coming out, I learned Lesbian pride."[5]

The next big turning point for Sue came when she published her book, *Staying Power,* the first nationwide study of long-term lesbian couples who had been together ten years or more. In 1985, Sue had just gotten together with a new partner (her current partner, Connie—they themselves now qualify as a long-term couple), and they went off together to the University of Hawaii for Connie to do graduate work. "I thought we were going on our honeymoon," said Sue, "but she seemed to think she should *work* on her graduate program." So Sue started thinking, "Man, what am I going to do with myself? I'm married to this person who likes to work really hard and now she's off! I've been abandoned." At around that time, she came across a book called *Married People: Staying Together in the Age of Divorce,* which of course was about heterosexual couples. As she read, Sue began thinking, 'Somebody ought to write a book like this for lesbian couples.' That was as far as the idea went. Then she started out on another tangent. She looked back at her own history of two long-term relationships—ten years and nine years—and began to worry. The evidence showed she had considerable staying power, but her relationships didn't keep going on and on; they weren't permanent. And she thought, "God, I'm with this perfect person, but given both our histories, how are we ever going to stay together?" That was when she decided to go and talk to the experts, lesbian couples who had stayed together, and ask them how they did it. That was the motivation for her book.

University women's studies programs were flourishing at the end of the eighties, and the National Women's Studies Association (NWSA) annual conference was an important event, with an extensive program, and lots of publishers there. Sue and her partner attended one of these NWSA annual meetings just as Sue was beginning to look for a publisher for her book. At this point she'd done some of the research, but hadn't yet written a word. Her partner went up to the Naiad Press (a lesbian press) booth and told Barbara Grier, the publisher, about Sue's idea. "Oh," said Grier, "send her over." So Sue went over, stuck out her hand, and said, "Hi, I'm Susan Johnson. I'm the person doing a study of long-term lesbian

"You discover that there are all these people who love you, who don't want you to die, who want to help you."

couples." And Grier said ("I always cry when I tell this story," says Sue.) "Hi, I'm Barbara Grier. I'm the person who wants to publish your book." That was it, and that was wonderful, said Sue, because then she knew that the book would be published, and she knew who the audience would be.

For almost thirty years, Sue's parents had been quite uncomfortable with her being a lesbian, though polite about it. That all changed in 1990 when she published her book. "That did it for my parents," said Sue. "All of a sudden the fact that I had written a book about it made the whole thing wonderful. It legitimized it. And that was the point at which they came out as the parents of a lesbian. My father would tell his men's group at the retirement community about his daughter and her book. It was a *big* turning point in my relationship with them." "Of course it might have had the opposite effect," I said. "Yes," said Sue. It could have been: 'Oh God, now it's all public, this is terrible, at least it was private before!' It might have been exactly the opposite reaction." We both laughed, and she went on: "I think it's a mark of how committed they are to learning and to books, and to that form of expression."

On April 25, 1995, Sue was diagnosed with breast cancer. "A diagnosis like that ... All of a sudden it's *Bam*, from one moment to the next. There's a huge shift," she said, "a before and after. The person that I was before this happened seems like a different person. The thing you've lost is that innocence, which is kind of a happy feeling, a really nice feeling, and you just don't have it anymore. You don't take anything for granted anymore. It makes you forever grateful for life."

After her lumpectomy, Sue went through *very* intensive chemotherapy—nineteen weeks doing a six-day-a-week protocol—and then after chemo, there was radiation. The whole process took from April 25, 1995, the day of her diagnosis, until December 12 of that year, when she completed her treatment. Connie (Sue's partner) did massive research on breast cancer, informing herself about all the special characteristics of Sue's case. "She had her wits about her," said Sue. "She had to read all that stuff. I don't know how she did it. She was fabulous, just wonderful. I was too scared." Terrible as it was, Sue also found much about her experience with breast cancer that was quite wonderful.

You're fighting for your life," she said. "You're really focused. If you didn't have a spiritual life—which being a born Unitarian, I more or less didn't have—you get one. Even light candles. And you meditate. You do everything. You just pull out all the stops. A friend's mother who was raised Catholic had everyone lighting candles for me. Fine! Good! Excellent! I'm not going to pick and choose. This is not the time to be particular. Anyone who had any help for me, man, I was going to do it. And that's a wonderful feeling. You also discover that there are all these people who love you, who don't want you to die, who want to help you.

Sue was living in Anchorage, Alaska, at the time. One day she was in a women's bookstore there, telling the two women who owned it about the diagnosis. Another lesbian woman, someone Sue knew only slightly, was there in the bookstore listening to the story. "She called me up later that same day," said Sue, "and she said, 'Susan, I would feel . . . I'm retired. I would feel it an honor if you'd let me, once a week, come and take you wherever you need to go, do whatever it is you need to have done. I would just feel wonderful about that.' Out of the blue. You get on these waves of love and concern and caring, and find help that you didn't know was there."

Josephine ("Josie") Donovan: "I had to take a stand"

Josie had finished her master's degree and was teaching at the University of Kentucky at Lexington in the spring of 1970, when Ohio National Guard troops shot and killed four student protesters at Kent State University. That was a big moment in the student antiwar movement, and campuses across America erupted in outrage. At the University of Kentucky, student demonstrations and confrontations with the police went on for two or three days. Then Kentucky Governor Louie B. Nunn decided to bring in the National Guard, fully armed, guns

JOSEPHINE CAMPBELL DONOVAN

loaded with live ammunition, bayonets mounted. "These were just kids that were in the National Guard," said Josie, "nineteen-, twenty-year-old Kentucky kids. They didn't know anything, had no idea how to handle those guns, so it was a scary situation." One day, Josie and about twenty other protesters were left standing, rather defiantly, out in a field near the student center. They saw a line of National Guardsmen moving toward them across the field, all wearing gas masks with tanks of gas strapped on their backs, carrying spray guns with long, tubular nozzles. "They came marching up," Josie said, "and we just stood there. Then they came at us, as if they were spraying insects." They shot out the tear gas full blast, aiming high and straight at them. It was a very toxic gas, of a type banned by the Geneva Convention. "The gas hits you in the face and then you run," said Josie. "So we ran, but then we circled back right away, and in ten minutes we were back there."

A photographer from the *Louisville Courier-Journal* caught the whole tear-gassing incident on film. "The next day, there I am on the front page," said Josie. "It's from the back, so you can't see my face, but there's no question it's me. At the time, I never had any thought about my position but, in retrospect, I was playing with fire, as far as keeping my job there. They could easily have gotten rid of me. I didn't have tenure, and it was certainly easy to identify me in that picture."

During the confrontation, a guardsman aimed his nozzle directly at Josie, coming within about eight feet. She felt no fear, she said. "I learned that about myself. These guys were coming at me with their bazookas and whatnot, and I just felt a tremendous rage, that this was completely wrong. There was something absolute about it. Being right there, face to face, there was no time to worry or fuss. You just had to stand there, and that was it. I felt completely that it was the right thing to do, and I felt comfortable doing it. I never had any trouble with that." She paused, and then added, "There are some things I wouldn't have liked. I wouldn't have liked being arrested. I wouldn't have enjoyed going to jail, and I never did [go], although many of my friends did. I just happened to avoid it. And I never would have used violence myself. I didn't approve of violence."

Josie was a pacifist from early on. Her father, an army doctor, was taken prisoner by the Japanese during World War II. Josie was only four years old when he came back, but she still remembers hearing those firsthand stories of atrocities. From 1953 to 1956, she lived with her family in Germany. That experience of being in Germany during the Occupation–the abandoned concentration camps and the terrible bomb damage–left a deep impression. "I've always felt that our generation was very much affected by World War II," said Josie. "I personally felt really haunted by the war and especially by the Holocaust."

In Switzerland during her junior year abroad, Josie felt that same tremendous sense of the war still hanging over things. There was nobody there who hadn't been affected by the war in one way or another. "I think in many ways that the knowledge of World War II horrors has been the motivating force in my life," she said, "certainly politically. It gave me the feeling that I *had* to take a stand against what I saw as political evil. Temperamentally, I don't think I'm inclined to be that political. I was pushed in that direction because of the historical period I lived in."

Like many of our generation, Josie spent her earliest years in a women-headed household, consisting of her mother and grandmother, while her father was away at war. "Our first awareness," said Josie, "was of competent women managing perfectly well without men."

Her mother went to Bryn Mawr (Josephine Devigne, class of '38), and that is the main reason that Josie went there. Her mother was, in many ways, more French than American; she went through school in France, a brilliant student, graduating from the lycée in Paris with an *A Prim. Philosophe*. After the rigorous French schools, Bryn Mawr seemed comparatively easy, and Josie's mother was very happy there. A couple of weeks after graduation, she met Josie's father, got married, and, as Josie tells it, that was the end of the story.

Josie herself was not happy at Bryn Mawr, especially at the beginning, and that created a bit of a problem with her mother, who had such positive feelings about the College. Years later, when she read Sylvia Plath's novel *The Bell Jar* for the first time, Josie felt a shock of recognition. That was what it was like for her, in those early years at Bryn Mawr, that sense of suffocation, caught under a dome of glass where she couldn't breathe. "I felt sort of alien there," she said. "I think it was too British, too tweedy, too something." She thought for a moment, then went on, "We didn't value other women," she said. "There was always this sense that the real action, the real excitement, was somewhere else, 'where the boys were' (so to speak). There was a devaluation because it was all girls, 'just a girls' school.'"

Josie lived in Rhoads Hall, where she soon found a few kindred spirits who were interested in politics, and this little group of five or six, almost all of them freshmen, started hanging out in the "typing smoker" in the Rhoads basement. "We all smoked like crazy," Josie remembered. "Oh God! There was just a haze of smoke in that typing smoker. We all spent our entire life there, smoking and playing bridge. We were very politically aware; I think that's why we were drawn to each other. By sophomore year, we'd all gotten rooms on the same floor. We kind of ran that whole corridor, and hardly anyone else used the typing smoker where we camped out."

The typing smoker group had their own song, which someone's father had picked up during World War II, "a totally dumb song," sung to the tune of *Stars and Stripes Forever.* It goes like this: *Hurrah for the George Junior High. It's the best junior high in Toledo. The boys and the girls are so fine. They are really a wonderful group.* "It became our anthem," Josie said, "a sort of anti-anthem. Everyone else would be singing *Thou gracious inspiration* (the official Bryn Mawr song), and we'd start *Hurrah for the George Junior High.*" Since then, the song has taken on layers of symbolism and meaning. In the 1962 class yearbook, each one of the group had a line from the song. For the 25th reunion booklet, a couple of women from the group wrote quite moving pieces, and their final lines were from the song. "There was a kind of pathos about it," said Josie, "calling to mind the sort of pathetic things that we cheer for in life. It also became a metaphor for Bryn Mawr. The last line of one of the pieces was 'It's still the best junior high in Toledo,' which of course meant Bryn Mawr.

"We talked a lot about politics," said Josie, "and formed wonderful friendships that, in some cases, have lasted our whole lives. Yet we didn't take it that seriously. It was always, 'well, this is preliminary and the big things of our lives will be later on,' the big things being that we'll get married and have families. We never thought of each other as being serious commitments or primary relationships. I think we all value it a lot more now than we did at the time."

In her senior year, Josie took a course called Europe in the 20th Century, taught by history professor Felix Gilbert. Gilbert came to the

United States from Germany in the thirties, and was at Bryn Mawr from 1946 to 1962. A small man, rather shy, even formal, he spoke with a soft German accent, and always wore a slightly rumpled tweed jacket and tie. He wrote on a wide range of subjects, including books on early American foreign policy, on sixteenth-century Florence, and a memoir, *A European Past.* "His was one of the greatest minds I've ever been exposed to," said Josie, "and happily I appreciated that at the time."

When Josie said she wanted to do "something on revolution" for her term paper, Gilbert suggested that she get hold of a journal that Lenin had published called *Iskra* ("the spark"), pick out Lenin's articles, and read through them to see if she could trace any evolution in Lenin's thinking during the period of a few years at the beginning of the twentieth century. The only library in the country that had this rather obscure journal was the New York Public Library, so Josie went up to New York City on her Christmas vacation. The journals were in a special collection of Selected Works of the Bolshevik Revolution, and had to be hand-delivered and returned when the library closed at night. Every morning, Josie would show up and ask for the issues of *Iskra* to be brought out, go into the reading room, and read and take notes. ("I fashioned myself as Marx working in the British Museum," she told me, with a laugh.) She discovered that it was in those years, in those articles in *Iskra*, that Lenin formulated the whole concept of the Bolshevik Party. He was wrestling with the question of whether the revolution happened spontaneously or whether you needed a leadership elite. By the end of it, he decided you need an elite to lead, to foment the spark of the revolution. ("Gilbert, of course, knew this, and expected it," said Josie.) So Josie charted the emergence of this crucial idea through these issues of *Iskra,* and put it all together in her term paper. "It was something I was discovering for myself," she said, "so it was a marvelous project. And not only that, it's such a crucial issue—it's always been a hot issue for the women's movement. In women's meetings in the early seventies, this was something that came up a lot, and I'd be able to say, 'Well, Lenin, in the early issues of *Iskra* . . . .'"

For Josie—and this was true for many of us as we graduated from Bryn Mawr—there was a real disjunction between her expansive sense of intellectual self-confidence and her extraordinarily limited imagination of what the rest of her life could possibly be. "I had the idea that I would marry and have children and live in the suburbs," she said, with a laugh, "and that this would happen in a matter of weeks after I graduated, which is precisely what happened to my mother. When that didn't happen, I thought, 'Well, what am I supposed to do now?'" At the time, Josie had a rather negative attitude toward having a career and being single. "I was just kinda drifting," she said, with a mock-dreamy lilt in her voice, "waiting for Mr. Perfect to show up."

While waiting for Mr. Perfect, Josie got a job as secretary to the city desk editor at the *Washington Post*. The woman in the personnel office told her straight out, "They never hire women as reporters." It was as matter of fact as "It's raining." And it was perfectly legal then, before Title VII of the 1964 Civil Rights Act, to discriminate against women in hiring and employment. Unfortunately, the job really was to be a secretary to the editor, and Josie had no secretarial skills and no interest in being a secretary. "I was getting very angry there," she said, "and I never understood why." A man from the Harvard class of '62 had been hired at the *Post* at about the same time, as a reporter of course, but it didn't dawn on Josie until much later that this gender discrimination was what was fueling her anger. Eventually the editor told her she had attitude problems, and she left. Next, she worked at *Time* magazine as a "copy desk girl." The men wrote the articles (no women were allowed to write articles), then gave them to women "researchers" to check all the facts. The copy desk girls, even lower on the scale, picked up the articles, took them to the researchers, then picked them up again and took them on to the editors. Again Josie didn't understand where her anger was coming from, and again her supervisor called her in and told her she had an attitude problem.

Josie had one other job in journalism, as a regular general-assignment reporter at the *Sun-Bulletin,* a small paper in Binghamton, New York. That was actually a very good experience for her, because she was taken seriously as a writer and a reporter. It was "rather an admirable little liberal paper in a fairly conservative area of the state," she said, "and they were pushing various liberal causes." Josie felt comfortable there and had some good, meaty assignments. They even let her write an antiwar piece, a quasi-editorial. But she didn't stay in Binghamton. At this point in her life, just twenty-four years old, she had no real motivation, no clear sense of her own identity.

After leaving the paper in Binghamton, Josie went to Madison, Wisconsin, where her parents were living at the time. In September of 1966, she decided on the spur of the moment that she wanted to do graduate work in comparative literature, walked down to the "comp lit" office on the UW campus and managed, on the strength of her Bryn Mawr degree, to get into the master's program. It felt good to get into serious study again—Josie realized that she had been frustrated by the lack of depth in newspaper reporting—and she connected with two extraordinary faculty women, Fannie LeMoine and Germaine Brée. (There were very few women on the UW faculty, as was the case at most universities at the time, but Josie happened upon those two.) Fannie LeMoine, who became Josie's dissertation advisor, had her PhD in classics from Bryn Mawr. "She shepherded me through graduate school," Josie said. "I don't know that I would have made it without her, to tell you the truth. She was an inspiration in every way, intellectually and emotionally." Germaine Brée, a very well-known French scholar, had an "enormous office up on a hill," and was "treated like a living legend at the university." (Brée had taught at Bryn Mawr in the thirties, and she came to speak at the College, while we were there as undergraduates.) She was on Josie's dissertation committee and became a role model for her, as a woman who was "very political and also did wonderful scholarship."

In 1967, at the time of the Dow demonstration, Josie was a teaching assistant (TA), and the TAs went on strike to protest police brutality. In her department, the TAs were quite militant. Some of the men looked like Fidel Castro, wearing army fatigue uniforms, with big, bushy beards, and broad, red armbands to show they were on strike. Josie, on the other hand, was still dressing more or less the way she had at Bryn Mawr, in knee socks or tights and skirts. She didn't have a red armband, so she pinned on a polite-looking little card that said *TA On Strike*. Going on strike, of course, meant refusing to meet classes and running the risk of getting fired. Luckily, the board of regents decided, by just one vote, not to fire them. "That was good," said Josie, "because it was my only source of income."

After a few years of teaching at the University of Kentucky—and the tear-gassing episode that put her on the front page of the *Courier-Journal* —Josie went back to the University of Wisconsin to finish her PhD. She was living in Madison, just a few blocks from the campus, in August of 1970, at the time of the Sterling Hall Army Mathematics Research Center (AMRC) bombing, a massive explosion that completely demolished the building. The blast woke Josie up at about three in the morning, and when she bicycled past later that morning, she was shocked to see such terrible devastation right there in the middle of the campus.

A physics researcher was killed in the blast. Many activists, looking back, said the AMRC bombing marked the end of the student antiwar movement.

A day or two after the AMRC bombing, an underground group published a statement in a little newspaper called the *Kaleidoscope,* claiming responsibility. Josie had kept her copy of the paper, and happened to look at it again just a month or so before we talked. It was only then that she discovered that that whole issue of the paper was supposed to have been devoted to women's liberation. All the material on women's liberation had been bumped to the back at the last minute in order to put the articles about the bomb at the front. Josie didn't even notice it at the time. "I was focused on the bombing and finding out who did it," she said. "To me, women's liberation was a frivolous, silly thing, some women in New York who decided not to wear their bras. I was into serious things like the antiwar movement."

It wasn't until Josie had finished writing her dissertation and was typing it, in the summer of '71, that she finally took notice of the women's movement. Taking a break from typing one evening, she turned on the local PBS television station, which was broadcasting a discussion about women's liberation. The participants were a Catholic priest, Miss Wisconsin, and a woman named Elaine Reuben, who was an assistant professor at the university. "Reuben was so articulate," Josie remembered, "just listening to her made me realize that there was something to this women's liberation." Then Josie picked up Kate Millett's *Sexual Politics,* and really became interested.

Sexual Politics, published in August 1970, gave us language to describe our experiences in the family and in the workplace. It made the personal political. Millett wrote that being a woman in the United States had political implications, politics being broadly defined as "power-structured relationships, arrangements whereby one group of persons is controlled by another . . . a set of stratagems designed to maintain a [patriarchal] system."[6] The August 31, 1970, issue of *Time* magazine featured "Kate Millett of Women's Lib" and her book in a cover story on the women's movement, crediting Millett with providing a coherent theory to buttress the "intuitive passions" of angry women, chapter and verse for an assault on patriarchy by the feminist movement.

After discovering Millett, Josie kept reading. At the time, there was an explosion of feminist books, books such as Shulamith Firestone's *The Dialectic of Sex,* and *Notes from the Second Year,* compiled by the New York Radical Women. "All the core ideas of the women's movement were there," said Josie, "plus a broader perspective, plus the idea—and for me this provided the lead-in and the connection between my antiwar-movement activities and the women's movement—the idea that war is a masculine activity. And once I got into that idea—that women have a culture and a history much less violent than men, which can serve as a source for the whole society to learn from—I became increasingly involved in the women's movement."

In the fall of '71, Josie was hired back at the University of Kentucky as an assistant professor, a regular tenure-track position. That was when she first became aware of women's studies. "I had never heard of the idea until then," she said. "I realized I had an enormous amount of reading to do. I had read practically nothing by or about women during all those years, certainly not at Bryn Mawr, and certainly not at the University of Wisconsin. And there was no effort on my part to include women; I didn't even think about them as a group. Again, it's one of those ideas that, once you think about it, just opens up all kinds of things." So Josie began reading, and, in the next couple of years, did what amounted to a second, self-directed PhD, catching up on all those women writers.

The first women's studies programs were developed in the late sixties at the University of California, San Diego; Cornell University; and Douglass College of. Rutgers University, where classmate Elaine (Cottler) Showalter was teaching. *Female Studies I,* published in 1969,

"These first feminist courses were unlike any I've taught before or since. It was truly a revolutionary period: everything was being questioned; everything was experimental. The excitement and energy were overwhelming."

counted seventeen courses in women's studies nationally. A year later, there were more than a hundred courses, and by 1973, there were more than two thousand. Josie offered her first women's studies course, called Women in Literature, in the spring of '72. The following year, she taught a course in feminist theory, a history of feminist ideas, beginning with Mary Wollstonecraft. She later wrote a book on the subject, still widely used as a text.

"These first feminist courses were unlike any I've taught before or since," said Josie. "It was truly a revolutionary period: everything was being questioned; everything was experimental. The excitement and energy were overwhelming." She held most sessions of her Feminist Theory course (just ten students, most of them not much younger than Josie herself) in her apartment, and ran it almost like a consciousness-raising session, an experiment in teaching that blurred the traditional boundaries between student and teacher, class and life, academics and politics. One day they took the first hour of class to picket and leaflet a Kentucky Wildcats basketball game, to protest the use of "Kentucky Kittens," women students who served as "hostesses" in the recruiting process. In retrospect, Josie considers some of these experiments mistaken—there should be some boundaries, some distance between teacher and student, she says. But years later, at the University of Maine, she was still teaching her women's studies classes in nontraditional ways, and students in these courses still seemed to feel a special sense of excitement and discovery.

The first women's studies courses had a profound effect on teachers as well. "I was in the middle of all this," Josie remembered. "Things were occurring to me in terms of my own life as we moved through the readings, and things were getting increasingly explosive, in terms of myself personally and also in terms of the women's movement nationally." In the spring of '74, Josie and some other women in Lexington formed a support group, which met once a week for about six months, to discuss the changes that were happening in their lives, and to connect them with feminism. There were six in the group, three married and three not married, all in their late twenties or early thirties, a mix of women from the community, including one faculty wife, but no faculty members except Josie, and no students.

In the course of these meetings, Josie and one of the other women in the group fell in love. They soon became a lesbian couple and began living together, a relationship that lasted fifteen years. Before then, Josie had always thought of herself basically as heterosexual. She continued to date men at least through the first half of the sixties. Later, she became preoccupied with the antiwar movement and her work. "In retrospect, I can see that I always had intense friends who were women," said Josie, "but it was so taboo that I never . . . . It was something I never would have considered for myself. What the women's movement did was to normalize it, make it acceptable. Once there's that shift in attitude, then you're open to it, and you can move in that direction yourself if you're so inclined.

But it's complicated. It's very difficult to figure out what can trigger these enormous changes in your life.

"For me, at any rate, the late sixties and early seventies were a period of just unbelievable turbulence and change," she said. "I think all those of us, in what we called the movement, were really in high gear during that period. It's hard to reconstruct the enormous excitement and passion that we all felt at that time."

Chapter Four

Interesting Times

ISABEL CAROLINE BRANNON

"I've been lucky," said classmate Isabel "Isa" (Brannon) Spencer. "I guess everybody in our class feels that way, that we've lived in interesting times." While Sue and Josie were involved with antiwar and lesbian/feminist movements, Isa was working as a journalist, covering the War on Poverty, urban fires and riots, and industrial plant closings. She was on the front lines of all these struggles: city hall reporter in Chester, Pennsylvania, police reporter for the *Philadelphia Daily News*, business reporter for the *Trentonian* in Trenton, New Jersey.

In the late seventies, Isa was city editor on a paper in Delaware, and one day she took a new publisher on a tour of the state. They were together the better part of the day, driving and talking. At one point he asked her, "Why did you get into the newspaper business?" "I wanted to save the world," she said. And he said, "Coming a little slowly, isn't it?" When she told me that story, we both laughed, and I asked whether her answer had been tongue-in-cheek. "No," she said. "I meant it. I did. By that time I knew I wasn't going to, but that is, simply put, why I went into journalism. I think I always felt that you could do that."

The late sixties were a time in which all authority was suddenly becoming suspect—the military, the police, the government, all those authorities that people had really not questioned before. Before, we all identified with the police, at least those of us who were middle class and white. We thought they were helpful. Then suddenly, they were beating people in the streets. On the other side, the idealistic, nonviolent protesters of SNCC and SDS gave way to armed, angry revolutionaries, the Black Panthers and the Weatherman group. This was one of the most violent periods in recent American history. Of course, in 1968 there were the assassinations of Martin Luther King Jr. and Robert Kennedy. In 1969, there were the Manson murders, the police shooting of Black Panther leader Fred Hampton, the Weathermen's "Days of Rage" in Chicago, and news of the My Lai massacre in Vietnam. "We felt that doing nothing in a period of repressive violence was itself a form of violence," said one former Weathermen member. "The Vietnam war made us crazy," said another. "When you feel you have right on your side, you can do some horrific things."[1]

In March of 1970, three members of the radical Weatherman group were killed when the bomb they were building in a Greenwich Village townhouse exploded. One was Diana Oughton, the daughter of a prominent Republican banker from Chicago, and a 1963 graduate of Bryn Mawr. Another Bryn Mawr graduate, Kathy Boudin, class of '65, was also there in the house, but she managed to escape, and subsequently went underground. (The group was renamed the Weather Underground.) Ten years later, Boudin resurfaced in New York City, and agreed to participate in the robbery of an armored Brinks truck, in Nyack, New York, with a group that called itself the Black Liberation Army. (Her role was to ride in the getaway car, a Ryder truck parked three miles from the robbery.) A Brinks guard and two Nyack police officers were killed, and Boudin was sentenced to a term of "20 years to life" in prison.

In August of 2001, just before I met with Isa Spencer, Kathy had come up for parole, having served twenty years for her role in the robbery. The parole hearing got a lot of press coverage, especially in New York. I was struck by the tone of much of the commentary—the outsized passion, the deep feelings of rage and resentment that still attached to what one columnist called "this snake of the sixties." To many, Boudin represents the worst of the sixties, antidemocratic (anti-American even) and violent. Class privilege was part of what made her (and most others of the radical Left) unsympathetic. Kathy Boudin grew up with all the advantages: daughter of Leonard Boudin, a well-known leftist lawyer; graduate of Bryn Mawr; and so on. Even sympathetic commentators noted Boudin's "overpowering moral hubris."

A lot of people from the class of '62 remember Kathy Boudin. "She had bright blue eyes, and a bit of a weight problem," said one. "She was very radical even then, with a sharp lawyerly intelligence." Kathy picketed Woolworth's while she was still in high school (Elisabeth Irwin, a progressive private school in Greenwich Village). In her freshman year at Bryn Mawr, she was one of those who went to see Miss McBride to agitate on behalf of the College's black maids and porters. In her sophomore year she organized the "Second American Revolution," a major conference on race relations in the United States. She went to Cuba one summer to cut sugar cane, and spent her senior year in Moscow. In those days, Kathy was one of the best, the star of the political science department. After Bryn Mawr, she joined the antiwar protests, and did community organizing among the poor, "feeling a responsibility to use the privileges of [her] background to help others."[2]

For many of us, Kathy Boudin's story is a cautionary tale, reminding us of how lucky we were to have graduated from Bryn Mawr just a few years earlier, shaped by different forces; how narrowly we escaped being swept up in the violence of those tumultuous times. Here again we are a generation on the cusp. We came of age in the Kennedy years, when everything seemed possible and we were all in it together. After Kennedy's assassination, that world of optimism and common purpose was gone. People began to take sides. The residue of that is still with us today, one of the chief legacies of the sixties.

When I first met with Isa in the fall of 2001, we talked about Kathy Boudin, and about the bitter anger she still inspires. Isa, of course, had seen the sixties from a different side than most of us, from the point of view of the police and city hall. A lot of the feeling about Kathy Boudin came from a sort of knee-jerk reaction, supporting the police, she said.

Two state troopers had been killed in that robbery, and there was deep resentment about these privileged kids who killed cops.

Isa and I met at an outdoor café in New York's Greenwich Village on a crisp September morning, loud clangs from a nearby NYU construction project punctuating our conversation. At Bryn Mawr, we both majored in European history, and both worked on the *College News*. Now these many years later, her voice was what seemed most familiar, the hint of a southern accent, and the tone of gentle, self-deprecating irony. "We really are not a class of great achievers," she started out, "compared to some of the other Bryn Mawr classes around us."

Isa grew up in Tryon, a small town forty miles south of Asheville, North Carolina. Her father was caught in the Depression, and had to leave college to go to work. Then war broke out and he joined the navy. He came home after the war and bought a farm, built a house—he was going to be a gentleman farmer and stockbroker. But he developed glaucoma, before they knew much about it, and couldn't go back to work. He was a semi-invalid for Isa's entire childhood, and they lived on the income from his stock trades and securities. "The great thing about that was that he was at home," said Isa, "and so was my mother. We had a beautiful house, I read the stock quotes in the paper every morning for my father, and we all played canasta." At the age of twelve, Isa was sent off to boarding school at Garrison Forest, a girls' prep school in Maryland. (Her father was rather an anglophile and thought, the sooner you put your children in a boarding school, the better.)

Later, Isa applied to "the usual women's colleges." She thought she wanted to be in the Boston area but didn't much like Wellesley or Radcliffe. Then she got snowed in while visiting Bryn Mawr. "I was there for over a week," she said, "couldn't get back to my school. It was Freshman Show weekend, and I just loved the whole thing so much. I loved the campus, the most beautiful of any of the ones I saw. And so for that *very* logical reason, I decided to go to Bryn Mawr." She went on, "The thing is, you don't know *why* you do the right thing. I have such a chronological mind and Bryn Mawr teaches everything, including chemistry, from an historical perspective. For me, that's the way my mind works. So I did the right thing, going to Bryn Mawr. I think I was very lucky."

Isa was in Rhoads, along with Josie Donovan, one of the typing smoker clique. In her freshman year, she took two courses that were hard for her, German and chemistry. I used to help her with German, and that was how we got to know one another. In chemistry, she struggled through, with the help of her lab partner Sue Zebley (Duggan) ('62). At the end of the year, Isa went to see Dr. Berliner, who was the head of the chemistry department and also ran the lab (a typical Bryn Mawr situation), and asked him whether she could take organic chemistry the next year. "No," he said. Isa loved chemistry, but she barely passed.

Twenty years later, Isa was working as an editor in Wilmington, Delaware, the chemical capital of the United States, where DuPont and a couple of other big chemical companies were based. "It was appalling," she said. "We had two full copy desks, because we had a morning paper and an evening paper, and there was no one on either desk who had ever taken college chemistry. So I became 'Miss Chemistry.' That's where you see that they knew what they were doing at Bryn Mawr. They plunge you right in; there's no 'science for artists.' But it was terrifying to know more than other people when I knew how bad I was in chemistry."

Isa joined the *College News* as a freshman, and was managing editor at the time of the Woolworth's demonstration, but she decided not to march on the picket line. "I think I was a journalist before I even knew that I was," she said, "because something in me . . . I never did demonstrations. I never marched at Woolworth's. I never did that because I was on the *College News*, and to me you didn't do that. I've never marched in my life." Like a lot of southerners, Isa was put off by the feeling of superiority that some students in the civil rights movement seemed to have. "I've never been a particularly conservative southerner," she said, "but I hated the way they wanted to tell other people how they ought to run their lives." The summer before the Woolworth sit-ins, Isa worked at a public library branch in Harlem. She saw all the problems they had right there in New York City, and she thought, 'Why are they telling other people, in the South, what to do?' Now, looking back, she says, "Of course I was wrong, You make a statement some place, wherever you can. It's not that other things are not a problem too. But you take advantage of the fact that attention is being focused on *this* problem. So I should have focused more on the fact that there *was* a problem, not on why aren't they solving the problem in New York."

When Isa graduated from Bryn Mawr, she knew she couldn't go back to her hometown—there was nothing there; her peers who stayed were bagging groceries. She wanted to be in the Philadelphia area, and needed a job. But like many of us, Isa had no skills. She could barely type. She tried an advertising agency first, then a book publisher, but no one would hire her. Finally she went to an employment agency. It turned out that the woman there had worked years before on the *Herald Tribune*. After looking at Isa's experience as managing editor of the *College News*, editor of the 1962 Class Yearbook, and editor of the literary magazine at Garrison Forrest, she said, "You should work for a newspaper." Isa hadn't even thought of that. Right away, the woman called Gilbert Spencer, editor of the *Main Line Times* (and later, Isa's husband): "Do you need someone? I've got just the person here." It turned out that he did. This was June 16, 1962, just ten days after our graduation.

At the *Main Line Times*, the sports editor was male, but the other four professionals there were all women, quite extraordinary at the time. *Mademoiselle* actually did a feature article on the *Times* while Isa was there, because of its "all-woman" staff.

Shortly after President Kennedy's assassination, Isa left the *Main Line Times*, which was a weekly, for a job as city hall reporter on the *Chester Times*, a larger, daily paper in Chester, Pennsylvania. She remembers one embarrassing incident when she was writing for the *Chester Times*. "I had to go down to a ship that was about to be launched, christened, whatever they do with those things. It was a horrible, freezing day. We went down and were shown around the tanker; then I went back to the paper and wrote up the story. When I handed it in, the editor said, 'Oh no. I want you to write a first-person account.' As if it were so incredibly unusual that a woman would cover a tanker launching. So I had to write about going out in my high heels, and how I was going over the ice. I hated stuff like that; fortunately, I didn't get stuck doing that very often."

Chester had everything—a Ford plant and a dry-dock company that made tankers. The biggest thing on the skyline was the water tower of the Scott Paper Company, in the shape of a toilet paper roll. "I lived in Philadelphia," said Isa, "and I would just pinch myself driving to work down that industrial highway, past the plants of every major American corporation. To me, coming from the woods of Appalachia, it was just amazing, seeing this American industrial might every morning as the sun was coming up, driving along in my little Volkswagen. Of course, I knew it was the twilight of this . . . that Chester was an industrial city that was on the rocks. By that time, Lyndon Johnson was president, and had started the War on Poverty. "If ever there was a place where the War on Poverty was being fought, Chester was it," said Isa. "I remember they built a couple of towers with housing for senior citizens. There was so much hope in the air."

The focus of the civil rights movement was still on the South, but Chester had one charismatic civil rights leader, and every Saturday, he and his followers would all go downtown for sit-ins and boycotts. Then the cops would come along, swoop up the demonstrators, and slam them into padded wagons, carrying them away. This went on for weeks, and Isa covered it all. She didn't get arrested, though one of the other reporters did. Isa was usually pretty careful, and they didn't like to arrest women. "They didn't quite know what to do with women in those days," she said, "so we got away with more." Months later, Isa was married and living in a little row house in Philadelphia. She and her husband were sleeping one night, when a noise outside woke them up. Her husband said, "What was that?" And she said, "That's a cop, hitting somebody over the head." She knew the sound, from her time in Chester.

Isa married Gil Spencer in early 1965, and moved from the *Chester Times* to the *Philadelphia Daily News*. "I got that job, which I normally would not have gotten," said Isa, "because of a woman named Rose Wolf, who was working on the *Philadelphia Inquirer* at the time. She was one of the few women they had, and a wonderful, wonderful writer. Well, the *Daily News* had no women. And they decided that they wanted to have a woman too." So they hired Isa as a police reporter, the first and only woman in that job. The guys at the police administration building told her they'd been practicing cleaning up their language for a couple of weeks before she got there. It was so remarkable to have a woman in the job of police reporter that *Editor and Publisher* did an article on Isa. "I like to cover hard news as it is breaking," she told them, "not women's features. The police beat is the best education for covering government or any other beats. This is where it all begins."

Those were the days when there were hideous, horrible fires in cities in the Northeast, most of them arson. People were living in too-tight quarters in flammable housing, and big industrial buildings were catching on fire, or being set on fire by their owners. The first fire that Isa covered was back in Chester, a terrible fire—a woman's girlfriends firebombed her boyfriend, his wife, and their eight children and killed them all. But in Chester, Isa worked in the mornings, and fires were caught sooner in the daytime. At the *Daily News* in Philadelphia, she worked at night, when the really big fires occurred. She remembered one blazing nine-alarm fire—at the time it was the biggest fire they had ever had in Philadelphia. A pier went up, and huge, burning logs went sailing through the air, starting other multiple-alarm fires down along the waterfront. "I had just gotten back from our honeymoon," said Isa. "In those few weeks in 1965, I ruined my entire trousseau, because, in those days, I wore cute little suits and dresses to work—it would have been out of the question to wear pants—and then went out to cover fires." It's hard to believe how primitive communication was at the time. Isa was a "leg person," which meant that she went out and covered a story, called it in, and then a rewrite man wrote it. She only wrote a couple of stories the whole time she was there, because she was out getting them.

While Isa was at the *Daily News*, two policemen were killed. It was a *huge* story. The last time a Philadelphia policeman had been shot and killed in the line of duty was something like fifty years earlier; it just never happened. "Now, when you consider how many policemen have been shot," said Isa, "you realize that it was just the beginning of something, a watershed event." Isa was home in bed when she got the call to go down to South Philadelphia, where this had happened. She remembers how her little Volkswagen wobbled down the trolley tracks in the center of the street—both sides were lined with parked cars, and the roads were slick, because it was winter, and the middle of the night. When she got down there, she found out that the command post was right on the street where the policemen had been killed. They thought there might still be snipers on the roofs. "It was one of the few times I was in a place where I didn't feel terribly safe," she said. "Most of the time, being a police reporter was really the safest job there was, because wherever you went, you were surrounded by police."

Another thing was the bank robberies. "The police would stake out the banks," said Isa, "and when a bank robber came in they'd shoot him dead, right there, boom, like that. The guy hands the note over, the woman (the teller, who was always a woman) hits the buzzer, the guys rise up from the balcony, boom, and you're gone. It wasn't that long ago that we were doing that." *We* were doing that? Isa went on to explain. "I believe that we all are the police," she said, "and we are the prison guards. These people are acting on our behalf. And when I say we were doing this, shooting the bank robbers, I meant that, in a sense, we're all responsible for what our servants do."

While students in the antiwar movement were beginning to think of police as the enemy, Isa saw another side, more complex. "The police were not trained particularly well on what to expect," she said, "having grown up and lived their whole lives as respected members of society. Actually, the guys in Philadelphia who ran the civil disobedience unit were wonderful. Of course, I know now that they were spying on people, but they did at least have some idea of not overreacting, and they knew the people; they knew everyone. A man named George Fenel headed the unit, and he would tell people, 'Listen, don't do that,' or 'If you're going to do that, tell me first.' They did really have a very good approach. I remember one day I went up to cover a Teamsters' strike. I was talking to Fenel, and starting to talk with the Teamsters, when some strikers went over and took my car and turned it upside down. And Fenel just said, 'Okay guys, pick up the car; put it back.' He didn't overreact."

In 1967, two things happened: Isa's husband left Philadelphia for a job in Trenton, New Jersey, and Isa got pregnant. She had a job lined up in New Jersey, but couldn't take it because they wouldn't take a pregnant woman employee. "They appreciated so much my telling them, but that was that." So Isa didn't work for a year, and then went back to work three days a week (by then, she also had stepchildren at home). She didn't go back to work full-time until her daughter went to kindergarten, the same year her stepson went to college. "Working part-time, I did get to keep my hand in," said Isa, "which I think is important. Although the more we know now, late blooming is okay. For some reason, I felt that continuity was everything, that if you bowed out completely you'd never get back. That was so much the way of thinking in those days."

In April of 1968, Isa was at home sitting in her bathtub, seven months pregnant, when Gil came in and told her that Martin Luther King Jr. had been killed. "I thought I was going to have a miscarriage, right there in the bath," said Isa. "I was just absolutely beside myself. Then of course Bobby Kennedy was assassinated, much closer to the time my daughter was born. But for some reason I didn't take it . . . I didn't feel physically the way I felt then. Martin Luther King was as if someone just hit you in the stomach."

When Isa went back to work full-time, it was as business reporter for the *Trentonian*, in Trenton, New Jersey, where her husband was editor. She had to persuade the publisher, saying, "Either I'll go into New York every day, in which case you'll have to make Gil's dinner because I won't be home, or you can let me come here to work." So Isa became a business reporter, self-taught. "It was rather difficult," said Isa. "The most important thing in journalism really is to understand the context, to know what the next question is; if this, then that—knowing what it means. I understand crime reporting. I understand court reporting. I understand any kind of government reporting. I know what to ask. But I didn't know so much about business. So there was a lot that I didn't get. But there was also a lot I did get, and I wrote on those things."

The main thing in those days was plant closings, rampant plant closings. The saddest of all these was the Roebling steel plant—these were the people who built the Brooklyn Bridge, who made the cable. When that plant went down, around 1974, it was a symbolic moment. "I wrote about that," said Isa, "and I wrote about the scavenger people, who were buying up these places and running them the rest of the way into the ground, raiding the pension plans, doing what they could to take every last drop of blood out."

It was the beginning of the energy crisis, and Isa covered the gas lines and the riots and all. She remembers the sudden huge jump in the price of commodities, of raw materials. "That just changed the world when it happened," she said. "And I remember it personally. My stepson had just gone away to college, and he ate maybe fifty percent of the food in the household, because he was an athlete. After that, our grocery bills stayed about the same so I didn't pay much attention. Then all of a sudden, he came home for Christmas, and I went shopping and thought, 'God, what has happened!' Prices had gone through the roof."

Sometime in the early seventies, Isa brought classmate Ruta (Krastins) Smithson (one of the Rhoads typing-smoker clique) onto the *Trentonian* as women's editor. "This was a time when women's pages were becoming much more interesting," said Isa, "and Ruta was just the person to lead us into that new world." They covered subjects no one else was writing about at the time, issues like rape and domestic violence, and stories about women in sports, in the professions, in politics.

In 1975, Isa's husband won the Pulitzer. "That's another interesting thing in our generation," said Isa. "To what extent are you responsible for what your spouse does? In the old days, it was just a given that the wife was a part of her husband's accomplishments. But now you're not. So you're constantly trying to make a name for yourself, something you can say is yours, when really probably the biggest contribution you make is this other person. I felt I had a huge role in Gil's work—we talked incessantly about issues, and I edited some of the editorials—but I can't put it on my résumé."

I talked with several classmates who were working in the same field as their husbands, and many of them said they always felt second-rate compared to husbands who were their seniors, and more accomplished. "I have to say my husband is a very important person in the business," said Isa, "perhaps not a giant like Ben Bradlee of the *Washington Post*, but not far behind. He's fifteen years older than me, but it wouldn't matter if I spent eighty more years; I'd still never be what he is. I know there's only going to be a handful of people who are really huge in that way. I'm as good as ninety percent of the people; I'm just not as good as these top guys. So I always went through life with a feeling of complete inadequacy."

Like most married women of our generation, Isa followed her husband, moving from place to place to accommodate his career moves. Sometimes, having a husband in the newspaper business was an advantage— Isa worked on the *Trentonian* and the *Denver Post* while her husband was editor. But much of the time it was a disadvantage because of concerns over nepotism. Shortly after he won the Pulitzer, Gil Spencer became editor of the *Philadelphia Daily News*, a Knight-Ridder paper where Isa used to work. "Once he got the job as editor, I couldn't go back there," said Isa. "So now the question was, what were they going to do with me? Terrible problem, terrible problem." Some Knight-Ridder people came up to her at a cocktail party and asked, "So what are you going to do?" And she said, "Well, I'm going to be looking for a newspaper job." And they said, "The wives of Knight-Ridder executives don't work." Isa said, "Well, the wife of this Knight-Ridder executive does." So they said, "Where would you work?" She suggested she might work in Camden, New Jersey. And they said, "Oh no, that's a competitor. You can't work there." So Isa was really blocked in all directions—she couldn't work for the same place and she couldn't work for a competitor. Finally, they persuaded the editor of the *Philadelphia Inquirer* to hire her and put her in Wilmington, out of harm's way. This was not a happy situation: Isa didn't mind commuting, but she didn't like covering people who were not the main audience of the paper.

While she was at the *Inquirer*, Isa inadvertently heard some insider information on personnel matters. She immediately resigned from her job at the paper. "This is where life is so confusing," said Isa. "I just get very confused by my own life. Because I think there's a certain point at which, if you are going to do certain things, you have to realize that there are limits on your rights. I do think this cuts against women, and I think that nepotism laws are ridiculous, because they don't cover girlfriends and boyfriends. It's not fair that people who are married can't work together and all the people who are living together can. But I also felt, realistically, that if my husband's the editor, I should not expect to go work for him. And I shouldn't be in a position where I know about personnel."

In Wilmington, Isa covered school desegregation, first for the *Inquirer* in 1976–77, and then for the *Wilmington News-Journal* in 1977–78. The Wilmington school district was working under a court order that required them to desegregate the suburban and city schools together, an exceptionally sweeping mandate. It was the Wilmington School Board that did it, not the NAACP or any other civil rights group. "It was such an interesting time," said Isa, "and we had the most wonderful federal judge, so firm on what he thought America should be. He made some things happen while I was there that were really amazing." There were court hearings, with experts giving testimony about how children learn and

"I never would have thought, when I got into the newspaper business, that it would still be as hostile to women as it is today."

how they get to feel like second-class citizens. A lot of intelligent people were working on the issue. Finally they came up with a plan, and put it into effect. Then, just as the schools opened, the teachers went on strike, because of issues over money.

An emergency school board meeting was called, and more than a thousand people came. The board president stood on the stage facing this huge crowd and pointed his finger down at Isa, sitting in the front row. "Isabel Spencer," he shouted, "I hold *you* responsible for this strike." Isa had uncovered a secret deal that the school board made with the man they appointed as superintendent, to give him more money, hiding it in some sort of pension arrangement. When the teachers found out, they were furious. That was what the board president was talking about, and why he was screaming at Isa.

The strike was over soon after that, and it seemed like a good time for Isa to make a change. In 1979, she became metropolitan editor at the *Wilmington News Journal*, and she has been some version of city editor ever since. At that time, Isa was one of only a dozen women nationwide who held that position at a large (over 100,000 circulation) newspaper. This was important, because city editor is the job that traditionally leads to managing editor and then to editor. "I never would have thought, when I got into the newspaper business, that it would still be as hostile to women as it is today," said Isa. "I feel that I've had a lot of opportunities, but I don't feel that women in general are getting them. At the talent end of the business, they get jobs, but at the managing end, it isn't happening. The top editors are still men, sometimes with a woman managing editor. When the chips are down, the guys just seem to all look to each other.

Young women think it's not going to affect them, but it does. And that just breaks your heart. I'm not a revolutionary, but I never thought my whole life would go by and things would not be that much better. I look around and I don't see young women moving ahead today.

"One problem is just the comfort level," said Isa. "There are very few men who really see women as people." (Her husband, she says, is a rare exception.) "The men like each other and they want to be together. They play golf and they have a great time. They laugh at the same jokes. It's hard to break through that."

In 1990, Isa moved to Denver, Colorado, and became Sunday editor at the *Denver Post,* where her husband had been named editor. A few years later, Gil Spencer retired, and everyone else moved up a level–the managing editor became editor, and Isa became managing editor. The new editor was actually younger than Isa, but he was an old-fashioned kind of person, she said, with a "businessman kind of mind," not someone who was likely to have many women friends. He and Isa became very close, and that, said Isa, was a great breakthrough. One reason this was possible, she thought, was that she was older, so his wife didn't have any problems with it. They could spend a lot of time together without his wife wondering if something was going on between them.

They had lots of executive retreats at the *Post*, and of course, Isa was always the only woman. She remembers once wrestling with "are we going to have it, *again*, at the golf club," thinking to herself, "if they do that I'm not going," because the club wouldn't take women members (still quite common, even in the nineties). If they were going to the golf club, she was going to put her hand up and say she wasn't coming. "Oh God, I don't want to have to do that," she thought. Fortunately, they decided to go to Vail, a Colorado resort town, instead. So they got to Vail, and all the men, of course, were heading right off to play golf. They were all good golfers; Isa couldn't play with them because she wasn't good enough. But this time, Neil, the editor, said, "I'm not going. You guys go on." He stayed behind with Isa, and they spent the afternoon just walking around Vail. "It was sweet of him," said Isa. "He was so thoughtful."

When Isa first started as a reporter, her approach was that there are two sides to every question, and she wrote every story to reflect that. But there was never any question about which side she was on. "I wrote like the *New York Times* writes today," she said. "If you read a *New York Times* news story, you realize that the other side is in the last four paragraphs. It's not that they're taking sides—a lot of people would say *that*'s bad—but I don't think taking sides is nearly as bad as presenting an unrealistic view of what's really happening." She went on, "You can't save the world if you just preach at people. That doesn't work as well. People already know what they think. The older you get, the more you realize people are just looking for information. They're not looking for you to tell them what to think. At least not in serious newspapers, unless you're a columnist.""

Isa was at the *Denver Post* in 1992, when Amendment II passed, forbidding any kind of state legislation to protect gays and lesbians. Everyone was preoccupied with other constitutional amendments on the ballot—especially Amendments I (spending limits), VI (sales tax for schools) and VIII (lottery money for parks)—so no one was paying much attention to Amendment II. "It was just under the radar," said Isa. Also, everybody was polling quite regularly, and there was no indication this was going to pass. "I remember that, on election night, when we saw that Amendment II had passed, we were just beside ourselves," said Isa. "We were so stunned."

"But wasn't part of the problem that people didn't understand what the amendment meant—that they thought it was giving preferential treatment to gays and lesbians?" I asked. "No," said Isa. "They did understand, and that was the terrible thing. People knew what they were voting for, and if they had it to do all over again they would vote the same way. It was just appalling."

Gil Spencer was still editor at that point, and he put Isa in charge of a project to follow up on the issues raised by Amendment II. That was right after the election, which was in November 1992, and the supplement didn't come out until the following September—it took them that long to put it together. It was only sixteen pages in the end, but they had to wrestle with their own feelings and their own sense of what they should do. "We all sat and just talked and talked and talked about how to do this," said Isa. "Then someone would write an article, but the tone would be wrong, and we would junk it and start all over again. Because you cannot preach at these people who have made up their minds. We had to get all that preaching out of us, just wring it out of us. And it took months to do that.

"What we tried to do was to say, here are some approaches other communities have taken, and here are the results. Here's what they've done there, and the world has not come to an end. And here's how your neighbors live. And here are some people that you didn't even know were gay. Some small towns that are really backwards treat people a lot better than you do. A lot of articles about the way things work when they are working. It wasn't strident. We didn't win any national awards, because the national prize committees wanted something that was much more strident. But we got some local awards, and I was very proud of what we did in the end."

In 1996, Amendment II was struck down by a landmark U.S. Supreme Court ruling, protecting gay men and lesbians from state-sanctioned discrimination. An attorney named John Roberts (now Chief Justice Roberts) provided invaluable strategic advice, pro bono, to the gay rights advocates who were plaintiffs in the case.

Part III
Career Paths

Chapter Five

The Groves of Academe

I had these aspirations.
I wanted to do something with my life.
What paths were open to me?
I went to graduate school.

More than 40 percent of the class (68 out of 159) went straight from Bryn Mawr into graduate school. Bryn Mawr graduates had always gone on to further study in much higher percentages than did their peers from the other women's colleges, especially in the sciences. In 1962, we were also part of a nationwide trend of increasing graduate enrollments, including more and more young men trying to avoid the draft and Vietnam.

Graduate school, for us, was the norm, the obvious next step after Bryn Mawr. We didn't want the lives our mothers had, staying at home. So we modeled ourselves on our professors, who were often the only independent, working women we knew. The best students were actively encouraged to continue into graduate school. Others made the decision partly because they didn't know what else to do. Anthropologist Sherry Ortner talked about "just kind of coasting into the graduate school option," not at all sure that she would succeed, or that she even wanted to be "an academic." In those days, a Bryn Mawr degree had a certain cachet, and Bryn Mawr graduates were accepted into all the best programs.

Here we follow three women from the class of '62 as they wend their way in and out of academia: anthropologist Sherry Ortner; geologist Priscilla (Perkins) Grew; and English literature teacher Ellen Zetzel Lambert. Of these three, Sherry is the one who had the most straightforward academic career, moving from one academic appointment to the next. Priscilla advanced in zigs and zags, spending much of her career in government and in academic administration. Ellen spent ten years off the academic career track, as a "faculty wife." By the time she got her first tenure-track teaching job, she was somewhat out of sync, considerably older than her peers. She finally decided to leave the academic (university teaching/research) track, to teach in a private high school.

In the early sixties, anthropology and English were both fields in which a fair share of American women went on to graduate school. Sherry's class at the University of Chicago was about half men, half women. It was the same for Ellen at Yale in English literature. Sherry, like many young women at the time, was attracted to anthropology by stories of Margaret Mead and Ruth Benedict, legends in the field. "That was very important to me," said Sherry, "this kind of Margaret Mead image of the intrepid young woman in the field with a tape recorder." But these female icons were the exception; the actual statistics of the profession were the same in anthropology as in any other field. There were no women on the anthropology faculty at Chicago. Ellen found that at Yale, there was just one tenured woman in the English department (Marie Borroff, a noted medievalist). It was a shock for these Bryn Mawr graduates to discover that, in the wider world of academia, women were still outsiders.

Ellen's professors at Yale were blunt, unambiguous, saying, "Why are you doing this?" or "It's a good idea for you to get this degree; we really need bright, educated faculty wives." Sherry's first advisor—later she switched—told her she would have to change her image if she wanted to be taken seriously: she smiled too much, was too bouncy, too friendly, and there was something about how she dressed. "I think he thought he was being helpful," said Sherry. "Of course, I was tremendously offended. I went home and cried. Like what am I going to do with my face?"

Sherry and Ellen got married to fellow students while they were still in graduate school, and both of these first marriages ended in divorce. "It's so hard in this culture for two people with professional lives to keep it together," said Sherry. "It's too bad."

Priscilla got married four days after graduating from Bryn Mawr. "It was the fifties influence," she said. "I remember turning him down at first, saying, 'I can't get married because I want to go to graduate school.' It seems so funny now, but I remember thinking it quite sincerely." In the end, she managed to get married, to follow her husband in his next career move, and also to go to graduate school. (She applied to Harvard and Berkeley, where her fiancé was applying for teaching positions, and decided on Berkeley when he got the job there.)

Berkeley turned out to be a good choice for Priscilla. The earth sciences program there was world class, one of the most selective in the country. And while, in general, very few women did graduate work in geology, or in any of the other "hard" sciences, there was a particular history of Bryn Mawr women in the earth sciences program at UC Berkeley. Priscilla was one of only four women out of about eighty graduate students in the program, but three of those four women were from Bryn Mawr. "That probably made it a more supportive environment than some," said Priscilla. "They were there to talk with when the going got rough."

Priscilla, Sherry, and Ellen were all deeply affected by the social and political upheavals of the sixties. At the same time they were trying hard to keep their lives and academic careers "on track." Priscilla was at Berkeley in the early and mid-sixties, during the Free Speech Movement and the early stages of student protest against the Vietnam War. "I didn't get arrested," she said, "but I went into Sproul Hall and I heard Joan Baez sing. I was at the first meeting of the Vietnam Day Committee. And I remember the B-52s flying over Berkeley, going west." In those years, she was very busy with graduate work. When her husband went south one summer to teach at black colleges, she stayed at Berkeley to work on her dissertation.

Sherry returned to the United States in the spring of 1968, after two years of field work among the Sherpas in Nepal. She settled in California, trying to write her dissertation–having trouble getting started–and working for Eugene McCarthy in the presidential primaries. In June, Bobby Kennedy came to California to campaign, and it was there that he was assassinated. "It was a tremendously confusing experience," said Sherry, "because I was working for McCarthy; I was working against Kennedy. I wanted him to lose, but I didn't want him to get killed. Then in August, we watched the Democratic Convention on TV, that horrendous convention. I had a sense of tremendous upheaval, of wanting to be involved. But at the same time, I had to write a dissertation; I wanted to keep my life on track."

Ellen was in her first years of marriage at the time of the Vietnam protests, living at the edge of the Bard College campus. She joined some local peace marches, but was also busy writing a book, based on her

SHERRY BETH ORTNER

Yale dissertation. "It was part of this two-track life feeling," she said. "I was going on with my professional life, but there was all this other stuff which was personal stuff, but increasingly political stuff, that really didn't enter in. I remember, as everyone of our generation does, where I was in '63 when I heard about the Kennedy assassination, and then in '68, the Martin Luther King, Jr., assassination. Somehow, my personal life seemed very connected with all those losses, national losses."

Both Sherry and Priscilla have had what anyone would describe as very successful careers.

Sherry is recognized well beyond the academic world as a feminist anthropologist, and has received numerous awards, including a 1990–1995 MacArthur "genius" award. Priscilla has had much high-profile success in academia and government, what a *Bryn Mawr Alumnae Bulletin* article characterized as a "rock-solid" career. Yet both women talk about the fragility of that success, how it could all so easily have gone another way. Priscilla describes moments when she might have just quit. Sherry describes her life as a series of lucky breaks.

Sherry B. Ortner: "I think of myself as lucky."

I met with Sherry in a coffee shop on New York's Upper West Side, near Columbia University, where she teaches anthropology. She still had the same bouncy, cheerleader energy that I remembered from college, and the same distinctive twang in her voice. Sherry had recently spent some years doing research for a book about her high school class, including interviews with classmates.[1] It felt strange, a little unsettling, she said, to be sitting on the other side of the table.

"I think of myself as really being very lucky," said Sherry. "I wound up doing so much of the kinds of things I love to do. This is the way I remember my life, as a series of lucky breaks. Not that I feel utterly undeserving or that I didn't work hard, which I did. But it all could have gone in a different way."

A first lucky break was the one that got her to Bryn Mawr. In her junior year in high school, she went to talk with the guidance counselor about college. The conversation went something like this:

Well, where are you thinking of going to college?

Gee, I don't know. I'd like to go some place with a big campus, and football teams, and all that . . .

"I'd seen it in the movies," said Sherry. "You know, literally that was what I was thinking. And he said—now this is going to sound egotistical, but it's a true story—he said, 'Well, you know, I'm looking at your PSAT scores . . .' The scores were not *spectacular* or anything, but maybe they were good by local standards. He said, 'You know, I think you might be able to do better than that.' 'What do you mean?' I said. And he said, 'Well, you know, there's these girls' schools (as he put it) . . . like, you know, Bryn Mawr and Radcliffe.' And this little bell went off in my mind. It somehow immediately felt like that's what I wanted. I felt like it was kind of a fluke that he mentioned this to me. And I went to Bryn Mawr and I loved Bryn Mawr, and I feel like it saved my life."

"I just feel like I could have wound up . . . the worst image I have is one particular lifestyle which a lot of my high school classmates wound up in—a lot of shopping, a lot of the country club, a certain kind of very materially oriented existence. I'm less judgmental than I used to be about all of that, but I'm glad I'm not in that life."

Sherry's father was a college graduate, while her mother had gone for a couple of years and then dropped out. Both expected Sherry to go to college, and were supportive. "I think they wanted me to have a good education because they just thought that was what the modern American girl should do," she said, "and it would get me the right sort of husband. I think they wanted me to lead a kind of average American female life, and they wanted me to be happy within that frame." They didn't really expect her to go on to a professional career, not that they tried to stop it, but it worried them. Her father, at one point, used the phrase "You're pricing yourself out of the market." He meant the marriage market. "Now, I think my father's quite proud of me," said Sherry, "but from their point of view, it's been all backwards, that I had this great professional success but a kind of checkered marital career."

Weequahic (pronounced wee-QUAY-ic) High, in Newark, New Jersey, where Sherry went to school, was very college oriented; about 80 percent of the men in her class went on to college, a very high percentage for a public high school. Sherry had always assumed that the percentage was more or less equal for men and women, and that the Jewish parents especially (her class was 83 percent Jewish) were pushing all their children to go to college. When she went back to do interviews and look at statistics, she was shocked to discover that only about 40 percent of the women in her class went to college. She found that the girls who didn't go to college, and even many of those who did, felt somewhat bitter, resentful that their lives were cut back. Many of them say that their parents didn't want them to go to college, that if there was a money problem and there was a brother, the brother *had* to go, and the sister had to hold back. Or the brother went to a fancy, private college and they went to Newark State or Douglass. The brothers were getting encouraged, supported, and the sisters were not.

Sherry's next lucky break came at Bryn Mawr, when she was deciding on graduate school. She applied to various graduate programs in anthropology, her undergraduate major, got in everywhere, and didn't

Sherry Ortner in Nepal

know how to choose. So she went to see one of her professors at Bryn Mawr and asked his advice. "Did you get into Chicago?" he asked. "Yeah." "No question," he said. "You have to go to Chicago." So she went to the University of Chicago, ended up with Clifford Geertz, a well-known anthropologist, as her advisor, and did field work for her dissertation in a remote Sherpa village in Nepal, a transforming experience.

In 1971, Sherry was applying for her first real, tenure-track position. She had powerful support from Geertz and others at Chicago, plus a year of teaching and another year of post-doctoral research. It finally came down to three job possibilities, at Swarthmore, Yale, and Sarah Lawrence. Swarthmore already had some women on the faculty by that time. The big issue there was not gender *per se*, but rather whether Sherry would be in residence, a presence on campus. In the end, they made the assumption (wrongly) that because she was married and living in New York, she wouldn't be able to move. She was not offered the job. At Yale, as at most major universities at the time, the anthropology faculty was all male. But there were some people who were trying quite hard to hire some women, to change things. The Yale anthropology professor who had invited Sherry to apply for the job told her afterward about the faculty meeting where they discussed her candidacy. "Apparently there was this kind of really old-fashioned, straight-up sexism," said Sherry. "It was that women had no place in a serious intellectual environment, that you would have these women with short skirts running around and distracting people. And this was 1971!"

At Sarah Lawrence, the faculty was about fifty-fifty male and female. The college had policies that were good for women—prorated pay and tenure for part-time teachers. The job there was advertised as a regular, three-year contract, a tenure-track position. Sherry was their third choice, after the first two choices, both men, had turned it down. But when they offered the job to Sherry, what they offered her was only a two-year contract. By this time it was already April, very late in the academic hiring season, and with no job, Sherry was getting worried. "They called me up and offered me this two-year contract," she said, "and I don't know what possessed me, because I really needed this job, but I said, very judiciously, 'Well, thank you very much; I'll have to think about it.' This was kind of amazing in retrospect, because I don't know what I was going to think about; I had nothing else!"

Then came another lucky break. Hilde Geertz, former wife of Clifford Geertz, was a friend of Sherry's. Around that time, she called about something completely unrelated, and asked, by the way, how the job search was going. Sherry said, "Well . . ." and told her the Sarah Lawrence story. Geertz was indignant. "Why are they offering you a two-year contract?" she asked. "I don't know," said Sherry, "but I don't have anything else." "Call them back and tell them you won't come unless you have a regular tenure-track contract." So Sherry called them up, and very

A MacArthur "genius" award in 1990 felt like the ultimate lucky break.

gingerly (because she was scared of losing the job entirely) said, "I thought it was a regular tenure-track position; I wonder if you could tell me why you're offering me a two-year contract." The person at Sarah Lawrence sounded embarrassed, hemmed and hawed, and said he'd get back to her. Then he called her back and said, "We're happy to offer you a regular three-year contract." "Great," she said. "I'll take it."

When Sherry got to Sarah Lawrence College, in the fall of 1971, there were already the beginnings of a women's studies curriculum, developed under the leadership of historian Gerda Lerner. Lerner was a generation older than Sherry, a refugee from Nazi Germany who came late to an academic career, a pioneer in women's history, and a forceful presence. In 1970, she had sent a note around to her colleagues on the Sarah Lawrence faculty, asking them to think about what they might contribute to a women's studies curriculum. Renaissance historian Joan Kelly-Gadol wrote back, saying there was nothing much she could do, given her subject. But Lerner wouldn't take no for an answer. And Kelly-Gadol discovered that everything looked entirely different once she saw it from the point of view of women–the Renaissance was actually quite a setback for women; they had more powers in the Medieval period. Sherry, like Josie Donovan and other classmates in academic careers, had not paid much attention to women's issues until sometime in the late sixties/early seventies, when the feminist movement began to take shape. "That was a kind of explosion for me," said Sherry, "because–I mean, this is going to sound bizarre, but it had never occurred to me to think about that problem."

In her first year at Sarah Lawrence, Sherry team-taught a course on "Women: Myth and Reality" together with Gerda Lerner, Joan Kelly-

Gadol, and comparative literature professor Eva Kollisch. A lecture that she presented in that course later became the paper "Is Female to Male as Nature Is to Culture?"[2] a groundbreaking study in which Sherry sets out to explain the universal fact of female subordination, as well as its various, often contradictory, manifestations in particular cultures. Her basic thesis is that woman is identified with nature, something that every culture devalues, while man is identified with culture, human consciousness and its products. "I wasn't really saying it was women's plumbing or genes that keep them down," said Sherry in a 2003 *New York Times* interview. "I was saying that because women's bodies are more biologically involved with human reproduction, they appear more mired in nature than men, who seem transcendent. And that general pattern still holds."

After Sarah Lawrence, Sherry's career took off. Recruited by the University of Michigan, it was there, in 1990, that she got word of having been awarded a MacArthur Grant, popularly known as the "genius" award. In a way, this felt like the ultimate lucky break. "It was pretty terrific, I must say," said Sherry. "It's really about the best thing that has happened." There were some hints ahead of time that she was being considered for the grant, but she tried to put it out of her mind. Her second marriage was disintegrating just then, so it wasn't that hard to forget anything else. Sherry spent most of that year at the Institute for Advanced Studies at Princeton, while her husband stayed home in Michigan. One day, she got back from Princeton, and found him waiting in the driveway to meet her. "I still remember," said Sherry. "Everyone remembers where they were when they got their MacArthur. I pulled in, and he said, 'Somebody just called from the MacArthur Foundation.' They do give you a personal call; you don't just get a letter. It was like that old. . . . Did you ever watch *The Millionaire* when we were growing up? My mother loved it and we used to watch it. The conceit of the series is that there's an anonymous millionaire. And every week the male secretary of the millionaire–we never see the millionaire–knocks on the door of some family. The story starts with the knock on your door. That's kind of the way it is with the MacArthur."

Priscilla (Perkins) Grew–A Zigzag Career

As Sherry was starting in at Sarah Lawrence College, Priscilla was just leaving her first teaching job at Boston College. "I had broad interests, I guess from Bryn Mawr," she said, "and I wasn't really happy just working in my little specialty in geology." In 1970, she attended a conference in Flagstaff, Arizona, where she met a UCLA professor who was just starting up a regional environmental assessment project, an idea that was completely new at the time. The study was focused on Lake Powell, the lake created when they built the Glen Canyon Dam in the sixties. Priscilla got interested in the Lake Powell project, and helped put together a big interdisciplinary proposal for the National Science Foundation (NSF). They wrote her into the proposal as executive secretary, with a year's salary at UCLA. A year later, the NSF funding came through, and Priscilla decided to sign on. "I left a tenure-track position in a geologic specialty to go on 'soft money' as an executive secretary," she said. "People told me I was crazy. And I'm absolutely delighted I did it. It was one of the best choices I ever made."

I spoke with Priscilla in September of 2000 at the University of Nebraska–Lincoln, just as she was preparing to make another bold move,

PRISCILLA CROSWELL PERKINS

from Vice Chancellor for Research back into the classroom, teaching geology. Priscilla swept into the lobby of the Cornhusker Hotel, in Lincoln, where we were meeting for dinner, white shoulder-length hair swinging, eyes sparkling, bursting with energy and enthusiasm. She had just come from a tutorial on how to use the PowerPoint controls in a multimedia classroom. "When I left the classroom, I was still teaching with chalk," she said. "I remember, when I first went to Berkeley, I took a course on the geology of North America. The professor was known for his drawings and maps, all hand-lettered and hand-drawn. They were absolutely gorgeous. He would go into the classroom about half an hour ahead of class and draw, in colored chalk. And we all ended up going a half-hour early to copy it. It was a tour de force. I feel as though I went to school in the nineteenth century!"

Geology at Bryn Mawr had a very special reputation. It started in 1885 with the appointment of Florence Bascom, who was not only the first woman to receive the doctorate in geology in America, but also the first woman to receive a PhD (in any field) at Johns Hopkins University. Bascom soon became a legend, both at Bryn Mawr and among American geologists. A male colleague was amazed that she always carried her own equipment "like a regular fellow." Her students remember having to "walk fast to keep pace with her," as she led them out into the field, dressed in a leather jacket, a skirt "well above the ankles," and stout shoes.[3] Bascom became the foremost woman geologist in America, as well as the first woman to serve as a geologist on the U.S. Geological Survey, the first woman elected to fellowship in the Geological Society of America, and the first woman elected as vice president of that organization. During her time at the College (1895–1928), Bascom trained a number of very remarkable students. In fact, until the mid-thirties, a majority of American women geologists came from Bryn Mawr.

Only two students in our class majored in geology, yet the department had a full-fledged doctoral program. "Professors would take us on field trips," said Priscilla, "and they would invite us home. You saw graduate students all the time; you were immediately in that environment and just took it for granted." In addition to the regular geology faculty, there were visiting professors. Priscilla was able to study with a professor of paleontology from Princeton, and to take a combination undergraduate/graduate summer course in "Recent Sedimentation" taught by a professor from Scripps. These professors encouraged her to go to graduate school, and helped her get an NSF Fellowship at Berkeley. "They were both terrific mentors," said Priscilla, "and both later became really famous leaders in their particular fields. I got to work with them because I was from Bryn Mawr and the Bryn Mawr geology department had the reputation it did."

"I really sympathize with people who haven't finished a degree or things like that. There are so many points at which I could have dropped out or given up."

Priscilla has charted a bold, zigzag career path. But like many in our class, she also went through times when she felt discouraged, and lacked confidence. She still remembers her first assignment in freshman English at Bryn Mawr— *read poems on pages three, four, and five, analyze them, and be prepared to discuss them in class tomorrow.* She remembers the panic she felt. "I had no idea what you were supposed to do to analyze a poem," she said. "I thought you either read a poem or memorized it." She felt the same lack of confidence when she first got to Berkeley. There were people in her entering class who had just come off a year with Fulbright Fellowships, doing geological research in New Zealand and Norway. "Starting graduate school was like freshman year all over again," she said. "I was just not competitive."

Priscilla left Berkeley before finishing her dissertation (following her husband, who got a job at MIT), and went to teach at Boston College. "I'm sure it was the Bryn Mawr and Berkeley credentials," said Priscilla. "I was hired on the basis of one interview at a national meeting, just a month before I started teaching. Now, it's unthinkable that you could get a job that easily." The first draft of her thesis came back to her in Boston with a note from the Berkeley professor saying, "Well, this really isn't what we would expect," and Priscilla cried her heart out, completely devastated. Finally, her husband gave her some perspective, and encouraged her. "It's just your first draft," he said. "It's like getting a paper rejected. You've got to get used to it." When she submitted a second draft, the professor was happily surprised at its quality.

"If my husband hadn't encouraged me, I could have just given up," said Priscilla. "I really sympathize with people who haven't finished a degree or things like that. There are so many points at which I could have dropped out or given up. I was confident in the sense that I did feel, I've got good grades, I got into good schools, I can do this sort of thing—you sort of psych yourself up. But it's an awfully competitive world out there; it's just that, at some points, it becomes more obvious to you." For most of us, the experience of Bryn Mawr cut both ways—we knew we had good credentials, we even felt a certain sense of intellectual self-confidence, but this self-confidence was still untested and rather fragile. Deep down, many of us were not quite sure we measured up.

The late sixties were heady times for geologists. In 1968, the first paper on plate tectonics came out, setting forth a grand, encompassing theory that incorporated earlier ideas of sea floor spreading and continental drift. "It was a scientific explosion," said Priscilla, "like discovering the earth is round." During those years, she was preparing and teaching new courses at Boston College, writing her dissertation, and dashing over to seminars at MIT and Harvard whenever she could to hear about the latest findings. "It was an incredibly exciting time," she said, "because of all that was happening. It's hard to explain. I suppose it's as though you were in Europe during the Enlightenment. It was the biggest scientific revolution *ever* in our field."

After leaving Boston College for the Lake Powell project, Priscilla made a series of brave, sideways (even backward) career moves. Her father, she told me, had done something similar in his career. He started out as minister of a large Congregational church in New York, then moved to a tiny little church in Arizona because of her mother's health. Next was San Antonio, Texas, where Priscilla grew up, again a tiny church. Both of these church communities in the southwest were very conservative, and her father was quite unhappy. Finally, he just couldn't take it. He decided to leave the ministry, earn a PhD, and go into university teaching instead. "It was a wrenching decision," said Priscilla, "and it was playing out right in front of me. Maybe that's why I've always been able to move around and change careers, because my father moved and made this big career change."

The Lake Powell project really led to everything else. A UCLA law professor who worked with Priscilla on the project later became the deputy secretary of resources for California under Governor Jerry Brown, and he recommended her for a position in the Brown administration. Brown appointed Priscilla as chair of the California State Mining and Geology Board. A year later, in 1976, he appointed her director of a newly created department of conservation, which included the state geological survey, the division of oil and gas, the soil conservation group, and some other entities. Priscilla had approximately three hundred employees under her, and a budget of close to $11 million. "I had never supervised anything," said Priscilla. "I wasn't even a Brown campaign contributor. I couldn't have gotten that job without the Lake Powell project, and I wouldn't have gotten the Lake Powell project if I hadn't gone to the 1970 meeting in Arizona, and I wouldn't have done that if . . . . So you see, all these little links."

Priscilla divorced in 1972, and married her second husband, a geologist, in 1975, while she was in California. He came out to UCLA after they were married. This was quite unusual, even as late as 1975. Normally, the pattern was for women to follow their husbands. For the next couple of years, Priscilla's husband was a "trailing spouse," and was also involved in international collaborations in Antarctica. Then, in 1977, he got a Fulbright grant to do research in Australia. At that point, Priscilla had been on the job at the California Department of Conservation for less than a year, but she decided that she would resign to go to Australia with her husband. The plan was for him to join an expedition to Antarctica, and then later meet up with Priscilla in Australia.

Soon after her husband's departure, the people in the conservation department had a going-away party for Priscilla. They even gave her a little gold watch. Then, the very next day, a big emergency came up, something about nuclear waste disposal and earthquakes. "I can't remember what it was exactly," said Priscilla, "but it was an all-nighter. By the next morning, I decided I just couldn't give it up. I thought I would be giving up *everything*. I didn't have anything to do in Australia; I wouldn't have a job; I couldn't have a job there. So I changed my mind, after the going-away party and everything." Her husband was incommunicado in the Antarctic; the first he knew about her decision was on the return voyage, when he got a letter from her, just two weeks before his ship docked in Australia.

Since 1977, Priscilla and her husband have been living apart, seeing each other on average once every six to eight weeks when her husband is in the country, much less often when he is overseas. Back then, it was phoning every day and frequent letters; more recently, these communications have been supplemented by e-mails. In 2007, commuting marriages are not unheard of, especially among two-career academic couples. But this was 1977. Her husband's parents were "totally livid," Priscilla remembered. "It was hard," she said, "but I think, in retrospect, it was the right decision. He has been willing to put up with over three decades of doing his own cooking and living alone, while I took the jobs that I really wanted."

The other big decision was not to have children. "I think I first started thinking about this back in 1962, when I got engaged," she said, "while I was still at Bryn Mawr. I thought that if you have a family, then you definitely can't work. I did spend a lot of time thinking about it: 'Should I have kids, shouldn't I have kids?' It was the whole fifties thing." Priscilla felt very strong pressure from her first husband's parents to have children. "They said, 'You're going to be lonely when you're old,' and all that stuff. We'd have these horrible sessions." Her own parents also had those expectations. There wasn't any point at which she made a clear decision, she said; it was always just that she wasn't going to do it right then.

In a 40th reunion questionnaire, sixteen out of ninety-one respondents reported that they had never had children, an exceptionally high number for women of our generation. Classmate and demographer Betsy Gould talked about her own thinking on this subject. "I've read a lot about fertility," she said, "and I know that people who don't have children early are less likely to have them at all. I know a lot intellectually about the subject, but as far as my own situation goes, if I were to answer the question 'Why don't you have children?' my only honest answer could be 'I don't know.' And this is not a satisfactory answer. I didn't set out to have children or not to have children. It just never seemed the thing I wanted to do right then. I never really said to my husband, 'OK, now I really want to have a baby. Let's do it.' And the model I got from my parents (and my husband got from his parents), was that men worked all the time, while women took care of the house and children."

After the California Department of Conservation, Priscilla served six years as a commissioner of the California Public Utilities Commission. In 1986 she took another "backwards" step in her career, and moved to Minnesota as director of the geological survey for the state. (In California, she had been the boss of the geological survey director.) The Minnesota survey is a unit of the University of Minnesota rather than state government, so Priscilla was simultaneously appointed as a tenured full professor in the School of Earth Sciences on the Twin Cities campus. Survey funding, however (including the director's salary), was a separate line item in the University's budget. In June 1991, newly elected Governor Arne Carlson decided to veto the entire budget line for the geological survey, thus threatening closure of the unit. Priscilla had just twelve months to work to save it. She talked with legislators and rallied all the survey constituencies. Finally, after a yearlong campaign of letter writing and supportive newspaper editorials, the legislature voted unanimously to restore the survey to its former status, to keep it (and Priscilla's job as director) alive.

Soon after getting the geological survey re-funded, Priscilla heard from a former student. She was calling, in her capacity as a member of the University of Nebraska search committee for vice chancellor for research, to ask if Priscilla knew any women who might be interested in applying. A new chancellor at Nebraska had just appointed the first woman vice chancellor for academic affairs, and people on the search committee were on a mission to bring more women into the administration. "I was happy where I was, in Minnesota," said Priscilla. "But then I heard her describe the job. It involved working in all different subjects, music to my ears. So I said, 'Well, *I* would be interested in applying.' There was a silence on the other end of the line, and finally, 'Oh, that's great!'"

Priscilla was appointed vice chancellor for research at the University of Nebraska–Lincoln, and that is where she is still. In 2002, she moved back into the classroom as professor of geology, and in August 2003, she took on another new job, as director of the University of Nebraska State Museum—the state's natural history museum.

Ellen Zetzel Lambert–"Composing a Life"

I met Ellen in the downstairs lobby of the Dalton School, a private high school on New York's Upper East Side, where she teaches high school English literature. She stepped off the elevator straight from her last class

ELLEN ZETZEL

of the day, tall, slim, and very elegant, with striking, angular features.

Ellen was somewhat unusual among our classmates in that she had a mother who was a professional. Actually she had two mothers and two different role models. Her own mother was a social worker, her father a doctor, a gastroenterologist. But her mother was not working when Ellen and her sister were young, and she died when Ellen was just six years old. "I was very aware of having a mother who later was very much idealized as a presence in my life, and as a homemaker," she said. Ellen's father remarried a couple of years after her mother's death, and Ellen acquired a stepmother who was a very prominent Boston psychoanalyst. "In the latter part of my childhood, I grew up certainly with the assumption that I would have a professional life myself," said Ellen. "That was kind of a given. But I always knew that just having a career was not what I wanted in my life. I'd gotten a good look at a mother (my stepmother) who was so wrapped up in her career that there never seemed to be time for the children or domestic life, and I knew I didn't want that."

Most of Ellen's friends at Bryn Mawr were in rebellion against their stay-at-home mothers, determined that their own lives would take a different direction. "They were rebelling against something I had never had and *yearned* for," said Ellen. "I used to be very envious of girls who would say, 'Well, my mother would show me how to make gravy and we made gravy together.' I thought knowing how to make gravy was just the be-all and end-all. This was something that I didn't know how to do. I was deeply resentful of the fact that my stepmother never cooked." Eventually, Ellen and her sister began cooking on their own. "I never really thought about it 'til this moment," said Ellen, "but I think we began by making challah, the traditional Jewish bread. I don't remember whether my own mother ever made bread, but we had the sense that this was what mothers were supposed to be doing."

Issues of identity have always been central in Ellen's life. "There was so much pretending involved in my childhood," she said, "pretending that my mother hadn't died, that my stepmother was my real mother; pretending that we weren't really Jewish but were WASPs like all my friends in those early years."

Ellen was "a little crazy and wild" at Bryn Mawr, she told me. She was drawn to boys from Founders third floor at Haverford, the neighboring men's college, boys who were wild and exciting, and also very smart. For Ellen, that was a magical world. A group of them rented an apartment in "Philly," where everyone went on weekends, with mattresses on the floor. "For the girls, I don't think that drinking or drugs were a big part of it," said Ellen, "but definitely sexual freedom, and breaking the rules."

Ellen wrote her senior honors paper on the image of the walled garden in Medieval literature. "I had this sense of myself," she said. "Bryn Mawr was my little walled garden. And then there was all this emotional life I was leading outside the garden. I had a very serious boyfriend my last two years, a Haverford boy who was a pianist and a composer, but quite unstable. He went off to Berkeley with a whole bunch of other people, and then they really did get into that whole drug scene. Later he had a terrible breakdown. When I found out about it, many years later, I grieved so deeply, and I think I was grieving also for some part of my life that had been lost, a sort of romantic, spontaneous, wild sense of myself as I had been at Bryn Mawr."

In 1967, Ellen fell in love with and married a fellow graduate student in her department at Yale, and a few years later, they moved to Bard College, in Annandale-on-Hudson, New York, where he had a teaching position. Ellen became a "faculty wife." She also finished her PhD, did some part-time teaching, and turned her dissertation into a book (her first book; the one on beauty was her second), no mean accomplishments. But being a professional woman wasn't what she was really interested in at that point in her life. Mostly, she spent the next ten years trying to have a child.

"I felt that I wasn't anywhere," said Ellen. "I wasn't having a professional life that was really meaningful. I wasn't being a mother. I was just being a wife. I remember someone saying, 'Ellen is the perfect wife.' I'm sure they meant it as a compliment. She's this smart woman, and here she is living at Bard all these years, dedicating herself to her husband's career."

Finally, after ten years of that, her husband said, "Well, I guess it's your turn." "It was such a different world in the seventies," said Ellen. "Now, *I* would have said 'It's my turn,' and *long* before ten years." By then her first book, based on her dissertation, was published. She got a tenure-track teaching job at Boston University.

Soon after Ellen went to Boston, she and her husband adopted a child, a daughter. After that, what had seemed a happy marriage began to fail. "Once I was working and once I had a child," said Ellen, "I had the two things I had been wanting for so long, and the marriage fell apart, because the marriage had been sustained by this sort of double vacuum in my life. I don't think I saw it in those terms then, but it sort of leapt out at me in retrospect."

In the seventies, Ellen was a model wife in a very traditional sense. She didn't have a job. She was trying to have a baby. In the eighties, when her marriage was falling apart, she looked around and saw, to her surprise, that the world had changed. Before this, she had lived in an academic setting, where the men were having affairs with younger women, taking a subservient wife for granted. But now, the women were leaving the men. It was happening all around her. By this time, Ellen was in her early forties, at the end of a twenty-year marriage. "That's how it was for a lot of women of our generation," said Ellen. "We were slow to give up on more traditional marriages. We stuck it out for a long time and tried very hard to redefine our marriages, to create a more equal kind of partnership, sharing child care and things like that. But the men we were married to just didn't have that flexibility." Ellen's husband put it clearly: "I'm sorry. I wasn't brought up for this," he said. "I can't deal with these eighties marriages." They separated in 1986 and divorced the following year.

Not all of us stuck it out as long as Ellen did. (I was divorced in the mid-seventies, after eleven years of marriage.) But we did try hard to "save" our marriages. We grew up in the fifties, nurtured on the ideal of the nuclear family. Our parents generally stayed together no matter what. We were supposed to *work on* our marriages, not let them fall apart. For women of our generation, divorce was not only a crisis, but also a personal failure.

For many of us, divorce was also an economic shock. Suddenly, we had to figure out how to pay the rent, put food on the table, and raise children. This was another time in our lives when some of us came up against the world in a way that our mothers did not. "I don't think that earning a living was part of the equation when we were at Bryn Mawr," said one classmate. "I didn't know then that you had to support yourself and support your family."

When I got my first real job, in the U.S. foreign service, I called home to tell my parents. My father asked me what the salary was–this was not a question my mother would have asked–and I had to say I didn't know. They hadn't told me, and I hadn't thought to inquire. Later, with a husband and three children, I paid more attention to money. But it was not until after my divorce that I was confronted with the reality of being on my own, working to support a family. In coping, I discovered a surprising new sense of independence. Several classmates described a similar awakening. "After divorce, I began to understand that there was a connection between economic independence and psychological and intellectual independence," said one. " I think our generation has learned that and did that, or at least some of us."

Soon after her divorce, Ellen was denied tenure. She was in an odd position at Boston University, a good ten years older than the people hired with her. The others were either not yet married or not yet into childbearing, and by then everyone wanted people who were "on track" and would make it without any detours. "I guess I never quite fit the mold of the BU professor," said Ellen. "I was raising my daughter more or less alone, and by then I was working on my second book, on beauty. I knew I wasn't writing it the way they wanted me to. The current thing then was feminist theory and structuralism and all that, and I wanted to write more in plain talk." The tenure decision was a crushing blow, but it turned out, in at least one respect, to be a good thing–it freed Ellen to write her book the way she wanted to, without feeling constrained by the demands of the academy. *The Face of Love* became a much more personal book, and was published by Beacon, a non-academic press.[4]

After leaving Boston University, Ellen decided to try a different kind of teaching. She took a two-year replacement position at Milton Academy, a private secondary school outside of Boston, and found that she loved the

"I think that in a sense we're lucky, as women, in that failure just isn't humiliating in quite the same way as for men. So, we're much more able to make something out of these failures."

job and the people at Milton. When her two years were up, she moved to New York, to make it easier for her daughter to visit her father at Bard. Then in 1989, Ellen started teaching at the Dalton school in New York City, where she has been ever since. Now she is working on her third book—one related to her present life as a secondary-school teacher, on reading poetry with adolescents.

In 1996, Ellen remarried. Her present husband is a political organizer, an activist, not an academic. But more important than all that, Ellen says, is that this time around, she chose someone who *wanted* a partnership marriage: "Someone, for instance, who would not be threatened if his wife were the one working and he were the one shouldering the bulk of domestic responsibilities (which is their current situation), someone who would enjoy cooking together and making a home together—without the old, sharply defined sexual roles. It's not that he is of a different generation than my first husband," said Ellen. "It's that he is an entirely different kind of person, more able to make changes in his own life."

We talked about two books: Carolyn Heilbrun's *Writing a Woman's Life*, and Mary Catherine Bateson's *Composing a Life.*[5] Heilbrun sees women's life stories as quest narratives—exemplary tales of overcoming obstacles, of achievement, ambition, and power. Bateson argues that women's lives develop in a different pattern, one that is seldom linear. Women move from one thing to another, she says, and discover things as they go along. "I felt judged by Heilbrun's quest model," said Ellen. "But Bateson provides another narrative that is much more how my life has been."

She continued, "I think that in a sense we're lucky, as women, in that failure just isn't humiliating in quite the same way as for men. So we're much more able to make something out of these failures. You know, I'd lost ten years. I was off the academic career ladder, and I wasn't going to be able to get back on the ladder. And then I thought, But it doesn't *matter.* I don't really have to think of it that way. And I feel that that's true for most of my women friends."

Chapter Six

Schoolteachers

When it came time for graduation, Ellen Corcoran had no idea of what she wanted do next. The one thing she was clear about was that she *didn't* want to go to graduate school. "I thought there must be something wrong with me," she said. "All my friends seemed to have their lives planned out—what they were going to do, and who they were going to marry—whereas I didn't have a clue." Then she heard that President Kennedy's new Peace Corps was recruiting volunteers to teach in Africa. "I had always wanted to go to Africa," she said, "and it seemed a good way to grow up, make up my mind about things, and just take some time out."

Barbara Powell had wanted to be a teacher ever since she was in fourth grade. She too started teaching in Africa, in a job she had gotten through the Africa-America Institute. As this was her first teaching experience, she hoped to find a place where education was not compulsory, where the students were there because they wanted to learn. And she thought it would be an exciting time to be in Africa, just as all the African nations were gaining their independence.

In the United States, at least since the nineteenth century, school teaching has been a profession dominated by women (except at elite boys' schools and in the upper ranks of school administration). In school teaching, there was no sense that women were outsiders, nothing like the shock that Sherry Ortner and Ellen Zetzel Lambert experienced in entering the academic world. What Ellen Corcoran and Barbara Powell faced was much more subtle, and in some ways more difficult. Ellen had to get rid of her own elitist attitudes. Barbara discovered that in the female world of school teaching, the outspoken, "can-do" attitude she got from Bryn Mawr was often perceived as arrogance. These are stories of comeuppance, and ultimately, of lessons learned.

When Ellen joined the Peace Corps to go to Africa, she had no thought of teaching as a career. In fact, her father looked down on teaching, and considered it a real comedown for somebody who had gone to Bryn Mawr. Ellen herself needed some "reeducation," a process that began as soon as she arrived at the Peace Corps training site in Berkeley. "I had some illusions about my worth as a Bryn Mawr graduate," she said, "and here I found myself with extraordinarily interesting, successful graduates from public universities all across the country, places I'd never even heard of. I got my comeuppance very fast."

Barbara remembers Bryn Mawr as the place where she acquired a love of learning and a sense of intellectual self-confidence. "You came out of Bryn Mawr knowing that you had a good mind and it was an important asset that you could use the rest of your life. Also with a sort of can-do optimism, what other people might consider arrogance, the arrogance of people who have been very well educated and haven't been stomped down by lots of little humiliations."

Some of this had to do with male/female roles and expectations. In those days, women weren't supposed to argue. Josie Donovan talked about this in relation to her work in the women's movement. At Bryn Mawr, she said, "we used to argue rather vehemently with one another, and nobody took it personally. If I try to do that now, I find that many women get emotional, they get hurt, whereas we could just say what we thought and argue, knowing that nobody was going to be demolished by it or feel personally hurt."

"There was a certain confident style, which might have been *perceived* as arrogance," said Barbara, "but I think, for women of our generation, that 'arrogance' was essential."

Twelve in our class (of 159) went from college into teaching jobs, while another four went on for higher degrees in education. For some, like Ellen, teaching was a default choice, a good alternative if you knew that you *didn't* want to go on to graduate school. It was also a good way to see the world–classmates went to teach in far-flung locations such as Hawaii, Latin America, and Africa.

Women from Bryn Mawr, like most other "seven sisters" graduates, lacked the certification required for public school teaching. Most had never taken an education course or done any practice teaching. Independent schools, and some strong suburban public schools, recruited from this pool of elite women's college graduates, while the vast majority of public schools recruited from state college and university teacher-training programs.

Bryn Mawr has a long and complex relationship to teacher education, dating back to the early years of the twentieth century, when the older and larger men's colleges were just beginning to develop separate professional schools. President M. Carey Thomas saw an opportunity for Bryn Mawr to do something similar in the "female" professions of teaching and social work, where graduate training was still practically nonexistent. Thomas felt that Bryn Mawr graduates were already well equipped to teach at the high school level. (This was before there had been much research on adolescent psychology or learning theory, and many educators assumed that high school teaching was just like college teaching, "dumbed down" a bit.) But she saw a real need to develop professional standards and training for teaching in the earlier grades. In 1913, Bryn Mawr opened a new graduate department of education, based in the psychology department, together with a model school.

Katharine McBride first came to Bryn Mawr as a graduate student in psychology, doing work in testing and educational counseling. One observer recalls seeing McBride "surrounded by a group of children of all sizes and kinds, all chattering and interested and quite at their ease as they lined up for a series of tests . . . a picture which not even long acquaintance with her as a College President can supersede."[1] Attitudes about high school teaching were not much changed. When Miss McBride asked Barbara about her plans after graduation and Barbara said she wanted to become a teacher, McBride advised her, "Above all, learn your subject. Don't take any education courses."

When Barbara and Ellen started teaching, they took their own school experience as a model. With no education courses or practical experience, it was all they had. For Barbara the model was Kent Place, a private girls' school. For Ellen it was the integrated, hands-on curriculum that she experienced in the seventh grade at Shady Hill, a progressive school.

In our mothers' generation, teaching was considered to be something that an educated upper-class woman might do for a few years before she got married, or before she had children. Even in our generation, classmates who went into teaching did not necessarily think of it as a long-term commitment. Both Barbara and Ellen went into their first jobs with the idea of testing out their interest in teaching, to see if they wanted to make it their profession. And while they both stayed in the field of education, eventually both earned MAT and EdD degrees, moving out of classroom teaching to work in teacher training, school reform, and curriculum development.

Barbara Schieffelin Powell–Three Generations at Bryn Mawr

I remember the first time I saw Barbara, back in the fall of 1958. She stood out, in those early days on campus, wearing a simple yellow-and-white-striped shirtdress, looking so enviably, utterly relaxed and at ease. To those who felt like outsiders at Bryn Mawr, Barbara was the ultimate insider. She was confident, open, interested in people who were not like her and in the larger world.

BARBARA JAY SCHIEFFELIN

Barbara's mother (Virginia Loomis Schieffelin, '30), and grandmother (Julia Langdon Loomis, class of 1895) both went to Bryn Mawr. Her great-grandmother was in the first class at Vassar, which had been founded before Bryn Mawr. So the idea of higher education for women was not a new concept in her mother's family. (The tradition was different in her father's family, where generally the men went to college and the women did not–though one college-educated sister also attended Bryn Mawr.)

I asked Barbara if her mother or her grandmother had worked after college. "Well," she said, "they worked. My mother worked a lot. But they weren't in the paid labor force." Barbara's mother founded Fair Housing in Short Hills, New Jersey, the town where they lived, and volunteered in settlement houses and in hospitals. But graduating in 1930, during the Depression, the prevailing sense was that if you were a woman and did not have to support yourself, you should not take a job from a man who needed to support a family.

Barbara comes from a long line of socially conscious, activist women. Her maternal grandmother had been a suffragette, and her mother was "an early, vocal, articulate and very well-informed activist" during the Vietnam War. "She got the idea from Bryn Mawr," said Barbara, "and also from family, that you were expected to make a contribution." Barbara's mother marched in an antiwar demonstration in Washington, together with Barbara and some other teachers. Barbara and her mother both signed the Bryn Mawr alumnae antiwar petition in the *New York Times*. And in 1967, after race riots broke out in Newark, New Jersey, Barbara's mother volunteered as a tutor in the schools. "She was quietly fierce in acting on her beliefs," said Barbara. "In different times, she would have been a teacher."

Of her two parents, said Barbara, her mother was the major intellectual. Throughout her life, Barbara's mother kept little notebooks, and every time she read something, she would note down a pithy comment. In 1980, she was reading Herodotus' *Histories*: "Gossiping, delightful, glee in cruelties and sexual excesses," reads the note, written in a small, neat hand. "Enormous interest in large known world. Frequently inaccurate– but who cares."

Barbara attended public school up through the sixth grade, then switched to Kent Place. It was small, with strong traditions and personal attention. Barbara sang in the school chorus, worked on the newspaper and yearbook, and participated in student government. "I loved my school," she said. "Working in school reform, I find that I'm often the only person at the table who had a positive experience in high school. And

I wonder what vision they have for school reform if they themselves have never experienced a really good, exciting school."

Her brother went away to boarding school when he was fourteen, but her two sisters were with her at Kent Place, and the three of them did a lot of things together as a family. Family was important to Barbara, not just her own nuclear family but the extended family. Her father was one of nine children; she has twenty-three first cousins.

Barbara applied to Radcliffe, Smith, and Bryn Mawr, and was accepted by all three. She decided on Bryn Mawr after the *Chicago Tribune* report came out with Bryn Mawr ranked as the top women's college. When I asked what difference the decision had made, Barbara talked again about her mother. "You're in college for four years," she said, "but you're with your mother for the rest of your life, or her life. It was wonderful to go back to reunions with my mother, to serve as her 'companion' when she was older and had Parkinson's, to be with all these cool friends of hers. I know a lot of people in the Bryn Mawr clubs of Boston and New Jersey who also knew my mother, so there's a nice sense of continuity."

Family opened up the world for Barbara. When she studied the Ottoman Empire, at Bryn Mawr, it was a summer trip to Turkey with her family that made that history come alive. I asked Barbara what she remembered most about her time at Bryn Mawr, and she talked about Gertrude Ely, a friend and alumna (class of 1899) of the college who lived at the campus edge. Railroads were the connection—Miss Ely's father had been president of the Pennsylvania Railroad at the same time that Barbara's maternal grandfather was president of the nearby Lehigh Valley Railroad. Miss Ely was in her eighties when we were at Bryn Mawr, very active in the community and the world. Barbara would often drop by at her house for tea or dinner, and she helped Miss Ely form a boys' club, to keep local boys active and involved. After Bryn Mawr, on her way to teach in East Africa, Barbara stopped off for about a week at the Schieffelin Leprosy Research Sanitarium, in Karigiri, India, founded by her paternal grandfather.

Barbara remembers getting off the plane in Nyasaland, now Malawi, carrying one suitcase—the contents of which lasted her for a year—stepping onto the tarmac, where an African minister of the Church of Central African Presbyterian in full black cassock was waiting to greet her. She arrived a couple of days before she was to begin teaching, and the night before classes began, she panicked. She remembers feeling furious at Miss McBride for advising her not to take any education courses. And she remembers walking into the house of one of the other teachers that night, and finally, after meeting his wife and lots of talk, blurting out her question: "Mr. Kadzombe, how do you teach?" And he said, "Miss Schieffelin, you are a graduate." That was the best thing he could have said. He and the other two teachers there, both Africans, had not gone to college. So Barbara thought, "Okay, I must know something. I can figure this out."

At the Henry Henderson Hudson Institute in Blantyre, Malawi, Barbara taught English, History of the British Commonwealth, and African History. She was also choir mistress and athletics mistress—she taught singing, put on student choral performances, and helped students mark out the playing field with a bag of lime and a ball of string. "It was a very, very good experience," said Barbara. "I learned so much. You're totally on your own, so you have to make all the decisions. I was suddenly submerged in a very different culture and a brand new profession for which I had no training. Everything I had *ever* learned in all of my formal education and from daily living could be put to use. And I learned so much about the unique and unexpected talents of my students. They could draw precise and accurate maps of Nyasaland and the African continent, with colored chalk on the blackboard. They could sharpen pencils to a perfect point with a single razor blade."

One day about three weeks into the school term, three white men in black suits walked into Barbara's classroom, sat down in back, took out notebooks, and began writing. She had no idea who these men were, but her students immediately recognized them as members of Her Majesty's Inspectorate. The students also knew exactly what the men were there for, and were instantly on their best behavior—they volunteered answers, they raised their hands, they were quiet when they should be. Afterward, the inspectors met with Barbara and went through everything she had done in class. "They gave me one of the best teacher-training experiences I've ever had," she said. They said, "You used the following eleven words, which were too difficult for this level," and "We thought the way you explained the ocean in *Treasure Island* was well done." None of Barbara's students had ever seen an ocean like the one in *Treasure Island*; they didn't have any concept of such a vast body of water. But she found somebody who lived in Monkey Bay on Lake Nyasa, and got him to explain what the expanse of water was like. The inspectors thought she handled that well. Then they asked her how long she'd been teaching, and Barbara had to say "three weeks."

Barbara stayed in Nyasaland from September 1962 to February 1964. At that time Nyasaland had self-government in internal affairs, but the British still controlled foreign policy and the military. The Malawi independence movement, led by Dr. Hastings Kamuzu Banda and the Malawi Congress Party (MCP), was rapidly gaining force. Barbara soon got involved, traveling with the MCP on campaign trips. She was impressed by the party's reach and organization. "In every village there is some kind of mud hut structure with posters of how to improve the cultivation of maize, pictures of Kamuzu [Dr. Banda], and a table," she wrote, in a letter home. "The party also has Land Rovers that rumble over the mountain roads. They have big loudspeakers, and the party leaders give rousing political speeches. Everyone is filled with so much hope, so much sense of 'we're becoming our own country.'"

While the country was on the cusp of independence, Barbara was also immersed in the universal challenges of her adolescent students: pregnancy, illness, family problems, drugs, exhaustion. And their charms: energy, motivation, eagerness, and appreciation. She returned to the United States convinced that she wanted to be a teacher, and entered Harvard University's Master of Arts in Teaching (MAT) program. It was a flexible program that enabled her to take courses in African history as well as education, and she did a teaching internship in a local public school.

Barbara told me about one "searing experience" that occurred just a few weeks into her first semester at Harvard, her first real encounter with sex discrimination. She needed a book, which was not available at the School of Education Library or the Radcliffe College Library. There was a copy at Lamont, which was the Harvard College Library. She'd been teaching that day, and was still dressed as a professional when she reached the library, in a dress, a black wool coat, stockings, and pumps. She walked into Lamont, and the librarian said, "May I help you?" She said, "No thanks. I'm just going to get a book." He insisted, "May I help you?" She repeated, "No, the book I want is here and it's not in the other university libraries." Then he said, "You're not allowed in there." This was the Harvard undergraduate library, Harvard undergraduates were all male, and Barbara wasn't allowed in because she was a woman. That had never happened to her before. And in a library! Her father worked for the New York Public Library. She could hardly believe it.

"I was just thinking," said Barbara. "This happened to me for the first time when I was already in my twenties, in graduate school, not being allowed to use a library because of my gender. Can you imagine if that happened when you were younger, on a daily basis? It would grind you down."

After finishing her MAT at Harvard, where she co-wrote a curriculum on Vietnam, Barbara spent three years as a junior high school teacher in a public school in Newton, Massachusetts. She enjoyed the teaching, but ultimately couldn't quite imagine spending the rest of her career in a classroom. So Barbara decided to go back to the Harvard School of Education to complete her doctorate and to explore other options in education.

When Barbara returned to Harvard, she was advised that there were three interesting people teaching at the Ed School. One of them was Art Powell, who later became the academic dean. At one point, Powell, who had written a slim volume titled *Educational Careers and the Missing Elite*, formed a panel of Ed School students to persuade deans from top-ranked liberal arts colleges to advise their college seniors to consider education as a career. Barbara was a panelist. Her first letter from him read: "Dear Miss Schieffelin, We'll have a preliminary meeting . . ." That was in the mid-sixties. They married in 1968, "between assassinations."

There followed a decade of having babies and developing curriculum. (The curriculum—"Exploring Childhood" and "The Role of Women in American Society"— echoed the times and Barbara's own stage in life.) I read through twenty years of Powell family Christmas letters, wonderful, long, newsy accounts of the life of a growing family. One big issue of 1980 was "The Question of Barbara's Career." Since the birth of her third child, in 1978, Barbara had defined herself as an "educational consultant," doing short-term, part-time jobs. While consulting had many advantages— interesting projects, flexible hours, and a lot of variety—it didn't give her any cumulative sense of a progressing and predictable career. So Barbara began to explore possibilities for full-time employment. In the spring of 1981, she was offered and accepted the position of headmistress of Dana Hall, a private, day-and-boarding secondary school of four hundred and fifty girls located in Wellesley, just outside of Boston. "Ever since I was at Kent Place," said Barbara, "I thought it would be interesting to be the head of an independent girls' school."

That summer, the Powell family moved from their home in Cambridge to the Dana Hall head's house in Wellesley. It was a huge adjustment, living in a girls' school, and Barbara was learning to balance "the fervid and often conflicting expectations of students, faculty, administrators, parents, alumnae, and trustees," which made for a "challenging and humbling year."

In the spring of 1983, on the afternoon of the Boston Marathon, Barbara was "asked to resign" from her job at Dana Hall, with two months' notice. It was "for the sake of her family," the chairperson of the board of trustees told her. Each of the Powell children had a special reaction to "Danagate." Ben, the oldest, saw the bright side: "Now we can live in our own house, be our own family, and take out our own trash." Allie said he would miss the Dana Hall soccer fields, but was glad he wouldn't have to act like a grown-up all the time. Julia, at age three and a half, wanted clarification: "You're not the headmistress anymore, right?" Right. "But you're still my mommy, right?" Right.

Barbara was never told directly why she was fired. She has thought of some reasons. One was inexperience. She also had a very difficult mandate from the trustees—to reduce the number of faculty while simultaneously increasing the number of classes each taught. (The faculty tried to unionize as a result.) And probably she had not paid enough attention to the "politics" of the situation. Some years later, Barbara was still on a fierce emotional journey. "Someone should write a book about the Stages of Being Fired: Rage, Blame, Avoidance, Despair, Change to a New Field," she wrote in our class 25th reunion report.

In talking with classmates, I found that quite a few of us had been fired from at least one job. It was one thing when this happened in the sixties—like Josie Donovan losing her job as "copy girl" because she had an attitude problem—or even in 1970, when another classmate was fired from her job as union organizer because she argued too much. That was a different world then, before the women's movement. But for Barbara and several others, including myself, it was more complicated. We were fired in the eighties and nineties, when we were already in our forties and fifties and had reached quite high-level positions. (None of us were actually fired—in academic administration you were usually "asked to resign"; as a professor you were denied tenure; as a journalist you were "reassigned," i.e., demoted—but whatever it was called, it felt like being fired.) We couldn't really blame it on sexism or gender discrimination—Barbara was head of a girls' school, where many of the trustees were women. We had to ask ourselves what we were doing wrong. Had we been promoted to a level that was beyond our competence? Did we lack the drive that was necessary to succeed? Were we just too casual about holding on to jobs? Perhaps we were too much in the mold of our mothers' generation, and still thought of work as "making a contribution," while others were more attuned to the "politics" of the workplace, more intent on holding on to their jobs and getting ahead in their careers.

"I think I'm a person of great imagination," said journalist Isa (Brannon) Spencer, "but sometimes you don't really understand about how other people feel until you go through something yourself." Then one day Isa got "reassigned" from her job as editor. "I demoted a few people along the way," she said, "but somehow I always felt that my own career was on this great upward trajectory. When I got demoted, I thought, 'They're so wrong about me. Was I that wrong about the people I did this to?'" As privileged people, we were awfully sure of ourselves. Getting fired made some of us realize what it's like to be on the other end of things, to be judged wanting.

I didn't see it coming when I was fired, and I dealt with it as one of those things that happen in life that you have no control over. You just move on. Barbara, on the other hand, sought out key people at Dana Hall and talked with them one-on-one, in an effort to figure out what had gone wrong, to learn something that might help her work more effectively in the future. (She asked the question, "In your judgment, what prevented me from becoming an effective administrator?") One of the things she learned was that other people sometimes perceived her very differently from the way in which she perceived herself. "What I knew to be feelings

"I know now that some solutions are not intellectual at all."

of uncertainty and insecurity," she said, "apparently came across to others as arrogance."

The experience at Dana Hall taught Barbara to "do her politics" better. Now, when she goes into a new job, she tries to get a sense of the context, "the players," and where the potential barriers, pitfalls, and opportunities are, so that she's not politically naive and therefore ineffectual. She has also learned not to rely so heavily on intellectual solutions. "I know now that some solutions are not intellectual at all," said Barbara. "The best heads of schools are not necessarily great intellectuals; they're people who have incredible political skills and can balance all the constituencies you have to balance when you run an independent school. The models we got from Bryn Mawr were all these explosive women who bludgeoned their way through life and managed to have everything fall before them. But in a school, as in most aspects of life, you need to have more collaborative leadership. You need to understand people, their hopes and their dreams. You need to bring up younger people. If you have a great vision for how an independent school could be but you don't have the personal and political skills to get there, it doesn't matter how brilliant the vision is."

We were not the only women to experience career setbacks in the eighties and nineties. "Glass ceiling" was a term coined in 1984,[2] just about the time that so many of us were getting fired. We may just have been among the first to crack up against that ceiling. And however painful it was to be fired, in retrospect most of us felt that it had turned out to be a good thing, opening the door to new opportunities.

Since the mid-eighties, Barbara has consulted on program development, teacher training, and evaluation in a number of different settings, ranging from a farm school for at-risk boys to a public radio program showcasing young classical musicians. Much of the time, she has been working in educational settings other than schools. At Polaroid, for instance, she designed courses for hourly workers to learn such skills as giving constructive feedback and making presentations.

In one class, after the line workers had practiced making presentations to their peers on ways of improving the workplace, she told them, "Next week your supervisors are coming to class to hear your ideas." "Oh, no," they said. "That wasn't part of the deal!" And the next week, the supervisors all sat in the back row with their arms folded across their chests. But then, as the students gained confidence, the supervisors began to take out their pads and start writing notes. Afterward, they buttonholed the workers, and said, "About that idea you had . . ." "It was very practical," said Barbara, "very empowering."

Over the course of her career, Barbara has taught curriculum development and pedagogy, and has done research on how the concept of understanding is interpreted by teachers and students and demonstrated in the classroom. Since 1999, four years before the American invasion of Iraq, she has been working on Exploring Humanitarian Law, a curriculum in international humanitarian law–principally the Geneva Conventions– sponsored by the International Committee of the Red Cross and Red Crescent. International humanitarian law protects the lives and human dignity of the vulnerable during armed conflict. The curriculum is designed for high school students (ages thirteen to eighteen) and is taught in ninety countries all over the world. It explores such topics as the dilemmas combatants face in combat; the protection of prisoners; the aftermath of war; child soldiers; and land mines. "It's an excellent curriculum," said Barbara. "It requires that teachers explore the material *with* their students, which is very challenging, especially in countries where teachers are supposed to be the font of knowledge."

At the end of pilot programs in Morocco, Thailand, and Jamaica, Barbara asked the teachers what they needed to be able to teach the course. On the basis of what they told her, she developed materials on discussion, role-playing, and using film, and had the teachers teach each other in training workshops. The teachers' guide includes something called the "no easy answer corner," which helps teachers deal with pesky questions from students such as "Why have war at all? Why do we have to have rules for war? Why don't you just outlaw war?"

Now, as the Exploring Humanitarian Law curriculum goes online at a "virtual campus," Barbara is helping to connect teachers from all over the world, coming from vastly different perspectives, to talk about the curriculum and their teaching. "I love my work," said Barbara. "I feel as though I'm at the culmination of my career, as though everything I've done has been leading to this."

In April 2005 I got back in touch with Barbara to set up another interview and a photo shoot, and she responded with an e-mail telling me about "two new things" in her life. One was the birth of her first grandchild. "It's a whole new feeling," she wrote, "to see the next generation come forth into the world, to realize that life goes on, and to fall in love with a baby all over again."

It was already summer by the time I got to visit Barbara at her home in Cambridge, Massachusetts, a rambling brick house set in a garden, a hushed, blooming oasis on a stifling June day. I found her looking remarkably fit, in spite of the heat and her still quite recent aneurysm and open-heart surgery. (That was the second "new thing" referred to in the April e-mail.). She seemed to have a new calm and seriousness. "My aneurysm was a huge jolt," she said, "a wake-up call. So now I think, what's going to change? One of the things you learn during healing is patience. I've always been kind of an up-and-at-'em type. Now I've slowed down. I'm beginning to discover a natural flow in life."

Ellen Corcoran–Taking One Step at a Time

Ellen's pattern in life has been to come at things very carefully, very slowly, taking one step at a time. "I can remember very distinctly not making a commitment to teaching until I had been at it three years," she said, "by which time I felt I knew enough about teaching and enough about myself to say, 'All right, I'm going to stay in this field. I don't know what it will look like, but I'm going to stay in this field.'"

I met with Ellen in February 2001 at the University of New Hampshire at Durham, where she had been on the faculty of the teacher education program since 1972. I discovered her in a small corner office, surrounded by a cheerful clutter of books and papers, a large golden retriever stretched out at her feet. The dog jumped up, barking, to offer me a soft, wet nuzzle. "That's Honey," said Ellen, "short for Honeysuckle Rose." She came over and gave me a quick hug, then went on: "Honey's a great protector here . . . . I don't mean my physical safety. She protects me from the toxic environment that I sometimes feel. It's amazing how handy it is sometimes to have to take the dog for a walk."

ELLEN PATRICIA CORCORAN

Ellen grew up as the youngest of five children, Irish Catholic, in Cambridge, Massachusetts. Her paternal grandfather came over with the Fenians, an Irish rebel group, in the 1860s or '70s, settled in Cambridge, and managed to start a small department store, which Ellen's father later took over. By the time Ellen was born, her parents were already older, both around forty (her father was born in 1899 and her mother in 1901 or 1902). She remembers her father being very involved with his work and civic responsibilities, while her mother gradually retreated from the world. Ellen did not want her own life to turn out like her mother's.

Ellen's mother graduated from college, then immediately went home to take care of *her* mother, who was sick. She stayed with her mother until she died, then married and had five children. After college, Ellen's mother never really had any life of her own. She never worked outside the home (Ellen's father would probably not have accepted it), didn't really have any friends, and eventually even pulled back from doing volunteer work. "I think my mother was quite lonely," said Ellen, "and bitter perhaps about the way her life turned out. I remember when I was still in my thirties seeing pieces of my mother starting to emerge in me. My response was to immediately go into therapy, because I was damned if I was going to become her, and I didn't know how to deal with that on my own."

Ellen went to the local public school through the fifth grade, then switched to Shady Hill, a progressive private school that had an integrated, hands-on curriculum. In the seventh grade they spent the whole year studying the American Civil War. Ellen remembers reading Steven Vincent Benet's *John Brown's Body*, singing a choral requiem for Lincoln, and doing her first major research paper. Her father happened to be a Civil War buff, and brought in rare books on loan to the class. Ellen still remembers her seventh-grade teacher, a Miss Caudill, from Tennessee. "She hadn't lost any of that marvelous cadence to her voice or the capacity to tell stories that seems to me to be distinctively southern," she said. "It was just a wonderful year. Miss Caudill taught me that it was okay to just ask for what you wanted, rather than be some sort of jerk and get attention and eventually end up getting what you wanted. That was very liberating for me. It put me in charge of my life, which I had never really felt before."

After Shady Hill, Ellen went on to Buckingham, a private girls' school (later merged with a boys' school as Buckingham Browne and Nichols), for the last three years of high school. Buckingham was a very traditional school, almost classically oriented, in contrast to Shady Hill. Ellen thoroughly enjoyed it, worked hard at the subjects she loved, such as Latin, and did all right with the others. When it came time to choose a college, she knew she wanted to leave home, and was fairly sure that she would do better with a women's college. Smith felt too big, Mount Holyoke didn't interest her, and Vassar was unacceptable to her father, who for some reason had a real hatred for Vassar. "Bryn Mawr captured me," said Ellen. "I'm sure the campus was a part of it, and I had the feeling, I think, that Bryn Mawr was academically the most interesting."

By Thanksgiving of her freshman year at Bryn Mawr, Ellen was ready to quit. "I felt overwhelmed academically," she said, "like a lost soul." Part of that had to do with being Catholic. Her freshman roommate was from a quite religious Jewish family. "Going to a Passover Seder at their house was a wonderful experience," said Ellen, "and her parents were very gracious and generous. But the two of us were so very different. She was really brilliant, which I do not consider myself to be. If I have an intelligence, it's of a different sort." Ellen was drawn to another freshman, a Catholic from Joliet, Illinois, who shared a lot of her sense of "misfitness."

It wasn't just going to Mass every week that made Ellen feel like an outsider. It was also the kind of world view that she had been brought up with. "The way I experienced Catholicism was that it was not a thinking kind of religion," said Ellen. "It was driven by obedience, a 'don't question authority' attitude. And that was a stance toward life that was actively discouraged, I think, at Bryn Mawr." Later, Ellen herself would begin to question Catholic doctrine and attitudes, and eventually she left the church, the only one of her siblings to do so. But that was later. At the time, at age eighteen, it was hard to sort it all out. She just felt different.

At some point in that first semester, Ellen's family got word to Bryn Mawr that she was exceptionally unhappy. Then something quite extraordinary happened: Miss McBride reached out and began to invite Ellen to dinner on a fairly regular basis, about once a month. And that continued through the next three and a half years that she was at Bryn Mawr. "I was very lucky," said Ellen. "That experience turned everything around for me. What an extraordinary woman!" A lot of students were terrified of Miss McBride and felt that she disapproved of them, but to Ellen she was always generous and caring. "I think she was probably a very shy person in groups," said Ellen. "I got no sense of her as an academic; we never talked that kind of substance. We talked a lot about Bryn Mawr, its structure, and what made it hard for some students to adjust to the rigors of Bryn Mawr. She was intensely interested in that." When I pressed Ellen to describe Miss McBride as she knew her, she paused, thoughtfully. "I'm going to say two words," she said, "but I'm not sure I can articulate what I mean. I felt that she was very caring, but not necessarily warm." Ellen went on to explain. "It wasn't an intimate relationship," she said. "But it was very caring."

Another big piece of Bryn Mawr for Ellen was the person who was assigned to her in her junior year as a "little sister," Kathy Boudin ('65), who later joined the radical Weatherman group and was a key player in the 1981 Brinks armored car heist. Ellen remembers going up to New York several times to spend weekends with the Boudin family. "I was very wide-eyed," she said. "That was my first experience of the New York intelligentsia. It was the absolute antithesis of anything I had ever known, a whole other ether."

By Thanksgiving of her freshman year, Ellen was ready to quit. "I felt overwhelmed academically, like a lost soul."

In the fall of 1962, Ellen set off for Ghana, West Africa, where she was assigned to teach sixth-form French at Mfantsipim, Ghana's oldest and most prestigious boys' secondary school, whose graduates include Kofi Annan, the United Nations Secretary-General.

"Talk about being turned upside down and shaken inside out," said Ellen. "That's what that first year in Ghana was like for me. There wasn't a single assumption I made that survived that transition." There were some big things, she said, like the whole concept of time. If you're a little late, or even a day late, it's not so important. "For the first year there was a lot of my having to deal with my impatience," said Ellen, "and beginning to see the beauty of the other way." Ellen was a highly visible minority at Mfantsipim—a white American woman in an all-male school in Ghana. It took her a little while to become comfortable with that. The other big thing was health, something she had always been able to take for granted. She wasn't well for the whole first year, and her skin was covered with funguses because of the constant humidity.

Teaching at Mfantsipim, Ellen had to learn to deal with the legacy of the British educational system. "It was a very exam-driven system, and these were very achievement-oriented students," said Ellen. "If you deviated even slightly, it was: 'Please Miss, that was not on the syllabus.' And they weren't kidding. This was serious business for them." It took her quite a while to figure out how to honor her students' needs and at the same time give them something more than rote learning. She found creative solutions, began bringing in folktales from French-speaking West Africa to supplement the curriculum, and her students had a good time reading familiar stories such as "Anansi the Spider Man" in French.

After more than two years in Ghana, Ellen found it very hard to come back to the States. Many returned Peace Corps volunteers had the same problem, coming back into all the turmoil and violence of America in the sixties. "I wandered around like a lost soul," said Ellen, "looking for how to fit in, wondering if I even belonged in this country, really disillusioned. I just didn't want to be here. I talked a lot about wanting to go back and become a Ghanaian citizen." Her parents rode out the storm. They saw that she needed to find a new sense of direction, and gave her a year to do volunteer work in different kinds of social agencies, to explore different options.

She worked as a social worker in a YMCA in Chicago, and taught in a preschool program in Roxbury in Boston. As she did that, it was like a narrowing spiral. "It became clear to me that working with kids was a big piece of what I wanted to do," said Ellen. "Then the logic of it was, if you want to work with kids, a place where you can be guaranteed of finding them is schools. It wasn't really 'til then that I thought about teaching as a career." She discovered the Teacher Corps, a program created in the mid-sixties with War on Poverty funding. The program provided an opportunity for liberal arts college graduates to receive a stipend, study for a master's degree in teaching, and do an extended internship, all at the same time. Ellen joined in the spring of 1966, ending up in a group made up entirely of returned Peace Corps volunteers. "The Teacher Corps rescued me," she said. "I began teaching in East Harlem and working on my master's at New York University (NYU) and then just kept going."

Ellen was one of a team of five Teacher Corps interns at Junior High 45, located right at the foot of the Triboro Bridge, in East Harlem. The school was 60 percent Hispanic and 40 percent black, with a handful of whites. (Just the Mahoney family, as Ellen remembered.) The school was organized in a very traditional way: Students were "tracked," according to their reading test scores, and each subject was taught separately. Ellen was assigned to teach seventh-grade social studies—five separate classes, meeting for forty-two minutes each.

Ellen found this system impossible. So she negotiated with the principal and was permitted to create an experimental structure. It was experimental from their point of view, but she had lived it in the seventh grade at Shady Hill. She had one group of students all morning four days a week and all day for a fifth day, and she developed an integrated curriculum, which included every subject except for math, science, physical education, and home economics. The other thing that Ellen lobbied for was not to have a tracked class. So she had a heterogeneous group and stayed with them for two years, teaching them as seventh-graders and then as eighth-graders. "Once I had set up those conditions," said Ellen, "then I could really do something."

Ellen was teaching in East Harlem in April of 1968 when the news of Martin Luther King Jr.'s assassination came through. Her school was dismissed early, to get the teachers out. (School authorities thought there might be riots in Harlem, and that the teachers, most of whom were white, might be in danger.) Ellen lived downtown in Chelsea, which meant she had to walk all the way across town, right through the heart of Harlem, to get to a direct subway line. That day her students didn't want her to be alone in the streets, and a group of them decided to walk her across Harlem to the subway. "It's got to be one of the greatest memories I will ever have of that crew of kids," said Ellen. "As we walked, people in the street and in the windows of buildings all had loudspeakers. Some were playing gospel music, spirituals, *Amazing Grace* and things like that. Others were playing recordings of King himself, like the 'I Have a Dream' speech, and the sound was bouncing off the buildings as we walked along. My kids were all around me in a sort of phalanx, explaining to everyone who I was and why they were with me. It was truly an amazing experience to feel a part of that."

Soon after Ellen started teaching, the eighth-grade social studies curriculum was changed into urban studies, which gave her an opportunity to have her students do fieldwork in the neighborhood. Barring bad weather, they went out every day, studying a different city block each week. The students would do all kinds of measurement and mapping. Some of them would interview the people living there; others would take still photographs or film. Then they'd come back to the classroom with all this material and put it together to create a portrait of the block. The next week they would go out and do the same thing with another block. On Fridays, when Ellen had them for the whole day, they went on field trips to various city agencies. "I remember we once spent a day with the New York City cartographers," said Ellen, "all these little old Italian men with their ancient surveying tools and maps. It was great, great education, and a lot of parents were involved in those field trips, so it was really fun."

In 1969, the New York City Board of Education instituted a new policy of "community control" of the schools, and all the old-guard principals were forced out. That meant that Ellen lost her "privileges." By then, she had become very close to some of the other Teacher Corps interns; they had been getting together every week for dinner for years. When community control came along, four of the group, including Ellen, decided that life in these traditional schools was no longer bearable. They figured out how to get funding for an alternative school.

In 1970 they launched the Clinton Program, modeled after something called the Parkway Program, which had started in Philadelphia, and also went by the name of School Without Walls. They offered all the traditional subjects, which satisfied the state, but they had no requirements, which satisfied their own belief that students need to have some choice. In the mornings the students could take any of the traditional subjects, and in the afternoon they went out on their electives. These were entirely community-based, using the whole city, with apprenticeships at places like the Bronx Zoo and the Museum of Natural History. The Clinton Program ran successfully for several years, but it didn't survive the huge fiscal crisis that New York City faced in the mid-seventies. By that time, Ellen had already left for New Hampshire.

Ellen had supervised student teachers when she was in East Harlem and also in the Clinton Program. She found herself increasingly interested in these student teachers as learners, and started to look around for an opportunity to move into teacher education. Just then, in 1971–72, the University of New Hampshire (UNH) was searching for someone to help create a fifth-year internship program to replace the old undergraduate education major. It was a perfect fit, said Ellen. She moved to UNH in 1972, and has been there ever since.

Teacher education is one of six programs in the UNH education department, and oddly enough, it has the most senior faculty, "the old doddering types, such as myself," said Ellen with a laugh. "We're all products of Ivy League liberal arts colleges, all similarly educated, all have a shared vision. Basically I've been able to write my own ticket, to grow and move with the program. That's had the net effect of keeping me

"Honey protects me from the toxic environment that I sometimes feel. It's amazing how handy it is sometimes to have to take the dog for a walk."

intellectually engaged, never feeling like I'm doing the same thing twice. I also spend two days a week in the schools, which gives me grounding and credibility as a faculty member. People know I'm out there doing it."

Soon after coming to the University of New Hampshire, Ellen met Susan, who was teaching in the political science department. Susan was at Bryn Mawr in the 'fifties, married in her senior year of college, and got divorced just about the time that Ellen came to New Hampshire. They soon began spending a lot of time together, discovering they had a lot of things in common. They both enjoyed doing the same things, and both had a passion for traveling. Everything just fell into place. But it took several more years before they were ready to make a commitment to be together. "Before that I didn't feel as if I'd settled enough to know really who I was," said Ellen, "or what I was going to be doing with my life, or any of those things." Both of them had always wanted to live on the beach, so they moved from Durham, New Hampshire, to York, thirty-five minutes away on the coast of Maine.

Ellen got her first golden retriever (Honey is the second) at a time when Susan was having a heart bypass operation. "It was totally intuitive," she said, "the certain knowledge that I needed something young and totally healthy in my life if I were going to be able to work and be supportive to Susan. So I got a puppy, which is about the best decision I could have made."

Susan had already been retired for several years when I talked with Ellen in 2001, and Ellen had decided to retire as soon as possible so that they could both move down to their place in Key West, Florida, to live. Ellen's retirement came through in the summer of 2001. About a year later, she sent me an e-mail: "Having a lovely time in Key West and finding it very difficult to settle into a writing routine. I have hopes, however. Honey seems to be adjusting well."

These days, Ellen and Susan (and Honey) spend their winters in Key West and their summers (through the Florida hurricane season) in Cornucopia, Wisconsin, on the south shore of Lake Superior. I visited them there over Labor Day weekend, 2005. By this time Ellen was already at the end of her three-year "trial period" of retirement, long enough to begin to make decisions about priorities and how she wants to spend her time. "Most of the ingredients are in place," she said, "Susan, family and friends, the dog, painting, Key West, Cornucopia, travel. What's missing is some sort of public service."

"If you look back far enough, you see the seeds being sown," said Ellen. "If I wonder how I got into teaching, and even into this particular kind of teaching, I can see that all that was firmly laid out at Shady Hill. And I think probably my relationship with Susan was firmly laid out through my years at Buckingham and Bryn Mawr. Of course you don't know it at the time you're going through it, but then you look back and everything fits. It all seems to have a certain inevitability."

Chapter Seven

"Women Unwanted" In Law and Medicine

BARBARA HELENE PAUL

In September 1995, the New York City Bar Association celebrated its 125th anniversary, with Barbara (Paul) Robinson, of the Bryn Mawr Class of '62, presiding. A *New York Times* reporter noted the "evening's most striking tableau," at a cocktail reception before the speeches—Justice Ruth Bader Ginsburg of the U.S. Supreme Court huddled in a corner with City Bar Association president Barbara Robinson and American Bar Association president Roberta Cooper Ramo, the three women "trading war stories about their difficulties getting first jobs, and balancing the demands of new lawyering with new mothering."[1]

Barbara is the person we met back in Chapter 2, in the fall semester of her senior year, head of Undergrad, competence personified, confronting Miss McBride over conditions for the College's staff of maids and porters. In 2001, I went to talk with her at her offices at Debevoise & Plimpton, in midtown New York. She seemed essentially the same, except that the crisp blazer she favored in college had been exchanged for chic, understated corporate lawyer's garb, a dark fitted dress and pearls. In her portrait that hangs in the august halls of the City Bar Association, she is painted wearing a dress of vibrant purple, a startling flash of color in a gallery of dark-suited men.

We talked about the 125th anniversary celebration. "Of course I invited Justice Ginsburg, who had been very active in the City Bar

Association," said Barbara. "At first she wrote back and said she couldn't do it. So I tried again, saying, 'We have all these great women. (Other than Mayor Rudolph Giuliani it was an all-female cast, with Hillary Clinton and Chief Judge Judith Kaye participating in videotaped presentations.) You would be just the pièce de résistance.' She wrote back a second time and said, 'How could I miss company like that?'"

The 125th anniversary celebration was a striking demonstration of how far women had come in the world of law. ("It's a damn matriarchy," one man was heard to complain.) When the City Bar Association was formed, in 1870, its founders were all white Protestant men. Women weren't even allowed to join the Association until 1937. Its first Jewish president was elected in 1956; its first African-American president in 1990, and Barbara Robinson, the first woman president, took office in 1994. At the same time, on the national level, President Bill Clinton's attorney general, Janet Reno, and several of her top deputies were women, and two women sat on the U.S. Supreme Court.

Barbara herself was in the vanguard of this dramatic increase in the presence of women in the legal profession. Imagine being a woman entering Yale Law School in the fall of 1962. Yale not only dominated the town of New Haven, but at that time it was an all-male institution. All the undergraduates and most of the graduate students were male, and most of the institutions in town were closed to women. Barbara could not go inside the gym, she couldn't use the Sterling Library reading room, she couldn't go into Mory's (the place where the Whiffenpoofs singing group hung out), she couldn't go to the Elizabethan Club, she could not live in the law school dorms, and on and on. "Nobody now can understand that," said Barbara, "because of course now Yale is coed. It is such a change." At the time, a lot of the men at Yale Law had spent all their formative years in all-male institutions: boarding schools, boys' camps in the summer, and they went to Yale or Amherst, which were all-male then. They were really not used to seeing women Monday through Friday. Women were for Saturday. "I had come from Bryn Mawr and Haverford, where relations between men and women were very egalitarian, everybody was pretty relaxed," said Barbara, "and certainly we were used to seeing women who were in leadership positions. The first six months at the law school—I *loved* the law school—but the first six months I was there I would walk into

L-R: Ruth Bader Ginsberg, Barbara Robinson, and Roberta Cooper Ramo.

the lounge, and it would go silent, just go dead silent. You felt like–'Oh My God, I've done something obscene! What have I done wrong?' It was really odd, partly because it was so small."

This eventually changed, and things became much more relaxed, but there was a time when Barbara thought maybe she'd made a mistake. She went back to Harvard, to look at it again. "Cambridge was so lively," said Barbara, "but Harvard Law School seemed to me very stuffy and establishment. It had more in common with Yale College which, after all, was very preppy, had fraternities and all that, whereas Yale Law School was so liberal and open and different and imaginative. It really belonged in liberal Cambridge, but unfortunately it was located in New Haven." There were only seven women in Barbara's Yale Law School class, out of a total of about a hundred and seventy. Harvard Law School had about a dozen women in the class that entered in the fall of 1962, including two from Bryn Mawr. But Harvard Law was much bigger than Yale, with more than five hundred students in the class, and had only taken women for the first time in 1950. Until then, Yale was the only law school in the six

New England states that admitted women. They had women starting in the 1920s, said Barbara, not consistently and not in any numbers, but still way ahead of Harvard.

The small size of the Yale Law School was a big advantage for the handful of women students. At Harvard, you either had to work up the courage to raise your hand in a class of two hundred, or, in at least one professor's class, to speak up only on "ladies' day," one of the few days a year that were set aside to call on women students. At Yale, many of the classes were taught as small seminars, and that made it a lot easier to speak up in class. All the Yale law students ate their meals in the law school, and the men also lived there, while Barbara lived in the one women's dorm for graduate students.

She was apprehensive that first semester, seeing all these smart people taking lots of notes and raising their hands. "They make it terrifying on purpose," she said, "because they don't want you to think there's a right answer the way you were taught in college." There were exams, and at that time they also had grades (they don't anymore). Barbara did very well, and on the basis of her grades became a member of the *Law Journal*. "That was terrific," she said, "because I got to know the professors more."

In 2007, more than half of the students in medical and law schools are women. But in 1962, very few women thought of becoming doctors or lawyers, even at Bryn Mawr. In our class of one hundred fifty-nine graduates, eight went to medical school, and just five to law school. (A few more studied law or medicine later in life.) Most of us didn't even consider going to business school; it seemed too dull and materialistic, and the Harvard Business School, at least, did not admit women to their MBA program until a year later, in 1963.

On a 40th reunion questionnaire, classmates were asked if they had ever considered a different career than the ones they pursued. Seventy-one percent of respondents said that they had, and of those who named a profession, one-fifth mentioned medicine and another 20 percent said law. "I had wanted to go to law school," one classmate told me. "I always thought I'd go to law school. But I realized that I wanted a collegial kind of setting. And in those days there wasn't that. I was very friendly with a young man who was going to Penn Law School, and we started to talk about it. And I realized I would not even be able to . . . that he would be in some club that I couldn't join. I really admire Barbara and the others who went to law school. But they're smarter, and they can learn another way. I didn't think I could."

Barbara was on scholarship at Bryn Mawr, and also at Yale Law School. Unlike many of us, she thought about earning a living. Her mother was a very important person in her life and a role model, a woman who firmly believed that her children should be able to support themselves. She herself, with young children, went back to school and earned a graduate degree and had a career—very radical in the forties and fifties. "In some ways this was embarrassing in suburban America at the time," said Barbara. "It was almost as if my father couldn't adequately do his job to support her." Bryn Mawr was also important in Barbara's decision to go to law school—the college's attitude about its graduates, expecting everybody to go on and do something serious, at a time when not all the women's colleges were like that. It was Gertrude Leighton, a Bryn Mawr professor, who first encouraged Barbara to apply to the Yale Law School. Leighton had actually practiced law before she came to Bryn Mawr. She went to Yale Law School and graduated during the war years, when all the men were away at war and women had opportunities that weren't really "meant" for women.

When it came time to apply for a clerkship, Barbara ranked about fifth in her class. She was recommended for both a Supreme Court clerkship and a circuit court clerkship, went to the Supreme Court, and met Thurgood Marshall, who was then on the circuit court. But nobody offered her a job. Clerkships are never easy to get, she said, but the process then was not gender-neutral; it was definitely harder for women. "It would have been a great experience," said Barbara, with some regret, "and if I'd wanted to teach, not having a clerkship would have been a major gap. But I didn't really have anyone to push me. I didn't have a professor who said, 'You have to take this person.'"

If you didn't clerk, the next choice was to go to a large law firm. The idea was that you could build up your skills there, learn how to be a lawyer, then go on and do something else. So when Barbara interviewed for jobs, she interviewed only at large law firms. And law firms were probably the places most resistant to hiring women lawyers.

"Women Unwanted" was the headline in the December 1963 *Harvard Law Record*. "Do law firms discriminate against women? Most hiring partners admit that they do, and the girls [sic] agree." On a scale of plus ten (definitely does get job) to minus ten (definitely does not get job), 120 major law firms ranked women lawyers at minus 4.9. Only two groups were ranked lower: "lower one-third of the class," at minus 6.7, and "badly groomed," at minus 5.5. In the same issue of the *Record*, a Harvard law professor, who was a member of President Kennedy's Commission on the Status of Women, actually defended the prevailing bias against women: "Discrimination against women," he wrote, "unlike other forms of bias, is based partly on myth, but partly on relevant considerations. The firms know best how to run their own offices, and they are justified, if it is true that women tend to leave firms quickly, though no empirical study seems to have been made on this."

Classmate Marion (Coen) Katzive went to Harvard Law School, and had kept copies of the *Harvard Law Record*–fortunately, she's rather a pack rat–which was how that article came to my attention. At the time, it apparently didn't cause much of a stir. I checked with Karen (Willner) Ferguson, the other Bryn Mawr '62 graduate at Harvard Law, and she didn't even remember the article, though she did remember a woman law school classmate who came back from an interview at a major New York law firm in tears, having been told, without apology, that they didn't hire women.

The hiring process at Yale had several stages. First, the firms would come to the law school, where they had to take whichever students the law school gave them; they couldn't choose which students they would see. They would spend a day at Yale doing interviews, and then pick the ones they wanted to invite to New York. And that's still the way it works. Barbara remembers one interviewer who said, "You have a great record, and all that. You could come to New York and meet our partners. But of course we wouldn't ever let you meet a client. You could work in the library, I guess. You probably wouldn't want to do that." And she said, "No, I certainly wouldn't want to do that."

Law students typically spend the summer after their second year working in a law firm, and if they do well, they're expected to be invited back for a job after they graduate. Barbara went to one of the leading New

York law firms, which she described as *extremely* homogenous. "Their little office directory read like the Social Register," she said. "You would open the book and you would see Don Jones' boarding school, his college, his fraternity, his wife's maiden name, the names of his children, the country club he belonged to. . . . You know, the whole thing. I think it would have been a hard place even for a man, if he had gone to Fordham Law, or some place inappropriate like that. Never mind if you were a woman."

At the end of the summer, the firm held a dinner for the summer associates at the Harvard Club. At that time women weren't allowed to go in the front door of the Club, so Barbara had to use a back entrance. They sat in a private room, the older partners and associates, the younger summer associates, all men except for Barbara, of course. An old curmudgeon was invited as toastmaster, and everyone apparently thought he was very funny. He spent the entire evening saying, "Oh, if only a lady weren't in the room, I could tell this dirty joke." Then he proceeded to tell it anyway. He would say things like, the only women lawyers he'd ever met smoked cigars and wore pants. The whole evening was like that. Finally Barbara thought she needed to say something, to clear the air, although she would have preferred not to. "Well," she said, "I don't smoke cigars or wear pants. I might never exactly be one of the boys, but I would hope that in time I could just be one of the associates and that we'd all be more relaxed about it." That was a big relief to everybody. Afterward, they went back to one of the partner's houses, and then the young summer associates were invited on what was the traditional 'pub crawl.' "I have no idea if they were strippers' clubs, or even if I was invited," said Barbara, "but it was quite clear to me that crawling around in the bars with these guys was not what I was going to be doing." This firm did finally offer Barbara a job, rather grudgingly, after a long delay, and they were astonished and quite angry when she turned them down.

Barbara married her Haverford sweetheart—they met at Bryn Mawr at the beginning of her sophomore year, when she was all of seventeen years old—in 1965, just two days before her law school graduation. ("The degree was my dowry," said Barbara, laughing.) About a year after that, she ran into one of the men from her summer law firm. He said, "Well, you know, if you hadn't been engaged, we would never have understood how you behaved." Later, Barbara thought of what she *should* have said in reply: "You know, I don't mind being a pioneer, but I just think you're not really, *really* ready for women."

Luckily she had some other offers, which for a woman lawyer in those days was not to be assumed. When Supreme Court Justice Ruth Bader Ginsburg graduated from Columbia Law School in 1959, just six years earlier, not a single law firm in New York City would hire her. "I struck out on three grounds," she said later. "I was Jewish, a woman, and a mother." Barbara ended up joining Debevoise & Plimpton, where she is today. "It was a very lucky choice," she said. "I chose my firm with great trepidation, never having lived inside it, partly because I had a couple of friends from Yale who were going there, but more importantly because I thought the men in the firm were more diverse than in most." At the time most firms were really quite segregated ethnically—Jewish firms, non-Jewish firms, Catholic firms, WASP firms. But Debevoise & Plimpton at that time was Debevoise, Plimpton, Lyons and Gates, and Marvin Lyons, who was one of the main partners, was Jewish. "It was more WASP-y than not," said Barbara, "but it wasn't entirely WASP. And I was right, in hindsight, this was a very correct and important perception. I thought that if they could tolerate a little more difference among themselves, maybe they could be a little more relaxed about me. They'd even had two or three women, one of whom they really liked, who had quit when she had a child, so it wasn't that they'd never hired a woman."

Barbara's first child was born in 1967, her second in 1970. When she was pregnant with her first child, she asked for a "regular" five-day-per-week schedule, and got it, although she had to compromise by changing her specialty from a combination of corporate work and litigation to trusts and estates. With her second child, she worked part-time for a while, then came back full-time and asked to return to the partner track. She was the first woman at the firm to do that, and in 1976 she became the first woman to make partner. "I came back full-time sooner than I would have chosen to," she said, "because my sense was that otherwise I would never be considered for partner." Now, she tries to help younger women. "You waste a lot of energy beating yourself up," said Barbara. "Women can actually help each other, say, 'Of course you feel this way! It's all right; we've all been there. You can do it!'"

After Barbara had set the precedent, more women at Debevoise & Plimpton opted for part-time, but until the mid-nineties, none of these women stayed at the firm. "I was getting very discouraged," said Barbara, "because I think the signal it sends is that you have to choose between raising a family and having a career. Usually you decide to work part-time because you're raising a family, which means you're really doing two full-time jobs. But it's not your whole lifetime. Indeed it's the smallest period of your whole career. And so it seems a shame to lose people just because they get squeezed for a bit. That's why I'm so particularly happy that recently we've had many more part-time women in every department, even part-time partners."

(It is important to understand that these are "real" equity partners, with an equal share of profits. Debevoise & Plimpton is one of the few firms that has what's called "lock-step compensation," which means that as partner, you get the same as all the partners at your level of seniority, whether you work four hours or forty thousand hours, whether you bring in clients or not. This is very different from most firms.)

In the fall of 1995, just about the time of the 125th year celebration, the City Bar Association released a study of eight major New York City law firms titled *Glass Ceilings and Open Doors*. The report found that the doors had swung wide open for women in the legal profession—women constituted about half of all law school enrollments in 1995, and women at top law schools were getting great clerkships, and offers from all the best firms. But all the invisible biases that keep women out of top jobs (first dubbed the "glass ceiling" in 1985) were still firmly in place. A lot of law firm partners thought they had done "the woman thing," fixed the problem, but this report clearly demonstrated that the glass ceiling problem was getting worse, not better. An American Bar Association panel report issued about the same time found that at the highest echelons of the profession, whether in law firm partnerships, law school faculties, or on the bench, the percentage of women remained "inexcusably low, especially when measured against huge increases in the number of qualified women."

It may seem rather elitist to worry about women reaching the upper levels of major law firms, when the vast majority of working women are still clustered in low-paying "female" professions—secretary, nurse, librarian, teacher. But large law firms are important not just for the women lawyers who work there. Their influence extends throughout the legal profession and indeed throughout the larger society. "I have concentrated on the large law firms because I know them best," said Barbara, "but also because these are very wealthy, powerful institutions, and they advise the big guns in the world." Many of the nation's leaders in government and the corporate world have spent time in large law firms, and law firms shape the law by litigating cases and by sending their people to the state and federal judiciaries.

"If you have a chance to speak," Barbara's mother used to tell her, "make sure you say something important." The City Bar Association is extremely prestigious, and unlike many other bar associations, it has never viewed itself as an organization to promote lawyers. It has always seen its purpose, and a lawyer's purpose, as working to improve the law, to promote the best public interest. Barbara used her presidency to do the glass ceiling study, to focus attention on women in the legal profession. For many years she has also served on the board of Catalyst, an organization that works to promote the advancement of women mainly in the *Fortune* 500 corporate world, but also in the professions. Catalyst has a mission to help women working in large corporations and firms to succeed, to adapt to what is still essentially a male model of operating; and at the same time to try to change structures and practices, and indeed the whole culture of these institutions, to make them more accessible to women.

In 2002, women constituted almost a third of all lawyers, but only 15 percent of all equity partners in major law firms. In structure and culture, a firm is the ultimate old boys' club, a self-perpetuating partnership that is extremely resistant to change. The partners own the firm and share in the profits, while the associates are working their way up to partnership. Associates trying to make partner are judged not just on client service, but also on their demonstrated commitment, measured by the hours they put in—two thousand or more "billable hours" a year is normal in these firms—and on their success in bringing in new clients, which is rather quaintly termed "rainmaking." As Barbara explains it, "You can't just be good at servicing clients, you can't just do a perfect job, you have to bring in business. For women, developing business—in financial services as well as in legal services—is really hard. You've got to woo clients, and big high-

"When I was starting out, the discrimination against women was obvious. The stuff now is very complicated."

paying clients are what matter. It's hard for all young people to develop business, and harder for women to get the large corporate business controlled by men as clients. These men went to the same all-male schools, they know each other, they socialize, play golf. That stuff is alive and well and continues in grown-up life." Barbara is now working in a rainmaking network of women lawyers, figuring out other, more congenial strategies for bringing in new business, such as going to the ballet or the theater.

"What's hardest to get at," said Barbara, "is that it's mostly still men in control, men who are *judging* the associates in their firm, who really believe in their heart of hearts that they're good guys, who believe *profoundly* that their system is a meritocracy, and that it's not *them*. It couldn't be *them*. If you tell them that their judgment, their development of other young lawyers, their investment in young lawyers is skewed by their own expectations—(1) that women will quit and have babies; (2) that women won't want to do this—they don't want to believe it. The City Bar Association study found that 75 percent of the women who succeeded and became partners in those firms have children. So the idea that it's either/or, a choice between profession and family, and that women will quit, is just not true. Too often the expectations about women lawyers become a self-fulfilling prophecy."

The demands of rainmaking and billable hours create enormous pressure. "Everyone—men as well as women—is working harder for less," said Barbara, "and feeling very stressed." But for a woman, the real crunch comes when she decides to have children, because even today, taking care of children is probably going to be primarily her job, at least for a while, even with a supportive husband. "I think the difference is that when you and I were in college, nobody told us it would be easy," said Barbara, "and societal expectations were very different. A lot of the young women who are coming out now have gone to the Harvards and Yales and everywhere else, and have gotten the same As and the same opportunities, and get the same first jobs. They were brought up to believe that everything was essentially fair and equal, and when they run into barriers they feel angry and betrayed."

Some of the stories from the early days, of not being included, or clubs that didn't let women in the front door, now seem unbelievable, and quite funny. "It's nice that those stories are irrelevant," said Barbara. "I don't really tell them to young women because what's the point?" Then she told me another story, a true story, without names. This happened quite recently, in the late nineties. "A man announced at this meeting, 'Oh, Suzie Smith is a *wonderful* young woman lawyer. We would have *loved* to make her a partner. She was a *star*. But you know, she quit to stay home to raise her babies.' At which point one of the women—happily there are now a few women in the room—said, 'That's wrong. Suzie Smith is the primary and sole wage earner, the breadwinner in that family. She quit for a better job, more chance of advancement, better money, shorter hours. You know, not this crapshoot of a lottery where she's not going to make partner in the end anyway.'"

"When I was starting out, the discrimination against women was obvious," said Barbara. "The stuff now is very complicated."

DR. FRANCES CONLEY

Frances "Fran" (Krauskopf) Conley—Walking Out on the Boys

On May 22, 1991, Dr. Frances Conley resigned her position as tenured full professor of neurosurgery at the Stanford University School of Medicine, citing pervasive sexism. She was the first woman in the country to hold that position, and when she resigned, it was a huge story in local and San Francisco Bay Area media, picked up by *Newsweek* and network TV, a media storm that sent shocks through the medical profession.

The event that precipitated Fran's resignation was the appointment of a particularly obnoxious, sexist colleague as chair of the neurosurgery department. In a 1993 interview with the *Bryn Mawr Alumnae Bulletin*,[2] Fran talked about her twenty-five years of working with this man at the medical school, twenty-five years in which he regularly belittled her in front of colleagues (loudly remarking that she was "on the rag" if they had a difference of opinion), made sexual advances, and excluded her from meetings and interviews. "People want to know, 'When did you finally break down?'" said Fran. "Well, it wasn't like that at all. I can work with people who are hostile, who are sexist. But when you elevate people to leadership positions, you validate their behavior. I can work *with* him, but not *for* him."

In mid-October 1991, just a few months after Fran's resignation, an African-American law professor named Anita Hill sat before a panel of fourteen white male senators and made public her accusations of sexual harassment against U.S. Supreme Court nominee Clarence Thomas. Millions of women all over America were riveted to their TV sets and radios as the senators grilled her.

The senator from Alabama: "Are you a spurned woman? Are you a zealot civil rights believer? Do you have a martyr complex? Are you interested in writing a book?"

Anita Hill: "No, senator, no. I'm not given to fantasy. I can only tell you what happened."

Women generally believed Anita Hill–*I Believe Anita Hill* buttons sprouted on lapels everywhere–and they were outraged at the way Hill was treated by the committee. The only surprise was that this happened at the highest levels. Anita Hill and Clarence Thomas were both graduates of Yale Law School; Fran Conley was a brain surgeon at Stanford. In 1991, "sexual harassment" entered the general vocabulary.

Fran rescinded her resignation in August 1991, and won her case at the medical school–the offer to her obnoxious colleague to become chair of neurosurgery was withdrawn. Shortly after that, she was named chief of staff at the Veterans Administration Palo Alto Health Care System (VAPAHCS), an important position. Fran wrote a book about her experience at Stanford,[3] and has taken on a second "career," speaking out about the medical profession and mentoring young women. All these

"It was at Bryn Mawr that I finally heard for the first time that I had enough intellectual ability to do whatever I wanted to do."

"victories" have come at a high cost. "My career has been ruined by the stand I took," said Fran. "I'm considered a troublemaker now."

I met with Fran in December of 1998 in her office at the Palo Alto VA hospital. She was dressed in green cotton "scrubs," her hair cut shoulder-length, a slim figure with the easy stance of an athlete. "I think there's no question that I would not be doing what I do today had I not gone to Bryn Mawr," she said, "had I gone to Stanford instead. In terms of self-confidence and achievement and value systems, I just think that it would have been very different."

Fran grew up on the Stanford University campus, where her father was a professor of geochemistry. Her mother had a master's degree and taught junior high school, but didn't go back to work until Fran had gotten to the tenth grade. Before then she was a wife and mother (Fran is the second of four children) and ran a household, quite traditional family roles. The expectations for Fran's brother were clearly different from those for Fran and her two sisters. When the oldest sister turned sixteen, her parents gave her a sewing machine. A year and a half later, Fran turned sixteen, and she too got a sewing machine. "I still have that sewing machine," said Fran, "and it still runs. It's terrific. I made every stitch that I wore through high school, and most of what I wore in college. But when my brother turned sixteen, what do you think he got?"

"I don't know. A car?"

"No, he got a life insurance policy. He wanted a car. Absolutely. But the message, even from a fairly liberal, intellectual family, was Hey, somebody's going to be there to take care of you, the girls, and fellow, you're going to have to take care of somebody else."

Fran went to Palo Alto High School, then ranked as one of the top ten public schools in the country. But this was the fifties, and even in

Palo Alto it wasn't "cool" to do well academically, especially if you were a girl. "It was at Bryn Mawr that I finally heard for the first time that I had enough intellectual ability to do whatever I wanted to do," said Fran. "I had not heard that in high school and I had not really heard it from my folks, although I think they would say that they certainly tried to give me that message. But they were not pushy people. They didn't want any 'my daughter the doctor' type of thing. They just wanted us to be happy, to be fulfilled. Education was extremely important; they expected all of us to get a college education. Beyond that, it was whatever we wanted to do. In some ways that's a good environment to come from because then anything you do is self-motivated."

Fran's parents agreed to pay for all four children to go away to college for two years, with the understanding that they would then return to Stanford, where they had free tuition as faculty children. At that point, Fran wanted to get as far away from her family as she could. "I felt very constrained and confined," she said. "I wasn't allowed to go out for cheerleader or pom-pom girl, those things I really wanted to do. It seemed a good thing for me to get away to the East Coast, even though I knew nothing about it." By then Fran already knew she wanted to go to medical school and become a doctor, and of all the colleges she applied to, Bryn Mawr had the best reputation in science. So she packed her things in a great big trunk and set off to start her freshman year at Bryn Mawr, sight unseen. It took her about three and a half days to get there, sitting up through all three nights: one train into Chicago, another to Philadelphia, and finally the Paoli Local to Bryn Mawr.

Fran was not especially happy her first semester at Bryn Mawr, and found it hard to make friends, but she loved the science classes and she was fascinated by the all-female environment. All of a sudden it was women doing everything: in freshman plays, which we put on early in the semester, women played all the parts, women were the producers and the directors. It was eye-opening, said Fran, to see that women could do all this, that it was just accepted. She soon found her niche in competitive sports. "I joined the swimming team and found that was one thing I could excel at," she said. "And I met the people who became friends through that venue." After two years at Bryn Mawr, Fran transferred into a combined BA-MD program at Stanford, entering the Stanford University Medical School in 1961, one of just twelve women in a class with sixty men.

Statistics for women physicians parallel those for women lawyers. In 1964, only about 8 percent of medical students were women. In 1974, 20 percent were women; in 1994, slightly more than 40 percent. By 2000, most medical schools were about 50/50 men and women, but women physicians continued to be clustered in the lower-paying and lower-prestige areas of medicine. About 60 percent of all women practiced in five specialties: family practice, general internal medicine, obstetrics-gynecology, pediatrics, and psychiatry, compared with just 40 percent of men. In the more prestigious and high-paying procedure-based specialties there were still very few women. In 1993, women practicing surgery (including those in training) were only 6 percent of the total; in neurosurgery, only a little more than 3 percent. Academic medicine (which Fran says is *the* place for a physician to build a national and international professional reputation) and medical school faculties also remain very heavily dominated by men: in 1993 only 8.6 percent of full professors teaching clinical medicine were women.

Bryn Mawr has always sent a large number of graduates to medical school, because of its strong science programs. In his first President's Report, almost a year before the opening of the College in 1885, Dr. James Rhoads (himself a medical doctor), wrote of the requirements for the BA that students "must pass successful examinations in the elements of Chemistry, of Physics, of Botany, or of Physiology." Later in the report, Rhoads discussed the sciences in more detail, ending with the observation that "Beside their intrinsic worth as means of self-culture, physics, chemistry and biology afford a valuable preparation for the study of medicine, a profession to which an increasing number of women are successfully devoting themselves."

In the early 1890s, M. Carey Thomas and four other women formed a Women's Medical Fund Committee and raised $500,000 to enable Johns Hopkins University to open a medical school, with the stipulation that women should be admitted on equal terms with men. Their conditions were accepted along with their cash, and The Johns Hopkins School of Medicine opened in October of 1893. In Bryn Mawr's class of 1962, eight went to medical school. In the entering class at Harvard Medical School that year, out of just nine women, three were from Bryn Mawr.

The influx of women into medical schools is an important story. But there is an even more remarkable story about women and medicine—the growth of the women's health movement. *Our Bodies, Ourselves*,[4] published by the Boston Women's Health Collective in 1970, was one of the first and most important texts of the women's movement. At that time there was practically no women's health information easily available. Every fact in the book was a revelation, and it was even more of a revelation that a group of ordinary, non-expert women had done the research. The book helped spark other "ordinary" women to explore the health issues most important to them. By the early eighties, this grassroots movement had generated a wealth of information—research papers, books, health groups and centers, newsletters and journals. In rewriting *Our Bodies, Ourselves* for the 1984 edition, the Boston Women's Health Collective drew heavily on these resources. In the 1992 edition, *The New Our Bodies, Ourselves*, the emphasis is on "what women can do—for ourselves, for each other—in staying healthy, healing ourselves and working for change," while admitting that "we do need professional help with health problems, even when medical approaches are not always the best, with their excessive emphasis on drugs, surgery and crisis intervention."

A 40th reunion questionnaire for the Bryn Mawr class of '62 included several questions on health and health care, a growing concern as we enter our sixties. One question asked respondents whether they had ever been frustrated by their attempts to deal with the medical profession (for example, doctors didn't take complaints seriously, didn't provide enough information, or didn't treat patients with respect). Nearly two-fifths (39 percent) of respondents said they had had problems, including misdiagnoses and doctors who just wouldn't listen. "I was dismissed as a whining, neurotic annoyance when I tried to discuss well-documented, cyclical problems that disabled me for one to two weeks each month," said one classmate. "When it isn't an infection and can't be found on an X-ray, it can be hard to get treatment," said another. One woman, who asked about her son's prescription, was told by the pediatrician, "We don't need to know, do we, mother?" She changed doctors. Of those who reported positive experiences in dealing with their medical practitioners, a few mentioned that they felt that their status as an attorney, a PhD, or as a doctor's wife helped ensure good medical treatment. Fifty-three percent of respondents said they took hormone replacement pills, although there was a lively debate in the margins of some questionnaires about the benefits of this therapy. This was just a few months before the news came out about the high risks associated with HRT.

Fran's talk of "pervasive sexism" in the Stanford Medical School sparked several studies on sexual harassment in medicine, giving the rest of us a rare peek inside the hermetic world of academic medicine. An analysis of data from the Women Physicians' Health Study, a questionnaire distributed nationally in 1993 and 1994 to 4,501 female doctors, showed that experiences of sexual and gender-based harassment remained widespread, in spite of the large and increasing numbers of women physicians. And it was young women physicians who were the most likely to report being harassed, which suggested things were not getting any better. Male surgeons were the most frequent offenders.

An American Medical Association trustee acknowledged, with some surprise, that the study showed "that we weren't improving, that it wasn't necessarily a reflection of an older faculty that has older, more traditional ways." He suggested what was needed most was "more women in leadership positions–department heads, deans, provosts–because it starts from the top down." Female leaders would be role models, he said, and would help alleviate sexism in medical schools and training programs. There's some evidence he's right: Data released by the New York University (NYU) School of Medicine in May 2004 showed that, for the first time, a higher percentage of women than men in the graduating class chose residencies in surgery, a field long dominated by men. The NYU dean linked the increase to the female surgery professors the school has recruited, and the hiring of a female director who counsels students on applying for surgery residencies. In the same class, in other specialties, longtime trends persisted.

The 1992 *The New Our Bodies, Ourselves* points out the dilemma facing women physicians: "Wisely, few women are choosing the most grueling specialties; their preference is to live like human beings. Unfortunately, most of the influential leadership of medicine is not drawn from specialties women favor." Fran chose neurosurgery and academic medicine, and was willing to make sacrifices (not having children, for instance) to get to the top of a very demanding profession. I thought it would be useful to talk with some young women now in medical school—especially Bryn Mawr graduates and Stanford Medical School students—to see how things are changing, to gauge the future of women in medicine.

Rebecca Aspden graduated from Bryn Mawr in 2002, and went on to Harvard Medical School that fall, one of a class of about a hundred and sixty students, more than half of whom were women, with about 40 percent minority and international students. She was still in her first year of medical school when we talked, enjoying her classes. Rebecca reported only one slightly negative experience that seemed gender-related, in anatomy class. "I was on a team of two men and two women," she said, "and I didn't feel as though we communicated well. My experience with all-women groups at Bryn Mawr was better. At Harvard there was no sense of the group as a whole, making sure that everyone in the group is OK, is brought along. The other woman in the team had gone to Harvard as an undergraduate, so she was used to that dynamic. Now that I think of it, some of the people at Harvard Med I've most enjoyed talking to are those from women's colleges."

As in the legal profession, the real crunch for women comes when they decide to have children. It's even worse for women physicians, because there is such a long and grueling training period—a minimum of four years in medical school and another four years in a residency—which coincides with prime childbearing years. The key decision is choosing a specialty.

Cynthia Wang, a Stanford Medical School student, didn't definitively decide to go into medicine until she was thirty-one years old, and had her first child when she was thirty-three, not long after starting medical school. I spoke with her just after she had completed her first rotation, in surgery. "The work was fascinating," she said, "but it's probably the least 'family-friendly' specialty. I realize now that regardless of how intrinsically interesting I find a particular field, the culture of the specialty and the people it attracts are just as important. Surgery could be fascinating work, but from my limited experience, I decided early on that I could not work with surgeons day in and day out."

Family-friendly will certainly be one aspect of her decision, she says, but it's also finding "people you click with." "I'm interested in emergency medicine," she told me, "which isn't thought of as a particularly family-friendly field. But I've met some of the best people during my ER experiences. Rock climbing and running are two passions of mine, and many of the ER physicians I've met have similar interests. I want to work in Nepal and Tibet, and emergency medicine provides those opportunities. The specialty seems to attract individuals who have very full lives outside of medicine. The shift-work and flexible schedules allow people to pursue other interests."

Cynthia is full of praise for Stanford Medical School, which prides itself on its flexibility and its support of students who take an alternate route through medical school. But her experience as a medical student mom has been complex. "Since becoming a mom, my priorities have shifted drastically. I no longer strive to be the exemplary student. For me, I've decided to be the best mom in the world, and if I'm only a mediocre Stanford medical student, then so be it. It's true that women have to face this dilemma much more often than do men, and yes, it's unfair. But I really don't think about that too much. I've met some great female role models along the way, but I realize that few are living their lives the way I hope to live mine. I think most choose to sacrifice some level of involvement in the lives of their children, in order to pursue their careers. And most of those who are enjoying motherhood have lowered their expectations for themselves in their careers. It feels like you really have to choose one or the other."

When I last spoke with Cynthia Wang, in the summer of 2006, she had decided to go into child psychiatry, and was in residency training in that field. "My decision was extremely complex," she said, "and I'm quite certain that if I didn't have children I never would have found myself in this field." She explained:

> *Psychiatric patients have always been interesting to me, but the stigma attached to psychiatry, still considered, in my opinion, a lesser specialty, would likely have dissuaded me from pursuing it. The fact that the training is less 'call-intensive' and allows me to spend time with my very young children may have been the deciding factor. Pediatric neurology was the top contender coming out of my clinical rotations, but the prospect of*

*every fourth night in-house call for at least three years made that completely
unpalatable. . . . I feel that having children is my excuse, in a way. Not to say
that I am not completely happy with my decision—each day of residency my
decision is reaffirmed by my fascination with my patients and the support of my
colleagues—but it's interesting the way that I arrived here.*

As Barbara Robinson said, when talking about women in the legal
profession, discrimination against women is no longer so obvious. Women
now constitute at least half of all law and medical school enrollments.
But young women in law and medicine still seem to face an impossible
choice—either to "live like human beings," or to pursue ambitious careers
and make sacrifices in their personal and family lives.

Chapter Eight

Uncharted Territory

The spring of '62 was a time of youth and optimism—the tone set by the new Kennedy administration—and we were right in tune with the times: young, even a bit cocky, with high expectations of life. We felt a responsibility to do something serious after Bryn Mawr, but most of us were not thinking concretely about jobs and careers. It was more a question of vocation, doing something you felt passionately about and making a difference. Bryn Mawr president Katharine McBride helped set the tone in her convocation address at the start of our senior year. The real point of academic work, she said, was to "become a person you would not have been without it," to prepare yourself to "make a greater contribution to the world."

We were eager to enter this brave new world, but the world was not especially eager to receive us. Only a few career tracks were open to women in those days, even for women coming out of the best liberal arts colleges. Besides graduate or professional school, the other options seemed to be marriage or a job. And there were really only two kinds of jobs available—secretarial and clerical work (at news magazines, women were hired as researchers or "copy girls," but it usually amounted to the same thing) or teaching in a private elementary or secondary school.

Then there was marriage. By the time we graduated, almost a quarter of the class (38 out of 159) were either married or engaged. In reporting on the plans of graduating seniors, the *College News* treated marriage almost as a *career* choice; anything else was secondary, adjunct to the graduate's primary role as wife. The *News* reported that one senior was going to Europe with her husband; another would work in Paris while her husband was at the Sorbonne. Nine of those getting married were planning further studies; sixteen planned to work (often to support husbands in graduate/ professional school); and several others were "beginning families."

But what about those who *didn't* want to go on to graduate or professional school, work as a secretary, teach, or get married? That was the question that faced Mary Beebe and Mimi Armstrong, who were roommates at Bryn Mawr. And the larger question, the one that interested me, was how these two classmates managed to forge careers and compose lives, creating their own paths in what was then largely uncharted territory.

Mary Beebe–In Brancusi's Sculpture Studio

Since 1981, Mary Beebe has presided over the Stuart Collection, an inventive, exuberant outdoor sculpture collection scattered across the campus of the University of California, San Diego. The collection reflects Mary herself and her brand of open enthusiasm, her willingness to think differently about things, and her flexibility and tact in working with the various constituencies at the university. In person, Mary is quite small, with a look of competence and energy, a spring in her walk, straight

MARY LIVINGSTONE BEEBE

near-white hair framing her face, clothes that drape and flow, a shawl flung over one shoulder. She is a free spirit and also someone who gets things done, a rare combination. The process of adding to the sculpture collection starts when Mary invites an artist to come to the campus, look around, and develop an idea in response to a specific site. "The whole reason we bring in artists," she said, "is to do something we can't imagine." In the next step in the process, the construction and installation of the work, Mary makes sure that meticulous attention is paid to detail and quality. Finally, the entire university community is invited to an "opening," gathering around to view the work and meet with the artist.

"It's important that the work stir up conversation."

I went alone to visit the Stuart collection, early in the morning, steering the large rental van cautiously through a thick, dripping ocean fog, armed with a descriptive brochure and a campus map marked with the locations of the sculptures. Most of the collection I discovered largely by chance, these wonderfully odd, intriguing objects emerging from the mist. And that seems to be the point—the pieces catch you by surprise, interacting in unexpected ways with the landscape and buildings. I found no identifying plaques, nothing to say that this is a piece of art you should look at. In a grassy field, blocks of pink and gray granite are scattered like ancient ruins or a construction site, suggesting an arch here, a doorway there, a lintel, a threshold. Translucent blue-violet "fences" in V shapes wander high above, through a eucalyptus grove, blending with the soft haze and dappled shadows of the trees. Down a dead-end service road full of "No Parking" signs, I parked, then scrambled up over an embankment, all slippery leaves and mud. There I came upon an enormous, brightly colored bird, a giant sculpture by Niki de Saint Phalle, standing 14 feet high atop a 15-foot concrete arch, wings spread, silhouetted against the sky. Dark green vines and a few flowers covered the concrete of the arch, rising up from the earth like a warm and irrepressible life force, and the morning sun was just breaking through the mist, burnishing the giant bird's crest a warm, glowing gold.

The last stop on my tour was the Central Library, a forbidding structure, all cold concrete, a vast geometric block poised precariously, boulder-like, over its terrace. At first I saw no way into the library itself, then found a sign that pointed down a set of stairs to the main entrance. A tall, skeletal eucalyptus tree stood alone in the entrance plaza, silhouetted against the sky, its bare trunk and branches preserved and encased in a skin of lead. A tree of knowledge? A reminder that trees have to be cut down to make paper for books? A quiet reminder that knowledge is fraught and shouldn't be taken lightly? I continued around to the side of the library, a softer, friendlier approach, and stepped right onto the tail of a serpent, a tiled snake path leading up to the library terrace. The end of the tail wraps around an existing concrete pathway, like a snake wrapping itself around a tree limb, and as you climb, the body of the snake gradually grows rounder—I could feel the slight swell under my feet in the middle of the path. At the side, a little further up, a monumental granite book is engraved with a passage from Milton's *Paradise Lost*: "Then wilt thou not be loth / To leave this Paradise, but shalt possess / A Paradise within thee, happier far." I followed the path to where it flattened out to circle a miniature Garden of Eden, before rising again, the body still thickening, up to the broad head and flashing serpent's tongue at the library terrace. The snake path is by a Los Angeles artist, Alexis Smith, and the snake is part of what she calls her paradise series, so it's the serpent of knowledge. "When the library was being renovated, with a major addition being planned," said Mary, "I thought Alexis would be the perfect artist, because her work had often dealt with literature. So she did this great, 600-foot-long path as a snake."

These days, Mary leads a glamorous life, dashing off to Europe to meet with artists and collectors, commissioning artists, and nurturing and documenting the creative process as the works take shape. She has come a long way since she graduated in the spring of 1962, with *no* idea of what she was going to do after college. Entering the world after Bryn Mawr was quite a shock. "I remember that at Bryn Mawr we'd been taught to believe that we were women of the world, that we could do anything we wanted," Mary said. "But then you got out there after graduation and it wasn't quite true. Nobody wanted you unless you could type. It was like: *Wait a minute here!* It was kind of breathtaking." In the summer of '62, after graduation, Mary and a good friend of hers from high school enrolled in the Radcliffe College secretarial school, to learn to type and take shorthand. She was by no means the only classmate who went to secretarial school after Bryn

Mawr. Martha (Horsley) Hanrott, later a senior economist at the World Bank, told me that when she graduated, her father said, "Now that you've got a college education you should learn something useful." So she spent the summer learning typing and shorthand. "You know," she told me, smiling ruefully, "you can't get a job if you don't type." Looking back, it seems incredible that an elite women's college like Radcliffe *had* a secretarial school, and even more surprising that the best and brightest young women graduates spent their first summer out of college learning how to type.

"My friend Elisabeth had graduated *summa cum laude* from Smith and went on to Harvard Law School and is one of the smartest people I know," said Mary. "We both sat in the back of the room going 'What are we doing? I mean this is really grim!' It was *miserable*," she said, "and *I* was miserable, because my friends were all either getting married or going to graduate school, and Elisabeth and another friend were going to Europe at the end of the summer, while I hadn't a clue what I wanted to do."

At Bryn Mawr, Mary majored in sociology and political science. She thought she would like to be an ambassador, modeling herself on an aunt who had gone to Bryn Mawr and worked for the State Department (Mary later discovered that it was actually the CIA). "She was in Helsinki for a while," Mary remembered, "learned to fly, and obviously led a very glamorous life." Mary thought she might find work at the UN, UNESCO, or the State Department. She wrote letters and went around looking for jobs all through the summer of '62. But nothing came of her efforts. By the end of the summer she was beginning to feel quite desperate.

Then one of her grandmothers asked her what she would like as a graduation present. Mary suggested a new tennis racket, and her grandmother said, no, she really had something more in mind. What would Mary *really* like? At that Mary almost burst into tears. "What I really want," she said, "is to go to Europe with my friends." "Oh," said her grandmother, "I think we could manage that." So at the end of the summer Mary and her friends all got on the *Queen Mary*, in steerage, with footlockers full of clothes, and sailed to Europe. The price of Mary's roundtrip ticket, New York to Cherbourg, was $183.00. Three of the girls got off in Southampton; Mary and one other went on to Cherbourg and Paris.

Paris, for Mary, was a city full of art. She and her friend worked as au pairs to try to make their money go as far as it could—they wanted it to last a whole year—and spent all their free time going around to galleries and museums. One day, Mary went off by herself to visit the Musée d'Art moderne de la Ville de Paris on the Av. du Président Wilson. (This was before the Beaubourg was built, and all the contemporary art was still at the Musée d'Art moderne.) "There was a stairway that went down off a corridor," Mary remembered, "and I went down the stairs. There was nobody in museums in those days; I was all by myself. I went down, and I found myself *in* Brancusi's sculpture studio. It had been reconstructed *just as it had been left* when he died. And I nearly came *unglued*. It was really *incredible*."

After that, Mary and her friend got Eurail passes and traveled all over Europe, visiting museums and galleries. "I came home at the end of the year," said Mary, "thinking I'd do *anything* to work in a museum, if somebody would just hire me." She went to the Portland Art Museum and begged them for a job. A "wonderful, sympathetic woman," who was curator at the time, hired Mary as an apprentice for $250 a month. With her job at the museum, a $50-a-month basement apartment, and a bicycle, Mary was in heaven. "It was a small staff," she said, "and a great staff. I loved the company and I loved what I was doing." She helped to reinstall the Northwest Indian collection and organized the Japanese prints, along with sweeping the floor, making labels, and doing various other chores.

Portland, Oregon, was where Mary grew up, the oldest of five children, four girls and a boy, all very close. They all went to the Catlin Gabel School, a progressive school that had been started by people who came out of Black Mountain College. Shop and music and art were all very much a part of the curriculum. The arts were also an important part of Mary's family life—her grandmother was an amateur painter and her mother made sculpture. I asked Mary about her parents' expectations for her. "My parents were pretty good about saying, 'Fly with your own wings, do what you want to do, let your heart tell you where to go,'" she said. "My dad had expectations laid on him in the family business, and I think he hated the family business, so he didn't really set expectations for us." He did want them all to go to college in the East. Both of Mary's parents had gone East to college from Portland, and they wanted their children to do the same, to "broaden their horizons." There was also the very clear expectation that after college they would support themselves. "We were told, 'We're paying for you through college, and then you're on your own,'" Mary said. "'You're welcome here for vacations; we love seeing you; we love you and we want you to be around, but we're not supporting you from now on.'" The principle was clear—after college they were to be self-supporting, with no distinction between the sisters and their brother.

Mary's mother had gone to Bryn Mawr (Alice Biddle, '34, from a prominent Philadelphia family), and so Mary was absolutely determined *not* to go there. She and her friend Elisabeth wanted to go to college together, and Elisabeth's mother had gone to Smith, so Elisabeth was determined not to go to Smith. When they both got into Smith and Bryn Mawr there was a real dilemma—back and forth they went, not knowing what to do. In the end both of them sent back their postcards accepting the colleges where their mothers had gone. For Mary, it came down to a kind of instinct that she had. "I didn't want to be up in the woods," she said. "If I was going East I wanted to be near the cities, close to whatever was going on."

Mary remembers Bryn Mawr more for the friends she made than for any academic experience. Like many of us, she graduated with high ambition but no real sense of what she wanted to do next. Then came the epiphany in Brancusi's studio in Paris, and from that moment on Mary seems to have led a charmed life. After her first job at the Portland Art Museum she moved from one job to the next without visible effort, supported by strong women mentors all the way. "I've never had to look for a job, never been without or been desperately looking for a job," said Mary. "I've always just sort of landed."

From Paris to Portland to Boston: While Mary was working at the Portland Art Museum, she made a trip to Boston to visit her friend Elisabeth, who was then at the Harvard Law School, and Elisabeth suggested that she look for a job in Boston. "I went to the Museum of Fine Arts, and lo and behold I was offered a job in the registrar's office," said Mary. "The registrar didn't want to hire somebody who was trained in museum work or art history because he wanted to train the person himself, so I was a good candidate." A museum registrar tracks all the works that come in or go out of the museum, whether for exhibition or for sale, consideration of sales, or bequests. At the Museum of Fine Arts the registrar also served as secretary to the board, writing up the minutes of all the board meetings. Mary ended up working there for a year and a half, from 1964 to 1966. She got a good overview of museum activities and met a lot of people, everybody from the curators to the conservation people to the trustees. Then a job came up at Harvard's Fogg Museum, working for Agnes Mongan, a Bryn Mawr graduate (class of '27) who was curator of drawings.

Agnes Mongan was only the second woman ever hired by Harvard in a professional position—the first was someone at the School of Medicine—and by the time Mary got there, in the mid-sixties, she had been in her job for about forty years. Mary discovered later that Mongan was paid just *half* of what any man in her position would be paid. It wasn't until the seventies, when Mongan became director, that they finally acknowledged the pay discrepancy, and that she *demanded* the same salary as the previous director. She had realized before that she was being paid less, Mary told me, but always just accepted it as the way things were. Then feminism came along, and in the seventies Mongan said, "No! I've been here a long time, and I'm clearly qualified, and I'm the best person for this job, and you can jolly well pay me what you were paying Charlie Coolidge."

Mary was hired as Agnes Mongan's secretary, but after a few months in the job, she realized it was easier to make up responses to letters than it was to take dictation. "I wasted so much of Harvard's stationery at the Fogg Museum," she said. "Oh, it was pathetic!" (Years later Mary called to ask if she could change the job title on her résumé from *secretary* to *assistant*—Mongan said, 'Of course.') Mary made the most of her time at the Fogg. "Miss Mongan had an incredibly fine eye," she said. "It was great training in how to look." She also got to know a lot of graduate students who later became museum directors and scholars, as well as a few people in contemporary art in Boston. But after she had been at the Fogg for a while, she decided that either she had to pursue an academic degree or she had to get out and do something else. "Everybody there thought that Cambridge was the center of the world," Mary said, "but you were sort of a nobody if you didn't have an advanced degree. I considered the academic options and decided not to pursue them. Instead, I took off and went back to Portland."

In Portland, Mary once again landed in a great spot, working with a theater company at Portland State University. Her title was producer, and she ran a whole summer theater at the beach. It was a departure from the art world she was used to, her first experience working directly with a performing arts group. "It was quite a lot of fun," she said. "They were trying to start a professional theater group, so I was working with the board and Actors' Equity and all that. But everybody ran out of steam and the thing sort of came a little bit unglued."

Meanwhile, Mary's boyfriend had just bought a motorcycle in London. He took off to Morocco, across the Atlas mountains, into the Sahara and back. Mary flew to Athens to join him, then wired back to the chairman of the board at the theater company to ask if it was okay to stay for longer than the month she had originally planned. He said, "Absolutely. The board has decided not to continue; stay as long as you like." "That was great," said Mary, "because I was sort of burnt out." She and her boyfriend spent about four months riding around on the motorcycle, going from Athens all around Greece and Crete, then up through Yugoslavia and across Italy, stopping here and there whenever they felt like it, and having a great time. Then they took a few weeks in France before winding up by riding through England and Scotland.

While Mary was cruising around Europe with her boyfriend, most of us were leading more conventional lives, taken up with small children, work, and marriage. While most of us were a little too old to join the sexual revolution, we were the first generation of women to have some choice. We could decide *not* to get married or *not* to have children and still have a sex life. The birth control pill was approved in 1960, a real breakthrough for women in getting control over reproduction. Not only did women have greater access to contraception and abortion, but there was a different climate. "I think we were more adventuresome than our immediate predecessors," said Mary. "The pill and abortion gave us a kind of freedom, a kind of permission."

It is true that abortion was becoming somewhat more accessible by the time we graduated from college, but it was still illegal in 1962, and that didn't change in most states until 1973, eleven years later, as a result of the Supreme Court decision in *Roe v. Wade*. I heard from classmates who were able to get an abortion with a sympathetic doctor, but I also heard stories of frightening and humiliating experiences, and stories of traveling to other countries for an abortion–Switzerland, Yugoslavia, or Mexico.

Mary had one relationship–with the man on the motorcycle–that lasted more than twenty years, but they never married. She also had two abortions. "I don't regret my decisions," she said. "You know, you have occasional pangs and think 'what if?' and all that, but having a kid with my former mate would not have worked." Children have been a very important part of Mary's life; she is close to her eight nieces and nephews. Over the years they have spent weeks in the summer at "Camp Aunt Mary," and have traveled with her on European grand art tours and trekking in Nepal. "I think I'm better at being an aunt than I would have been as a mom," she said.

Not surprisingly, most of us are strongly pro-choice in the abortion wars. Mary has had a salary deduction for Planned Parenthood for her whole working life, raising it whenever she can. "I just really believe in Planned Parenthood, and I believe that it's outrageous that this should even be an issue today," she said. "It makes me more angry than almost anything, this whole abortion thing." She caught her breath, then continued: "Women really think about these decisions, you know, when they make them. And for people to be moralistic about these kinds of things, and try to impose their views on women. . . . It just makes me crazy!"

When Mary and her boyfriend came home to Portland after their motorcycle trip through Europe, it was back to the real world. "He had to shave his beard and find a job," Mary said, "and I also had to get my act together, find a job." She started working at a gallery; then a group of artists asked her if she would help them start a new contemporary arts organization. Mary agreed to do it, and in 1972 they opened the Portland Center for Visual Arts, which was one of the first real artists' spaces, artist-based, at the cutting edge of what soon became a nationwide movement to create such "alternative spaces."

All this started back in the fifties, when the Beats, Jackson Pollock, and Elvis began to challenge middle-class taste and standards. In the sixties, iconoclastic movements emerged in all the arts–the "happenings" and

Pop art of Red Grooms and Andy Warhol; random, spontaneous forms of music and dance pioneered by John Cage and Merce Cunningham; the electronic rock music of The Doors and Jimi Hendrix; the folk protest songs of Bob Dylan; the invasion of the Beatles and the Rolling Stones from Britain. Countercultural films such as *Easy Rider* and *Midnight Cowboy* began to address social issues, and experimental theater groups including La Mama, Bread and Puppet, and the Open Theater used drama as a form of political activism. Artists began working together across disciplines— dance, music, the visual arts, and film. In New York, Warhol had The Factory, The Velvet Underground, and Fluxus, and the Judson Dance Theater created an artists' collective where dancers collaborated with visual artists and filmmakers.

In the visual arts, the late sixties brought an explosion of new forms and overlapping movements—minimalism, post-minimalism, earthworks, conceptual art, body art, performance art, video. The National Endowment for the Arts (NEA) and the National Endowment for the Humanities (NEH) were both created in 1965 as part of Lyndon Johnson's Great Society. Through the next twenty years, into the Reagan administration, the NEA provided indispensable support for vanguard artists, new art forms, and new venues. By the late sixties, almost every American city had at least one experimental theater company. By the late seventies, most had alternative artists' spaces. An NEA grant enabled Mary to travel around the country in 1979 looking at earthworks, and the Portland Center for Visual Arts became very active, producing over a hundred exhibitions and installations by artists ranging from minimalists to Rauschenberg and Lichtenstein, and performances by Trisha Brown, Spalding Gray, Philip Glass, and many others. "We felt that just keeping one step ahead of the fire marshal was a major accomplishment," Mary said, laughing, "and that if we could find the money, we could do anything! We did a lot, for almost ten years."

It was clear that Mary had a genius for fundraising, as well as a special talent for working with artists. In 1981, some faculty members from the art department of the University of California, San Diego (UCSD) called Mary at her home in Portland, and asked if she would come and talk with them about a job. Mary was quite reluctant: She was strongly rooted in the Pacific Northwest and couldn't imagine moving to Southern

California. Finally she did agree to go and talk to the UCSD people and to the local businessman who was putting up the money to launch the Stuart Collection. Those conversations convinced her that there was a real possibility, an extraordinary opportunity for her to make a difference. So Mary upended her life and came to La Jolla. "I've never had any regrets," she said.

UCSD is a 1,200-acre campus, and a young campus. Being in Southern California, it doesn't have many indoor spaces suitable for large artworks. And the early eighties were a time when artists were just beginning to think about their work in the outdoors; art was coming off the pedestal. "We had the idea," said Mary, "that instead of buying work that had been completed in the studio, we'd bring the artist to the campus to look around and think about something that would be particularly relevant, a response to a specific site on campus.

"It's very satisfying to look back now at the university and see what a difference these projects have made," she said. "They become landmarks, and they also become a part of the history and traditions of the campus." UCSD students put on an annual festival around the Sun God, and the big

"When an artist has a grand idea, I feel you have to go with it."

bird has become a kind of emblem that shows up everywhere, on T-shirts and mugs, even on the campus phone directory.

When I talked with Mary in the summer of 1998, she had just gotten married for the first time. (Her husband is someone she met in La Jolla–the relationship with her Portland boyfriend ended about eight years after she moved away.) "He wanted to get married," she said, "but I was very resistant. Finally I decided, this is crazy, why shouldn't I at least try it?" Mary reflected on married life. "It's got its wonderful aspects," she said, "but learning to share decisions after you're used to calling the shots. . . . I'm finding I have to temper my impulses. But it's certainly worth it this time around."

In 1998, Mary was busy preparing for the installation of a new work in the collection, a fountain by Kiki Smith, at the School of Medicine, a bronze nude on top of a twelve-foot cast concrete tree trunk, with water coming out of her lower arms and hands, falling into a pond of stones. "It's quite beautiful," she said, "and I'm sure it's going to be controversial. It's important that the works stir up conversation." When I last visited Mary, in the spring of 2005, the new UCSD Engineering Academic Court was being readied for the installation of the Tim Hawkinson "Bear," a sculpture composed of eight granite boulders–the torso boulder alone is more than 16 feet high and weighs 201,000 pounds. "When an artist has a grand idea, I feel you have to go with it," said Mary. "The art has to have integrity."

Mimi Armstrong–"I should have been an engineer."

Ten years out of college, while Mary had just started the Portland Center for Visual Arts, Mimi was running a Sonoma County vineyard. "There I was," said Mimi, "an art history major, speaking Spanish to all the Mexican laborers and learning sociology as I went, and here was Mary Beebe, my college roommate, who had studied Spanish and sociology, running a museum. And I thought, wait, what's wrong here anyway?"

Mimi is someone you notice, very tall with powerful physical strength. She's always been a risk-taker, throwing herself into each new venture, extracting the maximum amount of joy out of life. At the vineyard, she was a hands-on manager, drove heavy equipment during the harvest,

MARY EVALYN ARMSTRONG

designed and built a lift for gondolas, and learned how to fix machinery and run giant systems. She took care of nine houses on the property and ran a small water company, learning all about hydraulics and wells. "I should have been a civil engineer," said Mimi. "Once when I took a vocational aptitude test, I scored higher than graduate engineering students. As a profession, engineering had all the things I needed—changing venues, different kinds of challenges, spurts of energetic physical work."

Mimi grew up in rural New Jersey, "more cows than people" New Jersey. "I had this enormous, very fast horse, for 4-H," said Mimi. "She was seven-eighths thoroughbred, a paint, a very showy horse. And I was fearless. My father had several heart-stopping moments. Nobody had hard hats where we lived. You would meet your friends and ride over the hills, teach your horse to stand still under the cherry tree, and pick all the cherries you could. And if the horse came home without you, the family didn't worry. They figured you'd come dragging over the fields soon enough. That happened a lot. And I can't tell you how many days I came home with my little dog hoisted up in front of me on the saddle, completely pooped."

The high school Mimi attended was not very academic—out of three hundred and sixty-five students in her senior class, only a handful went on to college. But Mimi had exceptionally high SAT scores, and was accepted everywhere she applied—Radcliffe, Swarthmore, Middlebury, and Bryn Mawr. She immediately felt at home when she visited Bryn Mawr, and knew that was where she wanted to go to college.

"Do you remember the picture of Mabel Lang in the bathtub?" Mimi asked me suddenly. "It's an image from Bryn Mawr that has stayed with me all my life." I did remember. Mabel Lang was a longtime classics professor at Bryn Mawr, and the photo Mimi was talking about appeared in an issue of the college alumnae magazine. Lang had just unearthed a bathtub on an archaeological dig, and she was sitting right in it, with a big smile on her face. "It was just such a wonderful picture," Mimi said. "Her feet were hanging out, and she was so thrilled to have found this bathtub that she didn't give a damn what she looked like."

When Mimi arrived at Bryn Mawr, just sixteen years old, she experienced a lot of surprises. "I had never really studied before I went to Bryn Mawr," she said. "It was a great shock to me to find out that you had to go to classes *and* read the books." It was her first experience with dating, and the first time she'd ever had a group of friends in a communal living situation. "To me, these were the delights of Bryn Mawr," she said. "All of these things were terribly exciting." Mimi lived in Denbigh Hall, together with Mary Beebe and Sue Johnson. They all used to dance, doing the twist. "I was spoken to, more than once, by the warden, told to tone it down," said Mimi. "It was certainly loud, but we couldn't resist." You didn't dance *with* somebody; you danced by yourself. It was Chuck Berry and *Roll Over Beethoven*, Fats Domino and *Blueberry Hill*.

Mimi and her friends used to go to nightclubs in Camden, New Jersey, to hear all the black blues singers. She had a boyfriend from Philadelphia who played guitar and rode a motorcycle. He would drive through the campus, full throttle, so Mimi could hear him as she was studying in the library. Then *whoosh*, she'd be gone, out the door and off with her boyfriend on the motorcycle, crashing through the woods and splashing through brooks. "Oh it was fun!" said Mimi.

But Mimi's experience at Bryn Mawr was not one of unalloyed pleasure. "In truth," she said, "I cannot remember any instance of a kind or personal word from any faculty member, except about what I was wearing." Her one experience of meeting with President McBride was horrible. "I don't think Miss McBride thought I was serious," she said. "I had the sense that she thought I wasn't really a Bryn Mawr sort of person. But nobody ever talked to me about it. Nobody ever said a word. Nobody ever asked me what I was going to do, what I wanted to become."

Bryn Mawr introduced Mimi to amphetamines–speed. She was tall and very thin at that age, and tended to black out when she stood up. So they sent her to the college infirmary and there, without any discussion with her parents, they put her on amphetamines. This was apparently state-of-the-art treatment at the time, and nobody questioned what the doctors did. "I had those little pink pills," said Mimi, "and boy! What it did was

"*I should have been a civil engineer. As a profession, engineering had all the things I needed–changing venues, different kinds of challenges, spurts of energetic physical work.*"

raise everything up for me, so that when I stood up I exploded!" It did cure the blackouts–she didn't black out ever again–but it also started her out on a lifetime habit of staying up three nights in a row, her sleep patterns destroyed forever. "They don't just keep you up," said Mimi. "They make your mind *race*. It's fabulous, that tremendous sense of power and the ability to get stuff done under pressure," she said. "I read all of Milton in two days and one night." Luckily, Mimi never got addicted, though she did keep on taking amphetamines for a couple of years after Bryn Mawr–and the doctors kept giving her prescriptions.

Mimi eventually found her academic niche as an art history major. In her senior year, she worked with Elizabeth Mongan, a well-known woman curator at the Rosenwald Collection of Graphic Arts in Germantown, Pennsylvania (and sister of Agnes Mongan, Mary Beebe's mentor later at the Fogg). This meant that Mimi had the only car on campus, an enviable status. By the spring semester of her senior year, she had already been accepted into a prestigious graduate connoisseurship program in New York, run jointly by Columbia University and the Metropolitan Museum.

Then, one day that spring, Mimi read an article about the University of California, Berkeley, and suddenly decided that she wanted to go there, to the biggest public, co-ed university in California, a state she'd never even visited. She applied and was accepted as a graduate student in art history, and that summer, Mimi and a Bryn Mawr classmate got in the car and headed west, driving all the way across the country until they finally ended up in Berkeley. "At that point," said Mimi, "I took off my shoes, picked up my guitar, and felt that I had come home. I just became a Californian." Again, Mimi talks of coming home, of immediately feeling at home—first at Bryn Mawr, now in Berkeley—another turning point in her life. Elizabeth Mongan, Mimi's mentor at the Rosenwald Collection, was terribly disappointed that Mimi didn't go to Columbia. Mimi herself doesn't quite understand all the reasons for her decision. "I think it was a sense that I didn't really want to be in the basement of the Metropolitan, to be an academic," she said. "I have a certain amount of energy that just needs to be diffused. But at the time I didn't have the brains to really look at things in a very structured fashion." I don't think many of us did.

Mimi was drawn to the open, welcoming, "anything goes" spirit of Berkeley when she first got there—this was before hard drugs, and before Berkeley became a mecca for runaways. When the Berkeley free speech and antiwar movements started up a few years later, she generally stayed clear of all the demonstrations and protests, even though most of her friends were political activists. By that time, she was writing her master's thesis, and trying to shut out anything that might distract her. Also, she was increasingly troubled by the escalating levels of violence and police brutality.

Mimi did decide to join some friends in an October 1967, march on the Oakland Armory. It was a turning point in the Berkeley antiwar movement—radicals wanted to raise the stakes, to stop the Vietnam War by closing down the induction center. But the police came in with clubs and wiped them out. "There were people beaten and dragged and handcuffed," said Mimi. "I saw one man shot." In the end, the Stop the War movement did succeed in shutting down the induction center, but that didn't stop even one young man from going off to war.

Mimi was just twenty-one, teaching and living in Berkeley, dating a man who was in his senior year at UC Berkeley and two years younger than she was, when she found out that she was pregnant. Her boyfriend had already been accepted at Harvard Medical School for the upcoming fall semester. He might have wanted to marry Mimi, but at that point he didn't want a baby. So Mimi agreed to have an abortion. She tried first in Berkeley. At that time in California, you could get an abortion if two separate psychiatrists testified that it was medically necessary for the mental health of the mother. Mimi went to see one psychiatrist and he laughed at her, literally laughed, and shooed her out of the office. She was already planning a summer trip to Europe, and she had read somewhere that abortions were legal in Yugoslavia, so Mimi decided she would go to Yugoslavia and have an abortion there.

Mimi was traveling with Michele, a good friend whose grandmother had given her money to go to Europe for the summer—another "fairy grandmother," like Mary's. They went first to the American Hospital in Paris, where Mimi had a checkup, confirming that she was pregnant. There was nothing they could do there, so they went on, heading toward Yugoslavia. By this time, Mimi was feeling quite sick. Her stepfather had given her a present of money that was specifically to be spent in three-star and four-star restaurants. So they stopped at a wonderful little hotel restaurant in the south of France. Mimi ordered its specialty, a crayfish dish, but when it appeared, she could not eat even one crayfish. She ended up with just bouillon. But Michele, who was quite round at that time, ate and ate. She ate steadily for two or three hours, one course after another. They were the only ones there, and the French waiters stood around watching, fascinated by this gastronomical indulgence. Mimi and Michele had arrived at something like 1:30 PM and ate 'til 5:00 PM, then went out and sat in the garden and had cognac. "I remember that just before we left the waiters applauded," said Mimi. "And I was so ill."

They went through the south of France, then through Italy. Mimi called her boyfriend from a pay phone in front of the Piazza San Marco in Venice, took him away from his dinner. She said, "Are you sure? Because this is getting more difficult by the moment, and I really would like to have this baby." And he said, "No. Absolutely not. Go ahead with the abortion."

And so they went through Trieste down to Split, where they stopped at a hospital, went in and found a doctor. They asked about an abortion, and the doctor said, "You can't. It's only for Yugoslavians." They went on to Dubrovnik, to try a pharmacy there. Yugoslavia was still behind the Iron Curtain then. It was a Communist country. But just that day, for the very first time, a Catholic priest had been allowed to come to Dubrovnik to celebrate Mass, and Mimi and Michele got caught up in the celebration. The priest had to turn around and go right straight back to Brindisi once it was over, and that night, Mimi and Michele went to a pharmacy, to talk with the pharmacist. Michele spoke better French, so she did the talking.

"My friend isn't married and wants an abortion," she said. "Can you help us?" He gave them a name–this was all cloak-and-dagger stuff–and they went out, in the dark of night, to one of the city's new apartment blocks, and up the back stairs. It was like a Russian novel. They met someone there who told them to meet him at what they call a "lying-in hospital" the next night, at midnight. He was a doctor, a gynecologist, and it was a French maternity hospital. Mimi still remembers every detail of what happened: "He brought me in. I had no anesthesia; I was given a piece of wood to bite on. He pulled up my dress, and then Michele had to go–I could see her through the door; she was hysterical. It was actually extremely clean, and they just used icy-cold water, did a D&C, and let me stay there for a bit. They gave me a prescription for antibiotics."

You couldn't get prescriptions filled in Yugoslavia then, but Mimi and Michele had already arranged to take the night boat to Brindisi in Italy. They were on a very tight budget, but decided they could just afford a cabin with beds in it. So they got on the boat, and Mimi lay down and rested. The next day they went to a pharmacy in Brindisi and got the antibiotics, and within three days, even less than that, Mimi was fine. "What an ordeal!" said Mimi. "But I had Michele. I was young and healthy, and without the anesthesia it was probably much easier to recover. And I don't remember. I remember pain. But you don't remember things. It was rather scary, but for some reason I had total faith in this doctor. And it was all very matter-of-fact." Nobody knew, Mimi came back to Berkeley, and that was the end of that relationship.

To support her second year of graduate work Mimi worked as many as five different jobs, including editing somebody's movie script. The ad said: *Must be able to use an electric typewriter, must have had experience editing scripts*. Mimi had neither of these qualifications, but she didn't let that stop her. She found her way to the scriptwriter's house, the door opened, and a giant man appeared, filling the doorway, and just looked at her. "It was probably my size," she explained. "You know, I'm an unusual size." "Do you know how to make a daiquiri?" he asked. Mimi said, "Certainly." And he said, "Come on in." She discovered later that the giant scriptwriter was someone named Judd Boynton, a Berkeley legend. He became a mentor, and Mimi found herself making daiquiris for Anaïs Nin and Timothy Leary and other luminaries, all gathered there to talk about using LSD as a therapeutic agent. "That was kinda over my head," said Mimi. "I was barely twenty-one at the time. But I knew enough to make daiquiris because I grew up in the right kind of family."

By the end of the sixties, Mimi had gone through one rather short marriage, to a man named Fred, and was married to her second husband, who as it happened was also named Fred. "My friends think that's very funny," Mimi said. "Freds 1 and 2, same exact initials, FWW. I didn't have to change the silverware, the linens, nothing." She had a four-year-old son from her first marriage and was hugely pregnant with her second child. She also had a master's degree, in counseling psychology, and was trying to finish her PhD in psychology at UC Berkeley while working full-time as an administrator in the public schools. About that time she realized that her second husband was an alcoholic. For Mimi, this was too much—it just wasn't possible to take care of her husband and her son, work, go to school, and have the baby at the same time. Something had to give, and finally she gave up on the PhD. She had finished the orals and written exams, doing better than ever before in her life, but when she was asked to make just a few minor changes in an article that she was preparing for publication, she couldn't do it, just couldn't make the few little changes required.

This was another turning point, the second time that Mimi turned away from pursuing an academic career. Once again her decision seems to have been driven by a strong, almost physical instinct for what was right for her. She could not force herself to revise the manuscript, just as she could not picture herself stuck down in the basement of the Metropolitan Museum of Art after college. For Mimi, these were probably the right choices. By giving up the PhD she opened the door to new ventures, more active and entrepreneurial. The first was the vineyard.

A few years earlier, Mimi's mother and stepfather had moved to California, bought some property in Sonoma County, and started raising purebred Holstein-Friesians. Then the tax laws changed so that gentlemen farmers couldn't take losses the way they used to, and her mother decided that the going thing was vineyards. So the cows went out and the vines came in. Then, just after they'd finished planting all the vines, Mimi's mother became ill, and they had to farm out the management of the vineyard to a commercial enterprise. That was when Mimi decided that

"We were living with the vines, right in the middle of the vineyard."

she would take her family back to the land, so that she could be there to take care of her mother and run the vineyard.

Those were halcyon days for the children, with ponies and friends and picnics and harvests. Mimi still remembers the sharp beauty of the landscape. "We were living with the vines," she said, "right in the middle of the vineyard. The truth is that you don't really know what beauty is until you've been out starting the sprinklers on a freezing cold night, seeing black foxes with red tails, undulations of skunks on the move, and shooting stars." She loved the hard, physical work of the harvest and the good company of the Mexican laborers.

When Mimi's younger son was two or three years old, she decided that she couldn't take him around with her anymore in the vineyard— he needed proper day care. So they bought an enormous building in Calistoga and turned it into a day-care center licensed for eighty children. Unfortunately there weren't enough children in Calistoga to fill the center, so after a few years they shut that down and turned it into a residential facility for the elderly. All this time Mimi was still running the vineyard. By the mid-eighties, she and her second husband were divorced. (His alcoholism finally got the better of him, and he died shortly thereafter, at the age of fifty.) Then Mimi met Michael, a charming European who would become her third husband.

Mimi has been married more often than most in the class. What was particularly striking about Mimi's marriages was that she had never been married to anyone who actually had a job. During her first marriage, which was the shortest one, she supported the family. That was Fred 1. Fred 2, the alcoholic, had some money of his own and was using it up at a horrid rate. Her third husband, Michael, thirteen years her elder, had enough money to live on and was interested in more esoteric things, so he decided that he would retire.

Michael was European, spoke fifteen languages, and gave Mimi a whole new perspective. "Michael taught me to slow down and examine life," said Mimi. "Before then I was headlong through everything." With Michael, Mimi began thinking about turning the home for the elderly into a spa. She went to look at all kinds of spas, got involved in European thalassotherapy, and became a real expert on spas. "French insurance pays for spa therapy," she said. "If you're arthritic, depressed, or just overworked and tired, you can have a mini-break at the spa. It's wonderful."

They never quite finished the spa project—the house was sold first, and by that time Mimi had also sold the vineyard. In 1990, she began another career, taking over a computer software company. Michael had been an investor in the company and it was rapidly going out of business, so he asked Mimi to step in and run things. She did, and by the time I met with her, eight years later, she had turned the business around and it was doing quite well, with eight employees and about five hundred clients. I asked Mimi how she had managed to learn about software. "I knew nothing about software any more than I knew about running a vineyard," she said, "but you know, one problem is very much like another. It's not brain surgery or rocket science. It's like managing any business."

Mimi is used to solving problems, finding money, experts, books, help, whatever it takes. However, none of this equipped her to deal with her eldest son's battle with schizophrenia. He was studying anthropology and went off to Australia, where he lived with aborigines, and when he came back, he was mentally ill. At one point he even attempted suicide.

That was in 1991, and it has taken almost a decade, step by step, for him to recover. For a time, Mimi's greatest fear was that he would wander the streets at night and, because of his size (6 foot 7 inches, close to 300 pounds), people would be afraid of him and he would end up dead. "When it's your own dear child . . . " Mimi said. "When you get out of abject, pathological fear, then you realize what huge expectations you have of your children and how many shocks it takes to get those expectations peeled away and to be able to just be with your child and see how it is. Happily, that son is now one of the sanest people I know," she said, "and maybe the most unconventional person I know. He's found his own salvation. He doesn't take any medications, but he's very telepathic and very sensitive, so he just avoids situations that bother him."

Mimi and I talked over lunch at Café Maxx, an elegant little California-style restaurant in Santa Rosa. It was December, a busy season for the software company, and Mimi was moving into a new house, merging households with her eighty-nine-year-old mother. She was upbeat and calm—doing too much seems to agree with her.

Mimi and Michael had divorced about a year earlier. While Michael had given Mimi a new, more thoughtful perspective on life and expanded her world, it eventually became clear that she was the more adventurous of the two. "What broke that marriage up," she said, "was that it was totally suffocating after a while. He's a fearful person, and I don't have any fears." They are still friends; they just couldn't live under the same roof anymore. Mimi told me that she was happier than she'd ever been, looking forward to a peaceful, creative part of her life.

In early May, 1999, less than six months after the lunch in Santa Rosa, I opened up a breezy, exuberant e-mail—*Subj: Rob and Mimi do Nevada*—announcing Mimi's fourth marriage. "Well my dearest friends," she wrote, "I've done it again! In Love's Lake Tahoe Wedding Chapel no less, I became Mrs. Robert Nichols Hamlin. We're doing everything backwards," she said, "marry first, and then work everything out. It's incredibly liberating to be able to fall in love when your kids are grown and gone and you can basically do anything that suits." Mimi's new husband was her childhood friend and neighbor—for years they practically lived in each other's houses, built snowmen and went ice skating, investigated creeks, rode the horses, went to the beach and played cards together, all the things she loves best. He's an engineer, vice president for research and development at a company that develops products with medical applications. "This man is solid and works for a living for a change," said Mimi. "It won't be just me with the schedule."

Part IV
Conclusion

Chapter Nine

"I Haven't Bloomed Yet"

*"Time and trouble will tame an advanced young woman, but
an advanced old woman is uncontrollable by any earthly force."*
—Dorothy L. Sayers

In the early nineties, a rash of books about menopause came out. Suddenly, the unmentionable "M-word" was on everyone's lips, and anthropologist Margaret Mead was celebrating "post-menopausal zest." This was the start of several waves of books about life's "third act," including at least one from the Bryn Mawr class of '62. In a 2004 book titled *My Time*,[1] classmate Abigail Trafford writes about this new stage of life, from ages fifty to seventy, calling it a "second adolescence," a time for starting new careers, new relationships, and figuring out "how to make the most of the rest of your life."

In the year 2000, members of our class celebrated their sixtieth birthdays—a new millennium, a new cusp, a new coming-of-age. In this new world, thanks to the recent longevity revolution, we are looking forward to a good ten extra years of "health span," perhaps thirty years of life after sixty. Retirement, in the old sense, is no longer an option. Some of us can't afford to stop working. And besides, many of us feel we are just getting going, just coming into our own. Once again, the women of Bryn Mawr's class of '62 are entering uncharted territory. In their fifties, and now in their sixties, these women are continuing to reinvent themselves, still intent on finding purpose in their lives and their work, still intent on improving the world.

After her marriage, in the spring of 1999, Mimi Armstrong sold the software company and went to join her new husband in Minnesota. Next I heard, they were off to Tel Aviv, Israel. When I finally caught up with Mimi and Rob in the summer of 2002, they were running a bed-and-breakfast in a stately New England country house located on the old Putney Road outside of Brattleboro, Vermont. Mimi seemed in her element, a gracious and efficient host. The B & B had become a prime destination for gay and lesbian couples and their families, coming from out-of-state to celebrate civil unions.

By that time, Rob and Mimi were already planning the next step in their lives. They wanted something that would not be as all-consuming as running a B & B, something that would take them back to Mimi's beloved West Coast. Mimi was looking for a project that would tap her creative energies. She thought about writing, perhaps stories based on her experience with all the couples and their families who came through the B & B.

In 2003, they sold the Vermont B & B and moved to Edmonds, Washington, north of Seattle, where they bought and restored a new home, which Mimi describes as "a kind of tree house overlooking (from afar) Puget Sound." Mimi enrolled in a yearlong scriptwriting course at the University of Washington, and started work on a film script about Rob's great-grandfather, Cyrus Hamlin. A full three decades older than anyone else in the class, she was bemused by the deference with which she was treated. Other classmates have made similar comments. "It's wonderful to be old," said one. "People look to you as a repository of wisdom."

Mimi told me her life had changed 180 degrees ("like Miss Elizabeth Bennett," in *Pride and Prejudice*, she said), not just in concrete ways—her marriage, where she's located, and what she's doing—but fundamentally, in how she sees herself, her new sense of purpose. Before, she always just picked up what came along. Now, for the first time, she is making choices, for herself.

While Mimi's story may be more eventful than most, she is not the only classmate making dramatic life changes. Fran Conley, the Stanford neurosurgeon, retired in 2000. She and her husband now live in what can

Fran Conley at Rancho del Mar.

only be described as a mansion ("It's too much, really," said her husband), built along the cliffs at Rancho Del Mar, on the coast north of San Francisco. The winds are constant, off the ocean, and the view is spectacular. Fran has a telescope in her study trained on the rocks offshore where gull chicks, just hatched, are flailing awkwardly in their nest. She takes the dog out at least once a day for a long run—Fran is frighteningly fit, and set a brisk pace on our "walk" along the coast. Her father had died recently, and she was busy sorting out his affairs. After that, she said, she wants to start writing a novel.

After Sue Johnson published her first book, *Staying Power,* about long-term lesbian couples, she came to New York City to do a reading and book signing at A Different Light, a gay and lesbian bookstore. Barbara (Paul) Robinson and Marion (Coen) Katzive, who were friends with Sue at Bryn Mawr, living in the same dorm, both came to the book signing, straight from their Park Avenue law offices. "They looked so different from everyone else," Sue remembered. "I just loved them for being there." "I was glad we went," said Marion, "even though we felt very conspicuous, out of place, dressed up in lawyers' suits." Everyone at the reading thought they were a couple. "Where do you live?" someone asked, looking at the two of them. Marion tried to explain: "I live in Scarsdale, and Barbara lives in New York City."

In 2000, Sue and her longtime partner left Anchorage, Alaska, and moved to Whidbey Island, north of Seattle. Sue is writing a book about her mother, and rents a writing studio downtown, which she has furnished with a comfortable stuffed chair, an oriental rug patterned in warm reds, shelves of books, files, a desk and computer, but no phone. It helps to get away, she says, and it means that her partner doesn't need to tiptoe around the house. Sue is just one of several classmates who, like Virginia Woolf, have understood the necessity of having "a room of one's own."

In 2001, after a long career in the newspaper business, Isa (Brannon) Spencer decided to leave journalism, to take a job as executive manager of the Annie Tinker Association for Women, a foundation that helps older women remain in their homes. There are currently about fifty Tinker "fellows," women who have worked mainly in the arts or related fields, who never earned much of a pension and whose families can't help out. They are living alone at home but can't quite afford it. The Tinker stipends are small—the group that came on in 2002 gets $150–$250 a month—but enough to make a real difference in quality of life. Some women who don't want to take money or help from a social service agency feel differently about Tinker because it is for artists. "We can take a woman on," said Isa, "and then press her to receive more substantial help from someone else."

Isa's new job is, in many ways, the antithesis of journalism—instead of informing and influencing a mass audience, she is working with individuals to help them. "Don't you feel that there are certain types of things we all start to do at certain times in our lives?" she said. "When you're younger you want to change the system. Now I think the system won't change. But I shouldn't be pessimistic; some wonderful things have happened in our lives."

Some wonderful things *have* happened, and we *did* change the system. But we have now come to realize that some things probably won't change, at least not in the near future. Like Isa, several classmates have shifted their focus, working to make a difference in the lives of individuals rather than trying to save the world. One classmate, a school librarian, told me: "I'm connecting a small number of students with good books, which I know is good for them. I have a larger number of students who couldn't care less. If I were twenty years younger, I would worry a lot about that. But now I don't take it personally. I'm no longer trying to change the world with my job."

At the time of our 40th class reunion, we were sixty-two years old, which at that time was the average age for men's retirement in America. But these Bryn Mawr women seem to be on the verge of deciding what to do with their lives. On a question about plans for the next ten years, everyone had a lot to say, the responses snaking out into the margins of the page. Travel was on almost everyone's list. And these were not old-lady travels; they were more like Graham Greene's "travels with my aunt," adventuresome, off the beaten track, to "exotic places," China, the Australian outback, to climb Kilimanjaro. Many planned to take courses, to learn languages, and to do creative work: painting, music, and especially writing. Money and health were two concerns—we hope that both hold out long enough for us to live fully and well.

I talked with classmates who were already taking their lives in new directions. A professor of Spanish literature spent a summer in Buenos Aires, where she took up the tango. A software engineer was getting involved in cultivating perennials. A senior economist at the World Bank was leaving the bank in order to write musicals, in collaboration with her new husband. One physician classmate had just launched a new, private practice, while another (the first woman to take the boards in oncology, in 1973) had recently gone part-time. "Now I'm into environment, education, Italian, sewing quilts," she said, "all these things I never had time for."

In this stage of our lives, we are intent on making a significant contribution, to our professions and to other people. At least a few of us are still thinking big: one classmate aims to "prevent war, hunger and pain." We want to do more volunteer work, and to nurture relationships, to make time to be with friends, with aging parents, children, and grandchildren. To "spend time in the wild," said one respondent. Another wants to "let [her] sense of spirituality bloom."

Joanna Underwood: No Time to Lose.

Classmate Joanna Underwood was a pioneer in the early environmental movement of the seventies, the founding president of INFORM, a not-for-profit environmental research organization. "Under her guidance, INFORM grew to be one of America's premier candle lighters, responding to toxic, energy, water and pollution threats with practical and imaginative solutions," said former EPA Administrator William K. Reilly. "As a prophetic environmentalist, Joanna has always been distinctly inclusive

JOANNA DeHAVEN UNDERWOOD

and positive in her approach, welcoming converts, and avoiding doomsday warnings."[2]

Joanna was a debutante, and came to Bryn Mawr from Rye Country Day, a private school. Her mother was a Bryn Mawr graduate (Helen Guiterman '28, a classmate and friend of actress Katharine Hepburn), a social activist who was a powerhouse in Planned Parenthood. I had arranged to meet with Joanna on September 17, 2001, in her (all-*green*) office, located a few blocks from the World Trade Center in New York City. As it turned out, we met at Joanna's house instead, and the first thing we talked about was September 11.

"I think September 11 has been a profound experience for young people who have felt upwardly mobile, protected and secure," said Joanna. "It's all been shattered now, and that is causing extraordinary rethinking."

> *This could lead to a new sense of community, a new sense of understanding that people need each other. It has raised new questions: How can we be a more caring and sharing part of a global community of six billion? The needs are so huge and we're really a small island of privilege. How can we play a different role in this world? I believe there are millions and millions of people around this country who are going through a process of rethinking. There's enormous opportunity here to try to draw out of this feeling of insecurity in people a sense of new possibilities, new solutions, new ways to live.*

Five years later, it is clear that what Joanna predicted has not happened, at least not on any scale that you would notice. The opportunities coming out of September 11 have been lost. The optimism and utopian vision of the early sixties, the practical idealism that characterizes the Bryn Mawr class of '62—all of that seems to have become irrelevant, out of tune with the times.

On May 22, 2006, the board of directors of INFORM issued a press release, announcing that "the organization's founder and President for 31 years, Joanna D. Underwood, has stepped down from her leadership at INFORM, and will be embarking on a new research and education initiative promoting sustainable energy and transportation for the U.S."

A few months earlier, Joanna had gone to the chairman of the board to propose a new role for herself, with less of her time devoted to fundraising and running the organization. "At INFORM, my interest was always in the mission," she said, "not in the politics of building an institution." Other classmates have talked about how good it is to be at this stage of life, when we don't have to care anymore about whether we are up or down, or how we are doing, when all the intrigue doesn't matter. Now that she has stepped down from her position as president, Joanna can make her own choices, for herself. She realized, she said, that she didn't have time to lose. She wants to focus on the issues she cares about—the transition of energy and transportation away from fossil fuels, and how to educate young people on the environment—and to spend more time with her husband.

When I last talked with Joanna, in the summer of 2006, she was already moving on, excited about new ventures, getting ready to go to Seoul, South Korea, on a U.S. Department of State program, to talk about sustainable development. "Having left INFORM, I've seen whole new opportunities opening up," she said.

In the spring of 2006, Joanna made two trips back to Bryn Mawr, once as keynote speaker for a major conference on environmental education, and once at the invitation of the Greens, a student group. "Let me tell you, the Greens

"I think September 11 has been a profound experience for young people. This could lead to a new sense of community, a new sense of understanding that people need each other."

are terrific!" said Joanna. And the Greens were inspired by talking with Joanna. "We were very impressed with Joanna Underwood," one student told me, "She persuaded us that there was a future in environmental work."

Waiting to Bloom

At our 35th reunion class dinner, Anna (Kimbrough) Morris took charge: "We'll go around the room," she said, "talk about what's going on in our lives." The conversation soon took an unexpected turn, a succession of fervent testimonies to marriage and family. It started out with classmates who were still with longtime spouses or partners–fifteen years together, thirty years, thirty-five years, they announced triumphantly. Others talked proudly of grown children, so much smarter and saner than we were at that age. We had gotten about halfway around the room, when this drumbeat of domesticity and good cheer was suddenly cut short. "I haven't bloomed yet," said classmate Laning (Pepper) Thompson. "I'm still waiting to bloom." There was a quick moment of silence after she spoke; then the next person picked up the conversation and we went on around the room.

After the reunion, I thought about what Laning had said, wondered if she were serious. I went to see her and asked what she meant. She had led an interesting, eventful life, I discovered, rather tough. Now in her third marriage, she had been the family breadwinner for most of her career, working for newspapers and doing freelance writing and editing. She wasn't discounting all of this, or suggesting that somehow her life had not been worthwhile. But she assured me that what she said at the reunion dinner was heartfelt and true. She hadn't bloomed yet. Like most of us, Laning had high expectations of life, coming out of Bryn Mawr. And now, thirty-five years later, she was still waiting to bloom, waiting to experience a real epiphany, a "eureka" moment when she would know what she wanted to do with the rest of her life.

Laning's quest takes on a new urgency, for her and for all of us who find ourselves in this new stage of life, our fifties and sixties and beyond. We are no longer struggling to build a career, and our children are grown up and on their own. The questions now are: Who am I? What do I want to do with my life? What would it take for me to really bloom?

Class dinners and questionnaires do not reveal much of doubts and anguish, even when questionnaire responses are kept anonymous, as ours were. But there are such doubts and anguish—worries about being alone, about losing our identity once we are no longer active and working, about getting old. "I look at my life as a failure," one classmate told me, "because I'm not okay. I cannot stand the idea of being old, being dependent. I know I'm doing too much for a sixty-five-year-old woman. I suppose at some point I'm going to have to cut back. But I don't know what I'm going to do. I'm really not okay by myself unless I keep working all the time."

Late Blooming and Ultimate Questions

Demographer Betsy (Barber) Gould and Rector Stephanie (Condon) Shoemaker count themselves among the many "late bloomers" in our class: Betsy was fifty-one when she got her PhD in demography, and Stephanie graduated from the Episcopal Divinity School at the age of fifty-

L-R: Betsy (Barber) Gould, Stephanie (Condon) Shoemaker, and Alison Baker.

HETTY STEPHANIE CONDON

five. I wanted to talk about late bloomers, and also about ultimate questions, and these two classmates seemed like just the people to give me some insight.

In the summer of 2000, Betsy and I went together to visit Stephanie at her home in Newport, Rhode Island. She met us at the front door, her two dogs barking excitedly, and, after big hugs all around, led us back to a screened porch looking out over the harbor. There we settled in for a three-way conversation: Betsy, a comfortable, rounded figure, energetic, with a high, breathy voice; Stephanie, dressed in semi-clerical black, warm, solid, and serene; and me.

We got straight to ultimate questions—the role of religion, or spirituality, in our lives, especially now, as we are getting older. "The horizon is getting closer," said Stephanie. "When you start to realize that this life will come to an end, then you begin to ask the questions that weren't really so interesting when you were younger: What does all of this mean? Is there something ultimate, beyond this?" She talked about love. By this time in our lives, we bring something to the table, the experience of relationships with children, lovers, friends, and family. "I think with relationships, your whole self is expanded," said Stephanie. "Love takes you out of yourself, and you begin to have a sense of something much greater, beyond yourself. In a way it's a better sense of who you are, so that you feel comfortable in this created world. It gives you a kind of serenity."

Stephanie herself has always felt grounded, she said, grounded in faith, really believing that there was a God, and that there was goodness. She was brought up as an Episcopalian and her father was a priest, so the language and context of religion were there, available to her. "It wasn't a moralistic, judging kind of religion," said Stephanie. "It was a sense of connectedness with the created order and the Creator, very personal, almost primal."

Stephanie had held various jobs in the years since Bryn Mawr, going from one thing to another. Her husband (an MD with a straight-arrow medical career) once asked, with some impatience, "Are you *ever* going to figure out what you want to do?" By the early nineties, she was running an art museum, also doing a lot of painting, drawing, and printmaking, a creative expression that she still loves. But she realized it wasn't enough. "It wasn't ultimate enough for me," she said. "I wanted to do something with more social significance." So she became a deacon in the Episcopal Church, then started volunteering at a battered women's shelter, trying to set up relationships between shelters and churches. At that time, nobody in the community trusted the clergy, the clergy didn't trust the shelters, and the battered women who went to church and were part of those congregations would never say anything about what was happening to them at home. Stephanie began asking some basic questions: How do you preach? How do you talk to groups so that people will feel free to come forward and tell you what is going on in their lives and get some help? It was her work in the parish that she really loved. "I loved working with groups in the parish, getting things up and running, getting people moving

"I'd really felt a call. There were several times when there were voices almost."

in their own directions," she said, "and I also loved the sacramental aspects of the church."

Being a deacon was still not enough, she realized. She needed to go to seminary. "I really felt a call," she said. "It's funny. I don't know how you explain it." So she went to the bishop and said, "Bishop, I just *know* I need to do this. I've tried to push it aside, because really, I don't want to go to seminary at this point in my life particularly. But I need to do this." The bishop, who was about to go off on a sabbatical, told her to come back and see him in six months. In those six months, said Stephanie, "I could *not* get rid of this nudge, this kind of pressure that would not go away. There were several times when there were voices almost. I just knew there was no turning back." And it was the right thing: After Stephanie made the decision, she felt as if the weight of the world had been lifted.

The bishop advised Stephanie to go to the Episcopal Divinity School (EDS). "It would be good for you to experience the wildness," he said. By the nineties, the EDS had a radical edge, pushing for gay rights and peace. It attracted a diverse student group, including a lot of middle-aged people—the oldest a seventy-year-old woman who had been teaching at the Bryn Mawr School of Social Work. After graduating from divinity school, Stephanie became an associate rector. Then, in January of 2001, she got her own small parish church in Saunderstown, Rhode Island, the Chapel of St. John the Divine. In the summer of 2004, when I saw her last, she seemed to be flourishing as rector. She had come into her own, as though everything else in her career had been leading to this.

Elizabeth (Barber) Gould

Betsy didn't really think about a professional career until she was in her late thirties, early forties. "My whole goal when I was eighteen was to leave Springfield, Ohio, and never come back," she said. She got married the Christmas after graduating from Bryn Mawr, worked as a secretary to put her husband through graduate school at UC Berkeley, went to the Australian outback with him to study the Aborigines, then followed again when he wanted to move to Hawaii. "He was the only one of us who had a plan," said Betsy. In Hawaii, she worked as an editor at a population journal, and got so interested in the subject matter that she decided to go to graduate school. (At that point her husband had just gotten a job teaching at Brown University, in Providence, Rhode Island, and Brown had an excellent program in demography.)

ELIZABETH BARBER

Graduate school was hard–"There's no process worse," said Betsy, "no process worse. I see that phrase: 'He took his PhD at Harvard.' I'm thinking, how did he take it? Did he wrest it away? But if I hadn't finished the PhD I would have felt like a Bryn Mawr failure; let's face it." Betsy picked up *Crazy Time,*[3] a book by classmate Abigail Trafford, about surviving divorce. "I read it when I was in graduate school and feeling that I would never get out," she said, "and I remember thinking, 'This is a lot like a bad marriage.' And Abbie's book really helped me through that."

Betsy got her PhD in demography in 1991, and since then, has been working mainly for the United Nations. "I feel very grateful that the UN continues to hire me," she said. "I do some freelance writing and editing at home for population groups, but I prefer to go to New York to work at the UN because it shows I'm a professional and I'm being paid for it. I would work practically for free for the UN. Fortunately I don't have to. But it validates your professionalism. It really does."

As a demographer, Betsy sees our class as part of a demographic cohort, just ahead of the baby boomers. "I think being in the baby boom would have been crowded, it would have been a crowded, crowded cohort," she said. "We've been just ahead of the baby boomers, and that's an interesting place to be. They've dominated the conversation from the time they were the student activists, and we're looking back and saying 'Well, if I were ten years younger, I might have made different decisions.' Now they're going to start retiring. It will be interesting to watch what's going to happen to retirement. They'll change it. We don't know how yet."

As always, the class of '62 is a step ahead, pathbreakers almost in spite of ourselves.

Looking Back

In the 40th reunion survey, there were questions about roads not taken, and about regrets. Almost a quarter of respondents said that if times had been different, they might have pursued different, more ambitious professional careers, in law, medicine, or engineering. "I vaguely wish that I had pursued a career," wrote one classmate. Another thought she would have liked "a *real* career." On the one hand, we feel that we have been lucky in life. We were the right ages at the right times, on the leading edge of the feminist movement. We played a role in breaking down barriers for women in the professions. Some of us went on to become the first and only woman in high-level jobs. On the other hand, we realize that when we graduated, in 1962, our possibilities were quite limited. Perhaps Mimi Armstrong *should* have been an engineer, but she really didn't have that option.

Some, if they had it to do over again, would have waited a bit to get married, to have children, or to enter graduate school. Overall, though, there were few regrets. Even bad choices had some good outcomes. "I shouldn't have married the person I did," wrote one classmate, "but then I wouldn't have had children, these particular children, who have so enriched my life." And perhaps regrets don't suit this group of can-do optimists. "What a terrible, useless thing is regret," said one.

What Does It All Mean?

First of all, this is about history—how we are shaped by the times we live in, and how we, in turn, shape history. It is mainly history from the bottom up, organized as a series of life histories, the personal narratives of individual women, each finding her own path through life.

As a group, the women of Bryn Mawr's class of '62 belong to a little-known generation that has gone through life just one step ahead of the baby boom. Through their stories, we are witness to more than fifty years of American history, through the last half of the twentieth century. These women were at Bryn Mawr as the Eisenhower fifties turned into the New Frontier sixties. They came of age in the Kennedy years, that extraordinary moment of optimism and idealism. Going out into the world of work, they were among the first to break down barriers for women entering the professions.

On the 40th class reunion survey, more than 80 percent of respondents felt that their lives had been significantly affected by their time and place in history. "We lived in a time of rapid social change, especially for women," said one classmate, "so we were pioneers in many ways." The survey went on to ask about particular historical events–the civil rights movement, the Vietnam War, the peace movement, the women's movement, the gay/lesbian rights movement, the sexual/reproductive rights revolution (birth control pill, legalized abortion, and so on)–a list that evokes the waves of social movements that swept through America in the sixties and seventies, when members of the class of '62 were in their twenties and thirties. "I wasn't an activist and I stayed out of protests and demonstrations," said one classmate, in a response that was echoed by many others, "but the women's movement and the reproductive rights movement affected all women of my cohort." "The reproductive rights movement kept me from having a baby a year, and the women's movement made my career possible," said another classmate. "I feel as though I was on the leading edge of the feminist movement. Birth control pills and law school were not available just a few years before I came along. It was also more difficult to move in the legal world when I became a lawyer (1974). There were no female partners in any law firm in the city when I graduated from law school." "I really feel we are on the cusp," said another classmate. "The classes before us, everyone had three babies before they were twenty-five. The classes after us had no babies at all."

In the survey and in interviews, classmates talk a lot about being "on the leading edge," part of a hinge generation, "on the cusp" of change. Most are too modest to claim much more than that. They were there, that's all, ready to seize opportunities as they appeared. They tell us what it was like, what individual women were actually doing in those years. It is an important first step, adding this particular group of women back into history. But if we only recognize waves of the women's movement once they become visible, we tend to underestimate the roles that individual women played in promoting social change. The march of history begins to seem inevitable, with recognized turning points and leaders. But there is nothing inevitable about these victories (or defeats). This is where the material of the oral histories is most valuable. It enables us to see the complex, halting *process* of change, and it enables us to see the ways in which women themselves were changed by their experience, sometimes in private, subtle ways. As Italian oral historian Alessandro Portelli put it, in a recent (autumn 2006) article, oral history, "brings history from above and history from below into the same text—as it were, to the negotiating table—creating an equal dialogue between the historians' awareness of broad spatial and temporal patterns, and the local narrator's closely focused personal narrative."[4]

"Mommy Wars, Round 587" was the title of Katha Pollitt's column in the July 2, 2006, issue of the *Nation*. Once again, the subject is upscale young mothers, with one camp telling them to "get to work," while the other insists that they should stay home with their children. Meanwhile, a survey of the Bryn Mawr class of 2002 showed 60 percent of graduates going straight into the workforce—the majority into finance, marketing, and management—and 16 percent going on to graduate school. These numbers were, respectively, the highest and lowest ever.

What does the class of '62 have to say to these young graduates, going out into such a different world, going into careers that we could hardly imagine forty years earlier? What does the class of '62 have to contribute, in round 587 of the "mommy wars?"

First, we can reclaim the history of American feminism, giving younger generations a fuller picture of their own history, as women. "Now I see how we got from June Cleaver to Bella Abzug!" said one young woman, after reading an early draft of this book. Second, by showing real women living real lives, we can begin to change the conversation. Instead of pitting women against one another in the mommy wars, these women from the class of '62 talk about helping younger women, especially in the crunch of balancing work and family. "We've all been there," says lawyer Barbara Robinson. "You can do it." The book provides a lot of different models of women trying to find satisfying lives and careers in times of flux and mixed messages. They show that you can have more than one career, that you may want to do different things at different times in your life. There is a lot of talk a lot about luck and the uncertainties of life. "The fact is, things happen that you have no control over," said one classmate. "It's how you respond that matters."

The women of Bryn Mawr's class of '62 were pioneers in opening doors for women in the professions. Many of us assumed that once the doors were open, that would do it. We thought that we and our successors from the baby-boom generation had completed the job. We were wrong. The doors have stayed open, but it turns out that open doors are not enough. Glass ceilings are a persistent problem. And while members of the class of '62 have tried, with some success, to make changes in their particular professions, the basic structures of family and work have not changed. For that you need a new generation of pioneers. And perhaps it is always difficult; perhaps it will always be a work in progress.

Notes on the 40ᵗʰ Reunion

On Friday night of the 2002 reunion weekend, we gathered around the steps in front of Taylor Hall for the traditional "stepsing," grouped by class, each with its own "songmistress," carrying a lantern in the class color. And the mistress of ceremonies, mistress of all the "songmistresses," was Anna (Kimbrough) Morris of the class of '62. Anna was resplendent in a flowing, purple robe, dangling earrings. She took command, moving us all across the quad into Thomas Hall when it began to rain, with brisk directions: carry your own chair, reassemble by class. Then Anna marked out the beat with her lantern (in dark blue, the '62 class color), up, down, to the center. She sang out, leading the songs in a loud, clear voice (a marked contrast to some of the other, more tentative songmistresses)—*Scarlet Ribbons*, our first class song (and "easy for the old girls to sing reasonably well," said Anna), and the traditional Lantern Night songs, *Pallas Athena* and *Sophias*, sung in classical Greek. Anna was our class songmistress during our early years at Bryn Mawr, and she is still whipping us into shape.

On Saturday, a memorial for classmate Jane (Hess) Flanders was held at the dedication of the Poetry Nook, a leafy bower alongside Pembroke East, with a slatted wooden bench, and a bronze plaque engraved with her poem "Mantises" set into a nearby quartz boulder. Poet, musician, and avid gardener, Jane died in April 2001 of a rare cancer. In our college yearbook, friends called her "our bard, our mapmaker."

Oddly, Jane and I talked of death, long before she knew about the cancer. She had invited me to her home in Pelham, New York, for dinner and a taped conversation.

Jane told me she was always writing poetry, but never thought of herself as a poet. "You went to Bryn Mawr and you knew who the poets were," she said. "They were Milton and Shakespeare, and maybe Marianne Moore. But you weren't a poet like that. You just wrote poetry." In 1971, Jane almost died after giving birth to twins. She had severe toxemia, and was in the intensive care ward for months. "I remember waking up," she said, "and saying to a nurse, 'I'm a poet.' And that was probably the first time I'd said that. I was realizing the things that were important in my life, which were surviving to raise three young children—the twins and a two-year-old—and that I was a poet. I came away with the sense that my brain had been absolutely cleared of nonessentials. I knew what was important to me. And somehow the poetry was something that I hadn't honored, and hadn't recognized, and it was a part of what I was, and who I was."

Later that evening, we were talking about what you put on your business card, how to answer the question, 'What do you do?' "Poet just doesn't seem like a career, like a doctor or a lawyer," said Jane. "It's not a profession; it's an obsession, or at least it was with me." We talked about obituaries: "I love the obituaries in the *Standard Star*, the local paper," said Jane. "Here you're reading the *New York Times*, and there are all these very impressive people, and then you pick up the obituaries in the *Standard Star*. There are lots of homemakers, and there was one who did crossword puzzles . . . whatever they did, right there in the headlines of these little write-ups. Perhaps I will be known for my early Sugar Snap peas, or 'had the earliest tomatoes' . . . "

On Sunday morning of the reunion weekend, we gathered for the traditional March of the Classes. The class of 1962 is getting toward the front of the line now. The 50th reunion class was out in force, ahead of us, with custom-designed silk scarves, a colorful, swirly maypole pattern, outclassing our modest yellow-and-white-striped umbrellas. When the signal came, we lifted up the long banner reading *Class of '62*, and stepped out, passing under the Pembroke arch to the skirl of bagpipes. At the entrance to the breakfast tent, our student helpers were waiting for us, leaping and dancing in a quick frenzy of enthusiasm. "Go '62!" they shouted. We all smiled and picked up our step.

Notes on Demography
by
Elizabeth Gould

Demographic indicators for American women reflect the sweeping social changes that occurred in the last half of the twentieth century. As women gained more opportunities in education and employment, female labor-force participation increased, as did the average age at marriage and age at the birth of the first child. The number of children—already lower for educated women than for the population in general—has declined, and a larger percentage of women have no children at all. One notable achievement in the twentieth century was the remarkable increase in life expectancy, from 47.3 years in 1900 to 68.2 years in 1950 to 76.9 years for a baby born in 2000. An American woman who turned 65 in 2000 could expect to live an additional 19.2 years. This brief note looks at some of the questions in two class reunion surveys (25th and 40th) and compares them with the United States population in general and trends during the last few decades.

Education

The Bryn Mawr sample, by definition, describes a population of women that was not typical of young American women in the fifties. Not only are we all college-educated, but we all attended Bryn Mawr, an elite women's college. The numbers are striking when compared with our national cohort (women who were 60–64 in 2000). According to the U.S. Census Bureau, 82 percent of women in this age group in the United States did not complete college, and only about 7 percent had an advanced degree. By contrast, more than three-quarters of the respondents to the 25th reunion survey reported that they had received at least one graduate degree, and nearly half (48 percent) had doctorates or medical or law degrees. (It should be noted that the survey results describe only those who chose to return the questionnaire, about half the class, and thus are not necessarily representative of the class as a whole.) Moreover, "late blooming" was not uncommon among our classmates: 23 percent of the postgraduate degrees were earned in 1977 or later, at least fifteen years after graduating from college.

Marriage and Children

In patterns of marriage and family, the Bryn Mawr group is similar in most respects to other educated women of the same age cohort. Three-quarters of the respondents to the 25th reunion survey said they were currently married, and an additional 18 percent were divorced, widowed, or separated. Only 7 percent had never been married. The figures were similar in the 40th reunion survey. Again, 75 percent of respondents reported that they were currently married, whereas 12 percent were divorced and 2 percent were widowed. The rest were single, separated, or living with someone. Nearly 95 percent of respondents said they had been married at least once, and nearly a third had lived with a man they were not married to. About 7 percent reported that they had been in a same-sex relationship. Of those married, 77 percent had been married just once, 18 percent had been married twice, and 5 percent three or more times.

Among American women in our age cohort, nearly two-thirds were married in 2000, with just over 30 percent widowed, divorced, or separated. About 4 percent had never been married. Compared with educated women today, we married young. (Compared with women in our own age cohort, we married slightly later.) The median age at first marriage for the class of 1962 was 23, and the median age of husbands was 26. About four-fifths of the women were married by age 26.

Eighty percent of respondents in the 25th reunion survey had children, and of those, 44 percent had two children. Twenty-eight percent reported three children, and 22 percent had just one child. Only 6 percent of classmates with children had more than three. Most childbearing was concentrated in a short time period, with the mean age at the birth of the first child being nearly 28, and the mean age at the birth of the last child just over 32. According to the National Center for Health Statistics, in 2000 the average American woman had her first baby at the age of about 25, an increase of nearly four years since 1970. This shift reflects both a decline in teenage births and rising birth rates for women in their thirties and forties.

Fully 20 percent of the Bryn Mawr respondents had no children. This was in sharp contrast to the percentage of childlessness among American women generally, which hovered around 10 percent up until the late seventies, when it began gradually to increase. We were ahead of the curve, more like young women today than our peers. Among the last cohort of American women to complete childbearing (those 40 to 44 in 2004), nearly a fifth had no children. This is partly a matter of choice, as women pursue careers and other non-family options, but some childlessness occurs because delaying childbearing increases the odds of being unable to conceive.

Work and Retirement

At the time of our 40th reunion in 2002, most women in our class were about 62 years old, nearing retirement age. However, the survey results showed that most respondents (71 percent) were still working in paid employment. Almost two-thirds of this group were working full-time, and the rest were working part-time or freelancing. We were much more likely than American women in our age group to be working. Data from the Bureau of Labor Statistics show that in 2000, just over 40 percent of women aged 60–64 were in the civilian labor force.

During the last half century, labor-force participation rates for men of all ages have fallen, while those for women have increased. For older men and women, the general trend has been toward younger ages at retirement, but the most recent data show a slight upward trend. This may reflect anxiety about pensions, health-care costs, and the solvency of the Social Security system. Or it may result from a healthy economy and the elimination of mandatory retirement ages. In any case, the decision to retire is a major one at this point in our lives, and responses to the 40th reunion questionnaire showed ambivalence about choices. When asked whether they were looking forward to retirement, many respondents (37 percent) weren't sure, whereas 24 percent could hardly wait.

Bryn Mawr women of our generation have been creative about striking a balance between work and family. The 25th reunion survey asked about "having it all," and about three-quarters of the respondents said they had tried to have it all. They described many patterns of combining our roles–taking them up sequentially or moving from one to another as time and needs dictate. By the 40th reunion, when most family and work choices were behind them, the majority of respondents to the reunion questionnaire seemed happy with their choices, at least with regard to family. In response to a question asking if they would make the same choices regarding work and family, two-thirds of the respondents felt they would make the same choices, whereas 21 percent thought their choices would be different.

Questions for Discussion

It's Good to Be a Woman: Voices from Bryn Mawr, Class of '62 is the ideal book-club book, dealing as it does with women's lives. Here are some questions to start off the discussion.

These women say that their lives have been significantly affected by their time and place in history, born in the war years (World War II) and coming of age in the early sixties with Kennedy as president. *When did you "come of age," and how has your life been affected by your time and place in history?*

Generations are usually defined in retrospect – the fifties generation of suburban housewives, the noisy rebels of the sixties generation – and the quiet in-between generation of women in this book. *Do you think of yourself as part of a specific generation? How would you define "your" generation?*

Anthropologist Sherry Ortner remembers her life as a series of lucky breaks, and goes on to say that it could all so easily have gone in a different way, *What does she mean by luck? What role has luck played in your life?*

Several of the women have had careers in the "male" professions – journalism, law and medicine – and played a part in breaking down barriers for women entering those professions. The doors are open now, even in business and politics. But there are still glass ceilings, and in many ways the professions are still quite hostile to women. The media are full of talk about the "mommy wars" and the difficult life/work balance for women. *What is the problem, in your view? What can we do about it, as individuals and as a society?*

Each woman in the book had to find her own path through life, and all asked themselves, again and again, two basic questions: "Who am I?" and "What do I want to do with my life?" *How do the women answer these questions of identity and purpose at different points in their lives? How do you answer these questions for yourself?*

The women in the book are now in their sixties, intent on "making the most of the rest of their lives." One says that she hasn't bloomed yet; while another has gone from a career as an economist at the World Bank to writing musicals, in collaboration with her new husband. *How do you think of this "third age" of life? What would it mean, for you, to bloom?*

If you have any questions or would like me to participate in your discussion, please e-mail me at alisonbak@aol.com. Visit my website: alisonbaker.info for more ideas and information.

Sources

The vast majority of my research, and almost all the quotations, are drawn from taped oral history interviews with classmates and others, most of whom are identified in the text. However, I also benefited greatly from written sources, especially for background material. I decided not to include footnotes, as too distracting in this sort of anecdotal, narrative nonfiction. This section will identify those written (and film) materials which are most relevant to each chapter, in addition to the sources for all citations.

Introduction

Class Surveys:

In the introduction, and in chapters throughout the book, I have drawn on three different Bryn Mawr 1962 class surveys—from the 10th reunion (1972), the 25th reunion (1987), and the 40th reunion (2002). I had various degrees of access and involvement as follows:

For the 10th Reunion Survey, done by classmate and sociologist Susan Johnson, I had the survey questionnaire as well as Sue's write-up and analysis of the responses. I did not have access to individual responses.

For the 25th reunion survey, done by classmate and demographer Betsy (Barber) Gould, I was able to consult the questionnaire, the individual responses, and Betsy's analysis and report.

For the 40th reunion survey, Betsy and I collaborated in designing the survey questionnaire—I added in some questions on history and feminism—and we both read the individual responses. Responses to all three questionnaires were anonymous.

Oral History

For readers who are interested in learning more about oral history, here are three books which will serve as a good introduction to the field. Grele's *Envelopes of Sound* includes contributions by Studs Terkel and Alice Kessler Harris, among others; while Gluck and Patai, *Women's Words* is a collection of essays by different writers.

Frisch, Michael, *A Shared Authority* (Albany, NY: State University of New York Press, 1989).

Gluck, Sherna Berger, and Daphne Patai eds., *Women's Words: The Feminist Practice of Oral History* (New York and London: Routledge, 1991).

Grele, Ronald, *Envelopes of Sound: The Art of Oral History,* (Chicago, IL: Precedent Publishing, Inc., 1975, 1986).

College Class Studies (fiction and nonfiction)

Horn, Miriam, *Rebels in White Gloves: Coming of Age with Hillary's Class—Wellesley '69* (New York: Random House, 1999).

McCarthy, Mary, *The Group* (New York: Harcourt Brace & Company, 1954).

Stimpson, Kate (Bryn Mawr, '58), *Class Notes* (New York: Times Books, 1979).

Chapter 1: Bryn Mawr College and the Class of 1962

For the history of Bryn Mawr College, and of the two college presidents, M. Carey Thomas and Katharine McBride, I consulted:

Horowitz, Helen Lefkowitz, *Alma Mater: Design and Experience in the Women's Collges from their Nineteenth Century Beginnings to the 1930s* (New York: Alfred A. Knopf, 1984).

————. *The Power and Passion of M. Carey Thomas* (New York: Alfred A. Knopf, 1994).

Meigs, Cornelia, *What Makes a College: A History of Bryn Mawr* (New York: Macmillan, 1956).

For information on geologist Florence Bascom and mathematician Emmy Noether, I read the Bryn Mawr College archives. On German refugee scholars generally, my primary source was Felix Gilbert's chapter, "Desirable Elements: Refugee Professors at Bryn Mawr in the Thirties and Forties" in *A Century Recalled: Essays in Honor of Bryn Mawr College,* edited by Patricia Hochschild Labalme (Bryn Mawr College Library, 1987).

For background on growing up female in the fifties

Coontz, Stephanie, *The Way We Never Were: American Families and the Nostalgia Trap* (New York: Basic Books, 1992).

Ehrenreich, Barbara and Deirdre English, *For Her Own Good: Two Centuries of the Experts' Advice to Women* (New York: Random House, Inc., 1978).

Halberstam, David, *The Fifties* (New York: Villard Books, 1993).

Life Magazine, *The American Woman: Her Achievements and Troubles,* special two-in-one holiday issue (December 24, 1956).

On feminism and women's history

Collins, Gail, *America's Women: 400 Years of Dolls, Drudges, Helpmates, and Heroines* (New York: Harper Collins Publisher, 2003).

Lerner, Gerda, *The Majority Finds Its Past* (New York and Oxford: Oxford University Press, 1979).

Schneider, Liz (Bryn Mawr, '68), "Our Failures Only Marry: Bryn Mawr and the Failure of Feminism," in Vivian Gornick and Barbara K. Moran, eds., *Women in Sexist Society: Studies in Power and Powerlessness* (New York: Basic Books, 1971).

For an overview of issues in women's lives today

Faludi, Susan, *Backlash: The Undeclared War Against American Women* (New York: Doubleday, 1991).

Macko, Lia, and Kerry Rubin, *Midlife Crisis at 30* (Emmaus, PA: Rodale/St. Martin's Press, 2004).

Orenstein, Peggy, *Flux: Women on Sex, Work, Love, Kids, and Life in a Half-Changed World* (New York: Knopf, 2001).

Pollitt, Katha, "Subject to Debate," *The Nation* columns, 2005–2006.

Warner, Judith, *Perfect Madness: Motherhood in the Age of Anxiety* (New York: Riverhead Books, 2005).

Marion (Coen) Katzive lent me her copies of the fall 1958 *Freshman Handbook* and *Class of 1962 Yearbook* (the source for most of the 1962 photos). She also allowed me to read and quote from the written text of her 2002 40th class reunion talk.

Anna (Kimbrough) Morris supplied the *Freshman Facebook* for 1958 photos of herself and of me.

Notes for Chapter 1

1. (pp. 8-9) Johnson, Susan, *When Women Played Hardball* (Seal Press, 1994).

2. (pp. 15-16) The description of Emmy Noether is quoted in the February, 2006 *Bryn Mawr Alumnae Bulletin* review of Patricia Emison, *Growing with the Grain: Dynamic Families Shaping History from Ancient Times to Present* (Lady Illyria Press, 2005).

3. (p. 22) Orenstein, *Flux* p. 97.

4. (p. 22) Macko and Rubin, *Midlife Crisis at 30* p. 35.

5.   (p. 23) Faludi, *Backlash* p. xviii.

6.   (p. 23) Warner, *Perfect Madness* pp. 260-261.

7.   (p. 24) Lerner, *The Majority Finds Its Past* p. xxvi.

Chapter 2: From a Fetish for Decorum to Marching on the Picket Line.

The main written source for this chapter is the weekly *Bryn Mawr College News*. I had a complete run of the *College News* from August 1958 through June, 1962, courtesy of Marion (Coen) Katzive.

For information on the civil rights movement as perceived by white girls growing up in the north, I looked at coverage in *The New York Times* for the period from May, 1954 (the Supreme Court decision outlawing segregated schools) to April, 1968 (the assassination of Dr. Martin Luther King, Jr.).

On the student movement (starting with student participation in the civil rights movement)

Frasier, Ronald, ed., *1968: A Student Generation in Revolt* (New York: Pantheon/Random House, 1988).

This is a very rich and comprehensive oral history of not only the American student movement, but also other student movements around the world. The American edition includes expanded material on the Woolworth's lunch-counter sit-ins and SNCC, as well as accounts of the Mississippi Freedom Summer, the Berkeley Free Speech Movement, SDS, and the movement against U.S. participation in the war in Vietnam, (used mainly in Chapter 3).

Notes for Chapter 2

1.   (p. 33) Steve Fraser, a student at the University of Wisconsin at the time, quoted in Fraser, ed., *1968,* p. 49.

Chapter 3: The Sixties (and Seventies): Turbulence and Change

In addition to Fraser's *1968,* I used several other sources for information on the student movement at the University of California at Berkeley, the University of Wisconsin at Madison, and in Paris, France, as follows:

Cohen, Robert, and Reginald E. Zelnik, eds., *The Free Speech Movement: Reflections on Berkeley in the 1960s* (Berkeley, CA: University of California Press, 2002).

FSM Archives (University of California at Berkeley libraries and online).

Berkeley in the Sixties (a documentary film by Mark Kitchell, 1990).

The War at Home (a film on the UW-Madison student anti-war movement by Glenn Silber and Barry Alexander Brown, 1979).

La Revolte des Etudiants. (ZOOM, 1968) A French TV special by Alain de Sedoy and André Harris, with the collaboration of Jean Paul Thomas.

On the women's movement

Rosen, Ruth, *The World Split Open: How the Women's Movement Changed America* (New York: Viking Penguin, 2000).

This is the first really comprehensive history of the American women's movement, taking readers on "an unforgettable journey through the last half of the twentieth century, charting the accomplishments and failures of a movement that transformed our politics, our culture, and our lives."

On the gay and lesbian rights movement

Duberman, Martin, *Stonewall* (New York: Penguin, 1993).

Johnston, Jill, *Lesbian Nation* (New York: Simon & Schuster, 1973).

Books/articles by Sue Johnson and Josie Donovan that are referred to in the text

Donovan, Josephine, *Feminist Theory: The Intellectual Traditions,* 3rd ed. (New York: Continuum, 2000).

Donovan, Josephine, "A Cause of Our Own," in Florence Howe, ed., *The Politics of Women's Studies* (New York: The Feminist Press of the City University of New York, 2000).

Johnson, Susan, *Staying Power: Long Term Lesbian Couples* (Tallahassee, FL: Naiad Press, 1990).

Notes for Chapter 3

1. (p 48) The description of Dr. Martin Luther King, Jr.'s "I Have A Dream" speech is taken from a front-page article by James Reston in the next day's (August 29, 1963) *New York Times.*

2. (p. 48) *FSM Archives.* Mario Savio December, 1964 interview with Doug Giles.

3. (pp. 49, 51) Dany Cohn-Bendit, quoted in Fraser, ed., *1968* p. 9.

4. (p. 53) Rosen, Ruth, *World Split Open*, pp. 201-202

5. (p. 62) Susan Madden, "I Have Four Coming Out Stories to Tell" in Julia Penelope and Susan J. Wolfe, eds. *The Original Coming Out Stories* (Freedom, CA: The Crossing Press, 1980) p. 128.

6. (p. 73) Millett, Kate, *Sexual Politics* (Urbana and Chicago, IL: University of Illinois Press, paperback version, 2000) pp. 23-25.

Chapter 4: Interesting Times

For background on Kathy Boudin and the Weathermen group, I consulted various New York press accounts from the summer and fall of 2001, when Boudin was first up for parole, as well as Elizabeth Kolbert, "The Prisoner:—Should Kathy Boudin go free?" in *The New Yorker* magazine, July 16, 2001 issue.

In 2001, Boudin was denied parole; in 2003 her case was reconsidered, and parole was granted. Among all the press accounts of fall 2003, I especially benefited from reading James Miller, "Return of the Weathermen: The unhappy afterlife of 60s' radicalism" in *The Boston Globe,* October 19, 2003, and from viewing a 2003 film documentary,

Weather Underground, a production of the Free History Project, produced in association with KQED Public Television/San Francisco and ITVS.

<u>Note on the My Lai Massacre:</u>

The incident occurred on March 16, 1968, but most Americans were not aware of it until after journalist Seymour Hirsch broke the story on November 12, 1969. Lt. William Calley was charged in 1969, convicted of premeditated murder in 1971, and sentenced to life in prison. He won his freedom, on appeal, by claiming that he was following orders.

Isa (Brannon) Spencer provided me with a copy of the September 1993 *Denver Post* special report on gays and lesbians in Colorado, which followed up on issues raised by the passage of an amendment which outlawed any state legislation protecting gays and lesbians.

<u>Notes for Chapter 4</u>

1. (p. 78) Quotes are from Naomi Jaffe, in the September 21, 2003 *Guardian Observer,* Brian Flanagan, in the 2003 documentary film, *The Weather Underground;* and James Miller, in the October 19, 2003 *Boston Globe.*

2. (p. 79) Letter from Kathy Boudin reprinted in the Summer, 2001 *Bryn Mawr Bulletin.*

Chapter 5: The Groves of Academe

<u>Notes on Chapter 5</u>

1. (p. 98) Ortner, Sherry, *New Jersey Dreaming: Capital, Culture, and the Class of '58* (Durham, N.C., and London: Duke University Press, 2003).

2. (p. 103) Ortner, Sherry, "Is Female to Male as Nature Is to Culture?" in *Woman, Culture and Society,* edited by Michelle Zimbalist Rosaldo and Louise Lamphere (Stanford, CA: Stanford University Press, 1974).

3. (p. 105) The material on geologist Florence Bascom comes from files in the Bryn Mawr College archives.

4. (p. 114) Lambert, Ellen Zetzel, *The Face of Love: Feminism and the Beauty Question* (Boston, MA: Beacon Press, 1995).

5. (p. 115) Heilburn, Carolyn, *Writing a Woman's Life* (New York: Ballantine Books, 1989) and Bateson, Mary Catherine, *Composing a Life* (New York and London: Penguin, 1989).

Chapter 6: Schoolteachers

For information on the history of the education program at Bryn Mawr, Cornelia Meigs, *What Makes a College?* was my main source. Alison Cook-Sathers, director of teacher education at Bryn Mawr, provided me with materials on the current Bryn Mawr–Haverford Education Program.

Notes on Chapter 6

1. (p. 119) Meigs, *What Makes a College?* p. 87.

2. (p. 128) The term "glass ceiling" was first used in a March 1984 *Adweek* article, then in a March 24, 1986 *Wall Street Journal* article.

Chapter 7: "Women Unwanted" in Law and Medicine

For background on women in the legal profession:

Epstein, Cynthia Fuchs, "Glass Ceilings and Open Doors," Fall 1995 report for The Association of the Bar of the City of New York Committee on Women in the Professions.

Fordham Law Review, "Essays–Responses to Glass Ceilings and Open Doors: Women's Advancement in the Legal Profession," *Fordham Law Review* 65 (1996).

Hope, Judith Richards, *Pinstripes and Pearls: The Women of the Harvard Law School Class of '64* (New York: Scribner, 2003).

Wellington, Sheila, and *Catalyst*, with Betty Spence, *Be Your Own Mentor: Strategies from Top Women on the Secrets of Success* (New York: Random House, 2001).

I am grateful to the staff at *Catalyst,* who opened their library and their files to me, enabling me to read widely in studies they had done on women in large corporations and law firms.

Notes on Chapter 7

1. (p. 141) Quoted from an article by Jan Hoffman in the September 14, 1995 *New York Times.*

2. (p. 153) Quotes from interview with Fran Conley in the Winter, 1993 *Bryn Mawr Alumnae Bulletin.*

3. (p. 153) Conley, Frances K., M.D., *Walking Out On The Boys* (New York: Farrar, Straus and Giroux, 1998).

4. (p. 157) The Boston Women's Health Book Collective formed in 1969, and put out a first version of *Our Bodies, Ourselves* in 1970, on newsprint. Since then, six editions have been published, in 1973, 1979, 1984, 1998, and 2005. For this book, the 1984 and 1992 versions (both titled *The New Our Bodies, Ourselves*) were my primary sources.

Chapter 8: Uncharted Territory

Statistics on the 1962 graduating class at Bryn Mawr are from the college archives and the *Bryn Mawr College News* 1962 graduation issue.

For a beautiful book of photographs, essays and interviews on the Stuart collection at the University of California at San Diego:

Beebe, Mary Livingstone, and Robert Storr (essays), and Joan Simon (interviews), *Landmarks: Sculpture Commissions at the University of California, San Diego.* (New York: University of California Press/Rizzoli International Publications, Inc., 2001).

Chapter 9: "I Haven't Bloomed Yet"

Notes for Chapter 9

1. (p. 187) Trafford, Abigail, *My Time: Making the Most of the Rest of Your Life* (New York: Basic Books, 2004).

2. (p. 191) William K. Reilly's remarks on Joanna Underwood were cited in the May 22, 2006 INFORM Board of Directors' press release announcing Joanna's resignation.

3. (p. 199) Trafford, Abigail, *Crazy Time: Surviving Divorce and Building a New Life* (New York: HarperCollins Publishers, 1982).

4. (p. 202) Portelli, Alessandro, "So Much Depends On a Red Bus, Or, Innocent Victims of the Liberating Gun," *Oral History* 34, no. 2 (Autumn 2006).

Index

About the Author

Alison Baker

Alison Baker is a writer and oral historian living in New York City, a graduate of Bryn Mawr College, class of '62, and the author of *Voices of Resistance: Oral Histories of Moroccan Women* (1998). She went through the decades after Bryn Mawr more or less in step with her classmates. In the sixties, she joined the foreign service, married and had children. In the seventies, she joined a consciousness-raising group, divorced, earned a PhD, and forged a career in academic administration. In the eighties, she lived with her children in Paris for a semester, and launched an "Academic Year in New York City" together with a colleague. In the nineties she went to Morocco, first as academic director of an American study abroad program, and then doing her own research on Moroccan women who were active in the independence movement.